The DAVID THOMPSON HIGHWAY:

A Hiking Guide

Jane Ross & Daniel Kyba

DISCLAIMER

There are inherent risks in hiking in wilderness and semi-wilderness areas. Although the authors have alerted readers to locations where particular caution is to be exercised, trail conditions may change due to weather and other factors. Hikers use this book entirely at their own risk and the authors disclaim any liability for any injuries or other damage that may be sustained by anyone using any of the trails described in this book.

The DAVID THOMPSON HIGHWAY: A Hiking Guide

Jane Ross & Daniel Kyba

Front cover: John Campbell on the last pull up Hummingbird Pass.
Back cover: Cline Creek Falls overshadowed by fall colours.

The publisher gratefully acknowledges the assistance
provided by the Alberta Foundation for the Arts and by
the federal Department of Communications.

COMMITTED TO THE DEVELOPMENT OF CULTURE AND THE ARTS

Published by Rocky Mountain Books
#4 Spruce Centre SW, Calgary, AB T3C 3B3
Printed and bound in Canada by
Kromar Printing Ltd., Winnipeg

ISBN 0-921102-38-0

Canadian Cataloguing in Publication Data

Ross, Jane, 1948-
    The David Thompson Highway

Includes bibliographical reference and index.
ISBN 0-921102-38-0

1. David Thompson Highway (Alta.)–Guidebooks. 2.
Hiking–Alberta–David Thompson Highway–Guidebooks. 3.
Trails–Alberta–David Thompson Highway–Guidebooks. 4.
Rocky Mountains, Canadian (B.C. and Alta.)–Guidebooks.*
I. Kyba, Dan, 1951- II. Title.
GV199.44.C22A45 1995   917.123'3043   C95-910415-1

CONTENTS

"To see the [Kootenay] Plains at their best, one should come over the Pipestone trail in August, and look down on the scene from the rolling hills of the south. Then the golden-brown of the ripened grasses floods the valley with light, for miles the river winds and twists from west to east, an occasional Indian shack comes into view, the faint ringing of a bell denotes that a few tiny specks on the landscape are really horses, and the white dots are teepees of the Indians."

Mary Schäffer: Old Indian Trails of the Canadian Rockies

Introduction

Stretching 83 km along Highway #11 from Nordegg to the Banff National Park boundary in west-central Alberta, the David Thompson Corridor is one of the few mountain areas in the province outside either a national or provincial park, or a wilderness area. The west end of the corridor is bounded on the north by the White Goat Wilderness Area, on the west by Banff National Park and on the south by the Siffleur Wilderness Area. North of Windy Point the corridor is defined on the east by both Abraham Lake and the North Saskatchewan River. The old coal-mining town of Nordegg to the north lies just within the corridor, while west of the highway the corridor is demarcated by the Bighorn Range. Lying within the boundaries of the David Thompson Corridor are the Kootenay Plains Ecological Reserve, the Landslide Lake Natural Area and the Big Horn Indian Reserve.

From the rolling foothills of the Nordegg area to the towering pinnacles of the main ranges, the David Thompson Corridor offers some of the most diversified scenery, flora and history in Alberta's Rocky Mountains. As awe-inspiring as the mountains are, they form merely a backdrop against which a tapestry of human emotions and accomplishments was played. Indians, fur traders, coal miners, travellers and tourists, developers and government, sometimes struggling against each other, but always struggling to control their own destiny in these mountains, wove a pattern dictated by the physical geography of the area. Today, the mountains and valleys continue to exert their hold over some of the same players. Stoney and Cree Indians come each spring to give thanks to their creator, while the popularity of the David Thompson Corridor among hikers, cyclists, hunters, fishermen and campers cannot be doubted by anyone who has witnessed their "invasion" each season.

With the introduction of user fees in the national parks, the appeal of and pressure on the David Thompson Corridor will undoubtedly increase. Already, the fragile ecosystem of the Kootenay Plains Ecological Reserve is under threat of inappropriate use. Primarily a hiking book geared for the day hiker and families (although some of the more popular short backpacks are included), the book also introduces the reader to the natural and human history of the area through four sidebars. Scattered throughout the chapters are route maps. Most of these maps are of areas large enough to encompass several hikes. So for your convenience each route is numbered. These numbers correspond to those given for each hike.

We walked all hikes described in this book. Many trails follow old mining, logging or forestry roads that are now closed to vehicular traffic. Other trails follow social paths, open ridges and creekbeds. Unlike within the parks, there are no signs, so it is especially important to follow the trail descriptions so as not to become lost in the sometimes confusing maze of trails. Lastly, we hope that visitors to the David Thompson Corridor enjoy their experience so much that they leave it as they found it, for others to enjoy.

AREA MAP

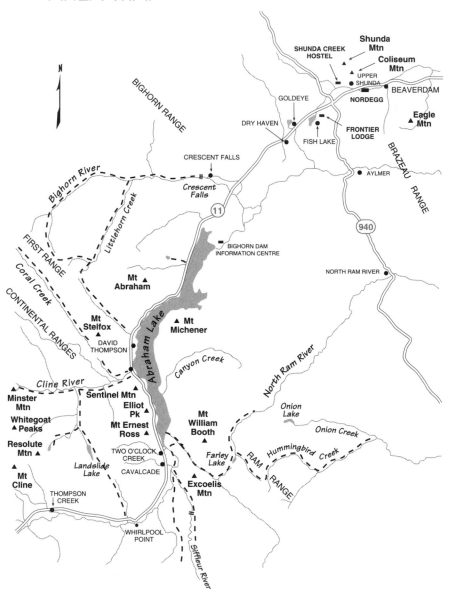

Nordegg Area

The forested hills of Nordegg offer both delightful family walks and more demanding hikes to open mountain ridges of the Brazeau Range. From the flora of the foothills to the black gold of the coal fields there is much of interest in this eastern part of the David Thompson corridor. It is an area, too, rich in history that is yours to be enjoyed and experienced on any one of these hikes.

Technically part of the boreal uplands ecoregion, the Nordegg area offers scenic lakes and rolling terrain that are associated with the foothills. White spruce and lodgepole pine dominate the forests, although poplar and trembling aspen are found in disturbed areas. Tamarack and black spruce are found in the swampy area around Shunda Creek. Plants such as Indian paint brush, yarrow and northern sweetvetch inhabit open meadows, while feather mosses and a variety of orchids form the forest undergrowth.

Rising above the green carpet of hills are the rounded bald peaks of the Brazeau Range. These peaks, along with those of the Bighorn Range found further west, are outliers of the Rocky Mountains. The "docking" of the continental plate to the North American plate 175 million years ago caused the edges of the two plates to buckle, forming first the west coast mountains. As the plates continued to grind past each other the buckling rippled eastward. The Brazeau and Bighorn Ranges represent the easternmost upheavals associated with the mountain-building phenomenon.

Thar's coal in them thar hills! Prior to the docking of the continental ship and the creation of the Rocky Mountains, much of what is now Alberta was a low-lying, tropical swamp. As plants died they were quickly covered by new plant growth. Over millions of years, the layers of dead plant material were compressed by mud and sand of successive inland seas into coal. Age and the amount of pressure to which the coal was subjected determine the hardness of the coal. In the Canadian west, the oldest and hardest coals are found in the mountains, with softer and younger coals found further east on the prairies.

Coal has long been used as a fuel for home heating and industrial purposes. With the introduction of the steam locomotive in the early 19th century, and the use of coal to fire those engines, there was a dramatic increase in the consumption of this fossil fuel. On the Canadian prairies, it was the soft, sub-bituminous coal of the Lethbridge field that was first used by the Canadian Pacific Railway to push its trains over the Continental Divide. The search for a harder, cleaner-burning fuel led to the discovery of bituminous coal at Canmore in 1890. Other mines opened in the Crowsnest Pass following the construction of the CPR's Crowsnest line in 1898. As hundreds of thousands of newcomers swarmed onto the prairies at the beginning of the 20th century, two other transcontinental railway lines spread their tentacles across the prairies and into the mountains. They, too, were in search of good coal fields.

Luckily for William MacKenzie and Donald Mann of the Canadian

Northern Railway, a source of excellent steam coal had already been discovered. In 1907, Martin Nordegg, a German scientist representing the Deutsches Canada Syndicate interested in investing in resource development in Canada, had staked thousands of hectares of land in the Bighorn and Brazeau Rivers area. Nordegg, though, had difficulty in attracting sufficient capital to begin development. The Grand Trunk Pacific was unwilling to commit itself before it had finalized its transmontane route and other foreign investors simply were not interested. MacKenzie and Mann, though, leapt at Nordegg's proposal and in 1909 with Sir William MacKenzie as President and Martin Nordegg as Vice-President, Brazeau Collieries Ltd. was born.

Setting out in the spring of 1910, Nordegg and his party conducted preliminary work throughout their leases. The South Brazeau area looked the most promising. If it hadn't been for a fluke, Nordegg

HISTORICAL FOOTNOTES

The Nordegg Mine Disaster

On October 31, 1941, 29 men were killed in the worst mining accident at the Nordegg coal mines. Until then, the mines at Nordegg had had an excellent safety record.

The immediate cause of the incident was an explosion of coal dust and gas seepage from exposed coal faces. An inquiry held afterwards attributed the disaster to the negligence of Brazeau Collieries, the company operating the mine. The inquiry found that the mine's pit bosses regularly failed to test for gas before firing the explosives that released the coal from its seams. According to Justice A. F. Ewing, who headed the inquiry: "there was on the part of all officials actively engaged in the operation of the mine a general disregard for safety provisions of the Mines Act and a general indifference to, and contempt for the dangers incident to gas accumulations in the mine."

Following the disaster, Brazeau Collieries eliminated the dangerous practice of blasting coal with explosives and became the first operator in Alberta to convert to the pneumatic pick.

The memorial to the Nordegg mine disaster is located next to the Nordegg Heritage Centre.

would have developed the South Brazeau and the history of the Nordegg area would have been very different. It was in the autumn as Nordegg and his party were en route to Rocky Mountain House that he saw an exposed coal seam near present-day Nordegg. Nordegg realized that millions could be saved by developing these coal seams, which lay further east than those of the Brazeau.

Very pleased, Nordegg threw himself into the development of the Nordegg Coal Basin. Two log houses and a log cookhouse were built first. Miners were hired and tunnels driven into the two thickest seams. Surface support is critical to any mining venture and during the winter of 1911-1912 Nordegg had mining equipment—boilers, generators, forges, tipple machinery—skidded along the North Saskatchewan River to the site. Meanwhile, construction of the Canadian Northern Railway from Stettler proceeded apace. When the first locomotive chugged into the new town of Nordegg on August 18, 1914, Nordegg more than lived up to his promise of having 100,000 tonnes of coal ready for shipment.

War has an odd way of turning former friends into enemy aliens. Martin Nordegg, a German citizen, found himself to be a *persona non grata* after the outbreak of World War I. In June 1915, he was asked to leave Canada. He spent the war years in New York City and when he was allowed to return in 1918, he discovered that control of the mine had been taken out of his hands. Embittered, he sold the German development company's interests in Brazeau Collieries. The war years were difficult ones for William MacKenzie and Donald Mann's empire as well.

Overextended financially, the Canadian Northern along with the Grand Trunk and the Grand Trunk Pacific were taken over by the federal government and merged into a Crown corporation, the Canadian National Railways.

Despite the upheaval in management, the mine itself did well during the 1920s. Some 800 people were employed by the mine and production skyrocketed to 500,000 tonnes. The Great Depression of the 1930s, though, had a predictable impact on the mine and the town. Miners were laid off and production plummeted to 150,000 tonnes. Even the installation of a briquette plant in 1936 did little to salvage the fortunes of the colliery. Only another world war brought a temporary halt to the mine's declining fortunes when demand for coal brought production back to 350,000 tonnes annually. Much of this coal came from three open pit mines that were opened at this time. But it was not to last. The conversion of the railways to diesel after the war meant that all Alberta's coal mines faced oblivion. Brazeau Collieries ceased operations in 1955. Most of the remaining families were moved at government expense, although a core of optimists remained in the townsite. Some of the community buildings were moved to other towns. The miners' homes and most of the managers' homes were razed by Alberta Forestry, which felt that the abandoned wood-framed houses were a fire threat. The historic business core, though, remains largely intact, but vacant. It now lies behind the chain link fence that demarcates the Nordegg Correctional Institute.

11

THE NORDEGG GHOST TOWN AND MINE TOUR

Has your appetite and curiosity about Nordegg been whetted? To appreciate more fully the workings of a coal mine and the life of a mining community, consider taking a guided tour of old Nordegg. The modest admission charge makes this tour the best deal in town! The tour begins by hopping into your vehicle and following the tour guide through the Correctional Institute's grounds to the lower mine site. Here, you stroll through the miners' washhouse where each miner had two lockers, one for his clean clothes and one for his mine clothes. The next stop is the upper mine site with visits to the lamp house and Numbers 2 and 3 mines. You cannot go into the mines as the entrances have been plugged, but the guide explains how "room and pillar" was the only method of extraction that the miners could use on the 12 degree pitch of the seams.

A drive through the upper town where the managerial class lived is followed by a visit to the tipple and briquette plant. Here, you have an opportunity to clamber up into the briquette plant to see a complete set of briquette makers. Then it's down to old Nordegg's main street where most of the town's businesses were located. None of the buildings are open to the public. Sunday ecumenical services are occasionally held in the church at the top of the main street.

Operated by the Nordegg Historic Heritage Interest Group. Formed in 1984, this group promotes the preservation, protection and presentation of the Nordegg townsite and mine site.

Tour times ~ 1:00 pm every day from the May long weekend until Labour Day. Weekends from Labour Day until October. School or group tours can be arranged through the Nordegg Heritage Centre.

Depart from ~ The Nordegg Heritage Centre located on the main street of Nordegg one km south of Highway #11.

Admission charge ~ Check at the Nordegg Heritage Centre for current admission prices.

Note ~ Although you drive between stops, much of this tour is out-of-doors. This is a large site so sturdy footwear is recommended. Be prepared to walk up and down slopes.

The tour guide, a retired Nordegg miner, explains the function of a rotary dump.

1 Eagle Mountain – map p. 13

Duration ~ full day
Distance ~ 15 km
Level of Difficulty ~ long walk with some steep slopes
Maximum Elevation ~ 2,038 m
Elevation Gain ~ 750 m
Map ~ 83 B/5 Saunders

This is a fairly straightforward hike that offers great views for modest elevation gain. Quads are threatening to chew up the old logging road that is taken at the beginning of the hike, but once off the road and onto the open slope one cannot but help enjoy the climb up Eagle Mountain, a local name for the highest point in the Brazeau Range north of the North Saskatchewan River.

~

Access ~ Park your vehicle at the old Alberta Forestry woodlot nine km east of Nordegg on Highway #11. An unmarked gravel turn-off to the south is the old woodlot road. Follow the road for 30 m to where the track forks. There is an old Forestry sign warning of illegal removal of firewood. Take the right-hand fork to drive into the woodlot proper and park on the east side of the open field.

0.0	trailhead
0.1	Soussner Creek
1.0	cutline and creek
1.8	cutline and creek
3.2	creek
4.0	cutline
4.4	junction
5.1	cutline
5.2	cut block
5.5	top of cut block
6.0	open ridge
6.5	high point of ridge
7.0	lower shoulder on Eagle Mountain
7.5	summit of Eagle Mountain
15.0	trailhead

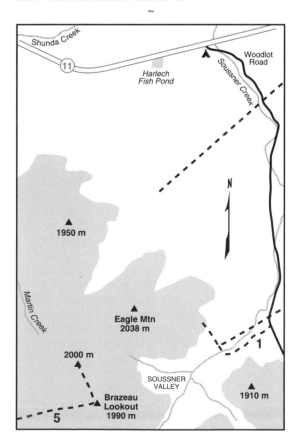

A view of the summit of Eagle Mountain from the open ridge.

The trailhead is the quad track on the east side of the woodlot near Soussner Creek. Within 20 m there is a T-junction with another track. Swing to the right and after a quick 100-m jog cross Soussner Creek. It is quite obvious that you share this old logging road with horses, mountain bikes and quads. If it has been raining recently, mud holes, which quad drivers see as a challenge, will span the entire width of the road. After nearly one km of walking through the forest, the road swings to the west toward Eagle Mountain. Cross a small stream. Just beyond the stream, a cutline joins from the right. Keep to the left, or on the old road and continue straight ahead. Finally, the road begins to break out of the bush, offering views of the Brazeau Range only to plunge back into the forest. The next reference point is an overgrown cutline on your left and a small stream where, to help you, some well-meaning souls have thrown across a couple

of logs. Continue along the old road to a rill small enough to hop across. Grass covers the old road making it easier for walking. Ignore another cutline that crosses your track at right angles. A short distance beyond this cutline there is an old corduroy road that, perhaps, a logging company laid down to bridge this particularly boggy section.

At last, the track leaves the forest behind to break out onto an old logged area. An old track joins from the right. Turn onto this track and follow it along the north edge of the cut block for approximately 500 m. Another cutline demarcating the south edge of an extension of the cut block joins on the right. Eagle Mountain is straight ahead beyond your immediate sight lines. To get there you must first bear right onto this cutline and follow it as it veers to the left and up into the cut block. Now comes the worst part of this hike—a bushwhack up the slope through thick undergrowth toward the top of the cut block. Cut logs and tree stumps hidden by the weeds and shrubs can make this walk rather treacherous, so be careful where you place your feet.

Once at the top of the cut block, find a game trail about 10 m to the left that leads through the trees to an open slope on the other side. The game trail goes up the slope for several metres, and then turns sharply to the left and angles up slope until it emerges onto the edge of the ridge. Having gained the open slope, turn right and follow it uphill. The slope is fairly open, and where copses of trees and bushes block the route, there are game trails that take you through. The scenery is quite charming, almost park-like, with the triangular peak of Eagle Mountain on the horizon drawing you ever forward.

Finish this part of the climb at the end of the ridge. Eagle Mountain and its lower shoulders are now to the left, so turn in that direction and descend to the base of the lowest shoulder. Most of the elevation gain of this hike is made between here and the summit of this locally-named mountain. As you climb the first spine the

GEOFACTS

Brazeau Erratics

As you climb the lower shoulders of Eagle Mountain you see scattered pebbles, cobbles and boulders. These are the Brazeau Erratics.

An erratic is a rock transported from its original location and deposited in another by a glacier. The most famous erratic in Alberta is the Big Rock at Okotoks. The rocks scattered across the Brazeau Range are much smaller than Big Rock, but they tell the same story: there was once a glacier here. During the Wisconsin glaciation— 40,000 to 10,000 years ago—the minimum thickness of glacial ice in the immediate vicinity of Eagle Mountain was about 2,100 m. So, as you admire the view from the top of Eagle Mountain, imagine ice so thick that it filled the valleys below you to an unknown height above you. Further to the west, we know the ice was thicker since erratics have been reported near the summit of Sentinel Mountain at 2,515 m.

If you look east from the top of Eagle Mountain you see what may be another glacial feature. Sprinkled throughout the forest below are small lakes. These may be kettle ponds. A kettle is a depression caused by a buried ice block. As a glacier melts and retreats, it leaves behind large blocks of ice that become surrounded or buried by deposits of gravel. As the ice block melts it leaves a depression in the gravel that in time may fill with water and become a small lake or pond.

A view of a Brazeau erratic (the rock underneath the author).

terrain becomes quite rocky, and on a sunny day you are buffeted by strong westerly winds. En route to the summit, there are a series of shoulders that give some respite in the otherwise steep walk up the hill. Then you come to what appears to be an impregnable cliff face that runs the length of Eagle Mountain. It can actually be breached quite easily on the left, and once up through the cliff a short spurt brings you to the top of the shoulder. The summit of Eagle Mountain is directly in front of you, so go for it and lope along the ridge to the base of this last pull to the top. En route, stop now and again to enjoy the unfolding vista of the Brazeau Range on the left and the jagged skyline of the distant snowcaps to the right.

On the rocky summit there is a sweeping 360 degree panorama from Coliseum and Shunda Mountains directly to the north past the rolling green-carpeted foothills of the Rocky Mountain Forest Reserve with its lakes, cutlines and roads, to the rocky peaks of the Brazeau Range and the mountains and glaciers to the far west. Directly to the west is the summit of the Brazeau Lookout hike.

Remember to add a rock to the cairn at the summit before returning the way you came.

HISTORICAL FOOTNOTES

Geological Survey of Canada

From the Brazeau Range west along the North Saskatchewan to the Banff park boundary are about 20 significant rock piles and cairns on nearby ridges and peaks. These constructions are souvenirs of the Geological Survey of Canada and its expeditions into the area between 1885 and 1915.

The first surveyors were R. G. McConnell and James White, who in 1885 undertook a topographical survey from near Calgary north to the North Saskatchewan River. In 1892 McConnell returned. He reached the Kootenay Plains via the Siffleur River on June 17, went east to The Gap, then proceeded to make a geological inventory of the North Saskatchewan River valley up to Howse Pass. Possibly because McConnell did his research along the south bank of the North Saskatchewan he missed the coal deposits along the Bighorn River. It was another surveyor, D. B. Dowling, who found them in 1906.

These surveyors were accompanied by local Stoney Indians who shared their geographic knowledge, and helped with the various manual tasks necessary on such expeditions: hunting, packing, brush clearing and the construction of survey markers. One of the guides during the 1885 expedition was a Stoney named James who drew a map outlining the North Saskatchewan River from the mouth of the Siffleur River to Haven Creek. The Stoney, due to cross-cultural misunderstanding and translation inaccuracies assumed initially that the surveyors were demarcating a reserve for them. By 1907, however, they realized that this was not the case. That year, when D. B. Dowling returned to the Bighorn River, a Stoney delegation including Silas Abraham, asked him to intercede on their behalf to establish a reserve in the area. Dowling could not, or would not do this and the issue of an Indian reserve remained unresolved for another 35 years.

These early surveyors have been gone for about a century, but their markers remain. There are two types. First are rock cairns, which are one to two m-high pillars of tightly-packed rock, sometimes with a post in the centre. They are found at the higher altitudes such as on Eagle Mountain. Then there are the rock piles, random collections of rocks set in a low pile, and found at lower altitudes such as at Windy Point.

2 East Bush Falls Loop – map p. 17

Duration ~ half day
Distance ~ 5.7 km
Level of Difficulty ~ easy stroll
Maximum Elevation ~ 1,450 m
Elevation Gain ~ 90 m
Map ~ 83 C/8 Nordegg

Old logging roads crisscross East Bush Mountain in a tangle of trails, tracks and roads. Although these old routes make excellent hiking and equestrian trails, do follow directions carefully so as not to become lost on the mountain. The waterfall on East Bush Creek is a pleasant bonus to this pretty hike.

~

From the Nordegg Heritage Centre walk up the main street 30 m toward the Nordegg Correctional Camp sign. Here, there is an intersection with a street on your left. Turn onto this side street. By the "No Exit" sign you will come upon a well-defined path on your right. The path leads up the slope past a haunting old graveyard surrounded by a picket fence. Just past the cemetery are several footpaths joining from the left. Stay on the main, broad path on the right as it climbs slowly through the spruce and poplar bush. The other paths return to the side street. At a second junction keep to the right. Almost immediately you come upon and pass under an old railway trestle

Access ~ Park your vehicle at the Nordegg Heritage Centre parking lot located one km south of Highway #11 at the Nordegg turn-off. The Heritage Centre is the yellow building on the right just past the golf course clubhouse.

0.0	trailhead
0.2	junction
0.4	junction
0.5	junction and trestle
0.6	junction
0.8	braid
0.9	junction
1.0	braid
1.5	cutline
1.6	cutline
2.0	stream and junction
2.1	East Bush Creek
2.3	East Bush Falls
2.6	East Bush Creek
2.7	East Bush Creek
3.5	junction
3.7	East Bush Creek
3.8	rail bed
4.0	junction
4.6	junction
4.8	junction
5.2	junction
5.5	junction
5.6	gravel street
5.7	trailhead

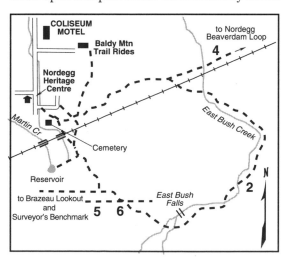

No one knows very much about this early cemetery. A number of the graves appear quite small. Perhaps some of the mining town's children succumbed to typhoid, a problem common in frontier settlements.

that once saw Canadian Northern, and later, Canadian National steam trains puffing their way into the old town of Nordegg to pick up coal from the mine. For a quick side trip, why not climb up to the trestle and follow the rail bed westward for 100 m to a second trestle? There is a fine view of the Martin Creek gorge at this point. To climb up to the trestle, take a small footpath that joins your main trail on the left. After viewing the gorge, return to the path below the first trestle and continue climbing.

Within the next 500 m a number of paths join the main trail. At the first junction, bear right. If you go left, you return to the railway track. At the second junction, also bear right. The trail on the left is a braid that will rejoin the main trail at one km. Keep to the left at a third junction. You will end up at the Martin Creek reservoir if you go right. The next junction is where the braid rejoins, so keep to the right along the main horse trail. By now, you are deep in the forested hills above Nordegg. The forest floor is overlaid with soft, feathery mosses that prefer this cool, damp environment. For amateur botanists there are elegant Venus slipper orchids to watch for. You might also watch for the telltale signs that you are on a bridle path. Step carefully!

Climb sharply to a cutline where you bear left. Cross a second cutline and continue to a small stream. Taking either cutline to the right takes you to the 12 Level Road. Now, begin to climb East Bush hill. Within 20 m of the stream crossing a secondary path joins from the right. Continue on the main trail, or to the left. Soon, you cross another stream. This time it's East Bush Creek. After this point the trail narrows. Within a few hundred metres you hear the dull roar of

East Bush Falls on your left. To view these pretty waterfalls, continue on the main path until it starts to descend, then scramble down the hillside to the left through thick, feathery mosses. The mosses hide the rocks and soften the profile of the hillside. If you stumble and fall, don't worry. The mosses are so thick you will have a soft landing. The waterfall is a short distance upstream. An idyllic scene greets you. A six m-high cascade plunges between rock walls into this secret garden of ferns and mosses.

Return to the path and continue down the hill to where you cross the stream to the left bank. After a short distance, cross to the right bank. Now, climb above the ravine to follow the creek downstream as it babbles its way between steep embankments. At a junction, keep left. The trail to the right leads to a cut block. You know there is yet another stream crossing when you begin to descend and swing back to the left toward East Bush Creek. Once across, the trail takes a 90 degree turn from the stream to soon intersect with the old rail bed. Continue straight ahead as far as a junction with an old cart track. Turn left onto the track. Bearing to the right takes you on the Nordegg-Beaverdam Loop. After 600 m a rough track joins from the left, but ignore it and continue straight ahead. At a fork, go to the right. Within 400 m there is yet another fork where you again turn right. As you approach Nordegg, the trail splits. Bear left and come out onto the gravel street. Turn left and walk out to the T-junction with the main street through Nordegg. Turn right to return to your vehicle.

WHAT'S IN A NAME?

East Bush Creek

East Bush Creek and Falls take their name from nearby East Bush Mountain. These unofficial names describe the mountain's former use and location.

East Bush Mountain was one of the sources of timber for the mining operations at Nordegg. All underground mines at the time required a great deal of wood to shore up the mine tunnels and roofs. Brazeau Collieries, then, obtained a timber lease from the federal government. The lease designated East Bush Mountain as Block "B," Timber Sale No. 16.

This was a bit of a mouthful and since it was located east of Nordegg, the 1,830 m-high mountain with its timber lease came to be called East Bush Mountain. The best view of East Bush Mountain is from Highway #11 above the Beaverdam Campground. East Bush is the tree-covered mountain on the west side of Martin Creek.

East Bush Falls.

3 A Nature Walk – map p. 20

Duration ~ half day
Distance ~ 5.6 km
Level of Difficulty ~ easy stroll with a stream crossing
Maximum Elevation ~ 1,340 m
Elevation Gain ~ 20 m
Map ~ 83 C/8 Nordegg

A stroll past Nordegg's historic golf course and Long Lake, a favourite nesting and staging area for many species of waterfowl, leads to Shunda Creek and beyond. For young families for whom 5.6 km is too much for little legs, there is an old roadway at the 1.5-km mark that will loop you back to your vehicle.

~

Walk along the gravel street past a row of mobile homes situated to the left. At the end of the street, continue along the track that skirts the edge of the golf course. This nine-hole course covers most of the land where the historic course was located. Continue along the track as far as the town's sewage lagoons next to the brown pump house.

Access ~ Park your vehicle at the Nordegg Heritage Centre parking lot located one km south of Highway #11 at the Nordegg turn-off. The Heritage Centre is the yellow building on the right just past the golf course clubhouse. Your trailhead is the gravel street on the north side of the Centre.

0.0	trailhead
0.3	end of cart track
0.5	No. 3 green
1.4	power line right-of-way
1.5	junction
1.6	Highway #11
1.7	AGT buried cable marker
2.1	Upper Shunda Creek Recreation Area road and footpath
2.4	Shunda Creek and bridge
3.1	Nordegg Recreation Association campground
3.2	junction
3.3	junction
3.9	junction
4.3	Highway #11
4.6	Shunda Creek
5.3	road and junction
5.6	trailhead

Walking beside Long Lake.

"Sewage lagoon" may evoke images and smells sooner forgotten, but these small ponds attract a variety of waterfowl such as mallards and blue-winged teals. At this point, keep to the edge of the fairway as you skirt Long Lake to #3 green.

Leave the golf course behind and pick up a footpath that leads along the edge of Long Lake. Despite its pretentious name, Long Lake is actually a marsh. With its shallow, languid waters it is an ideal habitat for Canada geese, mallards and other birds. Follow the trail as it swings in and out of the spruce forest and watch for the Canada geese nesting platforms in the lake and birdhouses along its shore.

The footpath ends at a power line right-of-way. Turn right and walk along the right-of-way for 100 m to a junction with another trail. If you wish to return to your vehicle at this point, turn right and follow the hard-packed track to the main road into Nordegg.

HISTORICAL FOOTNOTES

Bridge over Shunda

The first recorded mention of a bridge over Shunda Creek goes back almost 150 years.

On September 27, 1858, Sir James Hector of the Palliser Expedition broke camp near the Bighorn River, made his way along the bypass around the north end of the Brazeau Range and camped near the source of Shunda Creek. This was, according to Hector, a well-established trail. Next day he crossed Shunda Creek, perhaps near where the current highway bridge stands, by way of "a rude Indian bridge." This bridge is interesting since it is the first record of any bridge in the North West Territories west of Winnipeg. Father Albert Lacombe's famous "first" bridge at St. Albert was not built until 1862.

21

However, if you wish to continue, bear left. The trail ends at Highway #11. Cross the highway to an AGT buried cable marker. Find the old grassy roadway to the right of the marker and follow it to the Upper Shunda Creek Recreation Area gravel road. Cross the road and find the footpath in the trees. Bear left on the footpath paralleling the road as far as the bridge over Shunda Creek. Pick up the footpath again on the other side of the bridge. The footpath swings away from the road cutting through poplar and spruce forest then meadow to the Nordegg Recreation Association's campground. You have reached the southern loop of the ring road around this private campground. Bear right along the gravel road for 100 m to a trail leading to the right. Turn right onto this trail until you come to an intersection. Straight ahead takes you up Coliseum Mountain; the trail to the left leads to the Coliseum Trail Staging

Area parking lot. Turn right and follow the well-used path for about 500 m to a fork. To loop back to the trailhead turn right. To go to the left takes you on the Nordegg Ranger Station Walk. Follow the path to Highway #11. Straight ahead are the bald and imposing hills of the Brazeau Range, which overlook the swampy lands of Shunda Creek.

Cross the highway and continue the trek to the Heritage Centre by walking along the grassy abandoned roadbed. Shunda Creek poses a bit of a problem as the bridge has long since disappeared, but once across the creek it's a straightforward jaunt to the gravel road that, if you turned left, would lead to a limestone quarry. Turn right to gain access to the main road through Nordegg. Bear left along this road all the way back to the Heritage Centre and your vehicle. En route you pass the golf course and clubhouse on your right and the Coliseum Motel on your left.

FLORAFACTS

Yarrow

Scientific Name ~ *Achillea millefolium*
Other Name ~ Milfoil
Stoney Name ~ Pore Okporhnibin

Found in a wide range of ecosystems varying from grasslands to mountain passes, yarrow is identified by its flat-topped cluster of small, white flower heads atop a stem that ranges from 20-70 cm in height.

Yarrow's medicinal qualities have long been well known. The first medicinal use of the plant is accredited to Achilles, the Greek warrior, who made an ointment from the plant to treat the wounds of his soldiers during the siege of Troy 1250-1150 B.C. Since then, the yarrow plant has seen many uses. For example, its leaves and flowers were chewed by the Stoneys to make a pulp that was applied to stop external bleeding. They drank a tea made from the plant to treat everything from

internal hemorrhaging, constipation, tuberculosis, sore throats and liver trouble. This "aspirin" of plants was also boiled and drunk to relieve a woman's pain during childbirth.

WHAT'S IN A NAME?

Nordegg

Previous Names ~ Brazeau
Stoney Names ~ Watanozah (Where We Saw Loons) ~ Tasaktemna (Lake Mucky Swamp)

Nordegg is named after Martin Nordegg, who founded this mining community after he discovered coal in the area in 1910. The town was officially named Nordegg in 1914 with the arrival of the Canadian Northern Railway.

Nordegg was a planned community. Based in part on the town plan of Mount Royal in Montreal, Nordegg was laid out in a large semicircle centred around the railway station, company store, drugstore and hotel. Radiating out from this hub were the miners' cottages and other residences. "It was my intention to build a modern and pretty town," said Nordegg. He paid particular attention to the residences. "As the cottages all looked alike...I wanted to show a variance of colour...I selected soft pastels which proved very pleasing to the eye." Some cottages had sewer and water facilities. Nordegg even supplied flower seeds for the cottage gardens. Two churches, a school and a hospital were also built in town. Despite the community's isolation, living conditions were among the best of any Albertan mining town.

Shortly after World War I, the railway renamed its station Brazeau, after Brazeau Collieries Ltd., the owners and operators of the mine. The post office name, however, never changed. This caused considerable confusion. Mail addressed to Brazeau was either returned with the notation "No such post office" or redirected to Brosseau. Meanwhile, people seeking trail tickets to Nordegg were told that there was no such station. In time, the railway reverted back to the original name.

Nordegg is located near the upper reaches of Shunda Creek. This is a swampy region and forms the basis of the two Stoney names for the community, Tasaktemna (Lake Mucky Swamp) and Watanozah (Where We Saw Loons).

The miners' cottages at Nordegg, ca. 1916.
Courtesy of Provincial Archives of Alberta, #A 10,196.

4 Nordegg-Beaverdam Loop – map p. 25

Duration ~ day
Distance ~ 13.8 km
Level of Difficulty ~ long, steady stroll with some bushwhacking and a creek crossing
Maximum Elevation ~ 1,370 m
Elevation Gain ~ 40 m
Map ~ 83 C/8 Nordegg

Access ~ Park your vehicle at the Nordegg Heritage Centre parking lot located one km south of Highway #11 at the Nordegg turn-off. The Heritage Centre is the yellow building on the right just past the golf course clubhouse.

This hike has something for nearly everyone. For the amateur botanist the orchids of Beaverdam will be reason enough to take this walk. For the history buff, it's a chance to walk a kilometre or two along the historic rail bed of the Canadian Northern Railway that alone made the coal mines at Nordegg a viable operation.

~

From the Nordegg Heritage Centre walk up the main street 30 m toward the Nordegg Correctional Camp sign. Here there is an intersection with a street on your left. Turn onto this side street. By the "No Exit" sign there is a well-defined path on your right. The path leads up the slope past an old graveyard. Just past the cemetery are several footpaths joining from the left. Stay on the main, broad path on the right as it climbs slowly through spruce and poplar bush. The other paths return to the side street. At a second junction keep to the left. The trail to your right leads to East Bush Falls. At the next junction bear right along the trail. The trail to the left continues to yet another junction that can lead either back to Nordegg or to the Baldy Mountain Trail Rides headquarters. The trail rises and falls gently through the forest to another junction. Here, swing left; the trail to the right crosses the old rail bed of the Canadian Northern Railway. Continuing the walk through the open forest for another 600 m you come to yet another junction. Keep to the left to avoid joining the East Bush Falls Loop hike. Within a short distance you come to East Bush Creek.

Before crossing the creek look to your right. Above is the old rail bed, its trestle over East Bush Creek long since dismantled. You can see the flume through which the creek still runs. Cross the creek and continue along the path. You are now

0.0	trailhead
0.2	intersection
0.4	junction
0.5	junction
0.9	junction
1.1	junction
1.7	junction
1.9	East Bush Creek
2.1	junction
2.4	quarry road
3.9	junction and stream
4.0	stream
4.4	junction
4.5	junction
5.6	cutline
6.6	junction
6.7	Martin Creek and confluence with Shunda Creek
6.8	Beaverdam Recreation Area campground
6.9	bridge
7.8	Beaverdam overflow campground
7.8	Martin Creek and rail bed
10.5	first rock cut
11.1	second rock cut
11.4	third rock cut
11.5	fourth rock cut
11.6	quarry road
11.7	junction
13.8	trailhead

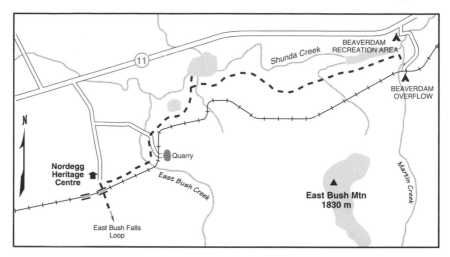

approaching the Nordegg Limestone Quarry. At the next junction keep to the left and do not go onto the quarry road. Your path soon ends at the quarry road, though. Cross the road and pick up the path on the other side. Once again you plunge into the forest, which offers occasional peeks at the surrounding mountains.

At a junction bear to the right. Or, if you are an orchid lover and do not mind an 800-m round trip to an old cabin and a beaver pond, take the road to your left. The Beaverdam area has been well named and the busy rodents have flooded much of the upper reaches of the streambed, including the area around the cabin. Of special delight are the purple-pink round-leaved orchids and the pale yellow Franklin's lady's slipper orchids, which can be found in great profusion by the edge of the beaver pond. Return to the junction where you will turn left.

Almost immediately you cross two small streams. Then bear left around the edge of the swamp until the trail becomes clearer. The trail swings to the right into the forest. At the next junction bear left to keep on the trail.

WHAT'S IN A NAME?

Martin Creek

Previous Names ~ Box Canyon Creek

Martin Creek is named after Martin Nordegg, founder of Nordegg. Locals give this stream the descriptive name of Box Canyon Creek. Their Martin Creek is a tiny rivulet that runs through the town from the old reservoir.

The original Martin Creek (the rivulet) appears as such on old townsite maps. It also appears on a 1914 topographical map. Because Nordegg was founded in 1914, it's clear that this designation has great local historical significance.

Why the name was later transferred to the larger stream to the east is unknown.

Martin Creek as seen from the Beaverdam overflow campground.

Examining some of the railway ties of the Canadian Northern Railway that carried daily coal trains and a passenger train three times a week during Nordegg's heyday in the 1920s-1950s.

The path then intersects with a cutline within 100 m. Continue straight ahead across the cutline. A short distance later you come upon what must be an old landslide. The trail winds between large, lichen-covered boulders, forcing you up, down and around. It's a pretty walk, the thick mosses softening the harsh outlines of the rocks.

The trail intersects with a cutline running due east. Turn onto the cutline. Cutlines rarely make good hiking trails and this one is no exception. Secondary growth has taken firm root making this part of the hike a bit of a slog. It also tends to be wet and boggy in places. But persevere. You are quickly approaching the Beaverdam Recreation Area as evidenced by the beaver pond that comes into view 6.4 km from the trailhead. At a junction, bear left along the cutline. Soon, you come upon the confluence of Martin Creek

and Shunda Creek just below a set of beaver dams. Shunda Creek is about 10 m wide here and is easy to cross though deep. Check out the sulphur springs that bubble out of the creekbed near the opposite side of the creek.

You are now at the Beaverdam Recreation Area campground, a pretty site just south of Highway #11 five km east of Nordegg. Picnic tables, a cookhouse and washrooms invite a long break before you start out on your return loop back to your vehicle.

Follow the road leading from the parking lot toward Highway #11. At an intersection continue straight ahead. The road on the left leads to the highway. Continuing straight ahead along the hard-packed road you cross a bridge and swing around to the south and west toward the Beaverdam overflow campground. This large, unattractive field with its gravel ring road has little to offer in the way of scenic beauty despite the excellent view of the Brazeau Range and Coliseum Mountain. Fortunately, you need not spend any time here. Rather, just before entering the campground leave the road and bear right across the open area to Martin Creek. The creek is not very wide and can be crossed with ease. On the other side is the old rail bed of the Canadian Northern Railway that was built to exploit the coal resources at Nordegg.

The tracks and ties were torn up years ago, making the old rail bed an excellent walking/bridle path. The old railway track goes through the bush for more than two km before entering the first of four dramatic rock cuts blasted out by the railway contractors, William MacKenzie and Donald Mann. While an expensive proposition, blasting was cheaper than rerouting the line up and around the hills. Certainly, the rock cuts make this part of the hike quite interesting. The first rock cut is at least 200 m long. Within 500 m, enter the second cut dominated by the red/brown weathering of the dark grey siltstone. The third cut slices through limestone, as does the fourth and last cut.

Leaving the last rock cut the rail bed soon ends at the quarry road, the one you skirted on the way to Beaverdam. This limestone quarry may be a good place to hunt for fossils, but you should not trespass as the quarry is privately owned and active. It is of some historical interest since it first opened for business just prior to World War I to provide ballast for the Canadian Northern Railway's spur line to Nordegg. All the limestone was quarried by hand, a hard, backbreaking business for both man and beast. Horses working on a

turntable were used to crush the rock. Today, the horses and hand picks have been retired in favour of trucks and shovels. Instead of being wasted in ballast this good-quality limestone is used in cattle feed and in the sugar beet industry at Taber.

Cross the quarry road bearing to the right approximately 20 m and pick up a path that will lead back uphill for a short distance to a junction. You should recognize this intersection as it is the same as the 2.1-km mark. Here, turn left onto the path and return the way you came to the trailhead at the Nordegg Heritage Centre.

FLORAFACTS

Orchids

Round-leaved orchid.

Among the most exquisite flowers to be found in the mountains are orchids. In the moist undergrowth of the forests, along streambeds or at the edge of bogs you can often find the magenta-speckled round-leaved orchid, the Franklin's lady's slipper with its egg-shaped blossom and the delicately beautiful Venus slipper orchid. These flowers have no ethnobotanical uses. In fact, the Indians knew that to pick an orchid was to kill it.

Railway Fever

The coal fields along the Bighorn River and the potential of Howse Pass as a route over the Divide made this part of the country attractive to financiers willing to back a railway through the area. The first serious evaluation of Howse Pass as a transmontane access was in 1871 when surveyors sought the best route through the Canadian Rockies for the Canadian Pacific Railway.

Between 1892 and 1912 almost a dozen charters were issued by federal and provincial governments for rail lines into the Bighorn River area coal fields and the Kootenay Plains. In 1898, the Western Alberta Railway Company proposed to build a line from the Alberta-Montana border north along the Front Ranges. The purpose of the railway was to provide western United States markets for Alberta coal producers. One of the promoters included a Calgary lawyer, future Prime Minister, R. B. Bennett. The most ambitious scheme was the Bella Coola and Fraser Lake Railway chartered in 1906. The company proposed to build a railway from Bella Coola on the B.C. coast east to Red Deer via Howse Pass.

Only one railway ever laid any track. In 1914, the Canadian Northern Railway reached Nordegg. The railway was as the result of an agreement between Martin Nordegg and the Deutsches Canada Syndicate, a German development company, and William MacKenzie and Donald Mann of the Canadian Northern Railway.

In 1908, Nordegg and two partners had chartered the Alberta and Brazeau River Railway. This railway was to access the Bighorn coal fields from Rocky Mountain House, then continue west to the Kootenay Plains and from there bear north to join the Grand Trunk Pacific Railway between Edmonton and Jasper. It was after Nordegg and his partners could not raise enough capital that he and the German development company entered into negotiations with MacKenzie and Mann. Nor-

degg paid a heavy price for the railway. In the agreement, MacKenzie and Mann controlled 45 percent of the stock in Brazeau Collieries Ltd. During World War I, Nordegg and the German company were forced from further participation in the affairs of Brazeau Collieries and the railway took full control of the coal mines.

Riding on the Canadian Northern Railway to Nordegg was an experience during the early years. The owners, MacKenzie and Mann, equipped the line according to the immediate traffic requirements and only made improvements when the traffic warranted.

Martin Nordegg learned firsthand the consequences of such an approach when he rode over the partially completed line in 1912. The road was not yet ballasted and the track was somewhat bumpy, causing a car to jump off the rails. No problem. The entire crew, in a very casual, practised and businesslike fashion, with heavy bars, lifted the car back on. The engine whistled; all aboard and the train was off—until the next curve when another car jumped the rails. Out came the crew, the car was lifted upright, the train continued until another car jumped the rails. And so on, again and again.

The engineer eventually decided to call it a day and everyone spent the night, sleeping as well as they could, in one of the freight cars. Not surprisingly with this unique mode of train travel, scheduling was not an exact science. By 1914, service had improved to the point that the train usually stayed on the tracks. But there were still a few problems. That year, a journalist from the Red Deer Advocate took the trip and reported: "the most aggravating feature is the utter impossibility of ascertaining from the railway men themselves when the trains may be expected to arrive or depart...even the telephone is generally useless to find out where the train is at any time."

5 Brazeau Lookout Trail – map p. 30

Duration ~ full day
Distance ~ 22.8 km
Level of Difficulty ~ steady walk with some long inclines
Maximum Elevation ~ 2,000 m
Elevation Gain ~ 570 m
Map ~ 83 C/8 Nordegg; 83 B/5 Saunders

At nearly 23 km this hike makes a very long day. Those people with mountain bikes will enjoy the terrain changes and long open straightaways. At the lookout there is an unobstructed view of the Brazeau Range and Eagle Mountain.

~

From the Nordegg Heritage Centre walk up the main street 30 m toward the Nordegg Correctional Camp sign. Here, there is an intersection with a street on the left. Turn onto this side street. By the "No Exit" sign there is a well-defined path to your right. The path leads up the slope past an old graveyard. Just past the cemetery there are several footpaths joining from the left. Stay on the main, broad path on the right. At a second junction keep to the right. Almost immediately you come upon and pass under an old railway trestle. Within the next 500 m a number of paths join the main trail. At the first junction, bear right. At the second junction also bear right. The trail on the left is a braid that rejoins the main trail at one km. Keep to the left at a third junction. The next junction is where the braid rejoins, so keep to the right along the main horse trail. Climb sharply to a cutline where you bear to the left.

At an intersection with a second cutline, turn right onto the cutline and follow it to the 12 Level Road that leads up from Nordegg. If you had followed the road you would have added a full kilometre to your hike. Turn left onto the road and walk up past two abandoned coal mines. At a fork past the second mine keep to the left. The right-hand fork leads to an AGT tower that offers no views. No vehicles travel past this fork since a series of ditches have been dug across the road. Continue past two cutlines and two side trails. At the next junction turn left off the gravel

Access ~ Park your vehicle at the Nordegg Heritage Centre parking lot located one km south of Highway #11 at the Nordegg turn-off. The Heritage Centre is a yellow building on the right-hand side of the street just past the golf course.

0.0	trailhead
0.2	junction
0.4	junction
0.5	junction and trestle
0.6	junction
0.8	braid
0.9	junction
1.0	braid
1.5	cutline
1.6	cutline
2.9	12 Level Road
3.3	strip mine #1
4.6	strip mine #2
5.4	junction
5.6	cutline
5.8	junction
5.9	junction
6.0	junction
6.2	cutline
6.5	East Bush Creek
6.9	pass
7.7	stream
8.1	Martin Creek
11.4	Brazeau Lookout
22.8	trailhead

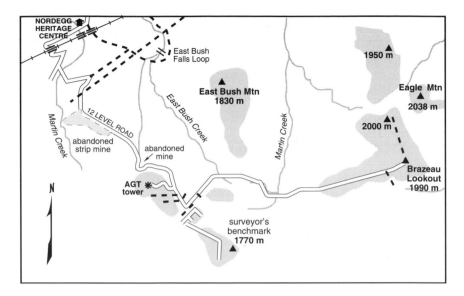

road onto a grassy, old road. Continue along this roadway, ignoring a cutline that joins on the right. This part of your walk is accompanied by wildflowers such as lupins, yarrow and paint brushes. Cross East Bush Creek and continue up over a low pass that separates the East Bush Creek and Martin Creek watersheds. Now descend slowly toward Martin Creek. The broad, grassy swath you are on is very wet with rivulets trickling their way downhill to Martin Creek. Find the horse trail that hugs the left side and follow it to the bottom of the slope. Then, swing to the right, cross the stream and find the old roadway on the other side. Within 300 m the road crosses Martin Creek and begins its climb toward the Brazeau Lookout.

You begin what is a long, and in spots, tough climb. For the next three km you ascend one ridge, then another, and yet another two, until you are finally at the top of the Brazeau Lookout. With each ridge ascent better and better views un-

fold below. Behind you to the west are the snowcaps of the Front Ranges and as you climb, the bald, folded outlines of the Brazeaus become visible on the right.

The road ends abruptly at the Lookout. Here, trail riders tether their horses and hikers take a break to enjoy the views that sweep in a nearly 360 degree arc. Eagle Mountain and its cairn on top can be seen at your one o'clock. If you wish to explore the ridge you are on, find a footpath to the left of the lookout. It leads through the bushes onto an open ridge interspersed with thickets of spruce trees. Views to the north take in the open slopes of the Brazeaus, Coliseum and Shunda Mountains. Some people may feel that they have the energy and time to cross over to Eagle Mountain. Mother Nature, though, has thwarted you, for below are sheer cliffs that run in a band along the entire length of the lookout ridge.

After puttering around, return the way you came.

WHAT'S IN A NAME?

Brazeau Range

Eagle Mountain from the Brazeau Lookout.

Previous Names ~ Near Range ~ Last or First Ridge of the Stony Mountains

The Brazeau Range is named after Joseph Brazeau, the postmaster at the fur trade post of Rocky Mountain House between 1852 and 1864. He was an American Creole from St. Louis who began his fur trade career in the United States by serving along the Yellowstone and Missouri Rivers. He later joined the Hudson's Bay Company.

Brazeau was a linguist who spoke six native languages—Blackfoot, Cree, Crow, Salteaux, Sioux and Stoney— and three non-native languages, English, French and Spanish. Sir James Hector appreciated Brazeau's assistance and spoke highly of him. Whether Hector named this range after the postmaster is unknown. However, the Palliser Expedition map of 1860 shows the "Brazeau or Near Range." Near Range is descriptive of its location, being the closest or nearest range to Rocky Mountain House.

The Brazeaus have been given other names. On an 1806 map by Jean Findley the Brazeau Range is called the "Last or First Ridge of the Stony Mountains." This again is descriptive depending upon whether you are heading east (Last Ridge) or west (First Ridge).

6 Surveyor's Benchmark – map p. 32

Duration ~ full day
Distance ~ 14.8 km
Level of Difficulty ~ steady walk on hard-packed roads
Maximum Elevation ~ 1,770 m
Elevation Gain ~ 340 m
Map ~ 83 C/8 Nordegg

A surveyor's benchmark at a high point behind Nordegg and the sweeping panorama from this vantage point are your rewards at the end of this hike. A straightforward walk, the hike is nonetheless punctuated with visits to two Brazeau Collieries' mines en route. For mountain bikers, this is a good introduction to the tangle of old roads and trails in the hills behind Nordegg.

~

From the Nordegg Heritage Centre walk up the main street 30 m toward the Nordegg Correctional Camp sign. Here, there is an intersection with a street on the left. Turn onto this side street. By the "No Exit" sign you come to a well-defined path on your right. The path leads up the slope past an old graveyard. Just past the cemetery are several footpaths joining

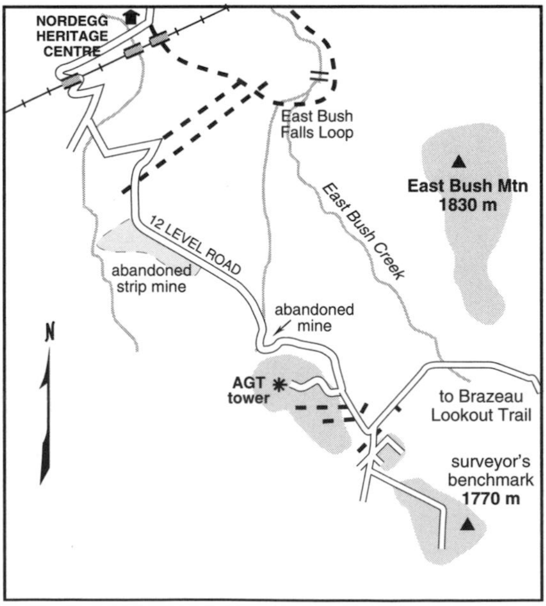

Access ~ Park your vehicle at the Nordegg Heritage Centre parking lot located one km south of Highway #11 at the Nordegg turn-off. The Heritage Centre is a yellow building on the right-hand side of the street just past the golf course.

0.0	trailhead
0.2	junction
0.4	junction
0.5	junction and trestle
0.6	junction
0.8	braid
0.9	junction
1.0	braid
1.5	cutline
1.6	cutline
2.9	12 Level Road
3.3	strip mine #1
4.6	strip mine #2
5.4	junction
5.6	cutline
5.8	junction
5.9	junction
6.0	junction
6.1	cutline
6.4	cutline and junction
6.6	junction
6.7	junction
6.8	junction
6.9	junction
7.1	junction
7.2	cutline
7.4	surveyor's benchmark
14.8	trailhead

Opposite: The benchmark.

from the left. Stay on the main, broad path on the right. At a second junction keep to the right. Almost immediately you come upon and pass under an old railway trestle. Within the next 500 m a number of paths join the main trail. At the first junction, bear right. At the second junction, also bear right. The trail on the left is a braid that rejoins the main trail at one km. Keep to the left at a third junction. The next junction is where the braid rejoins, so keep to the right along the main horse trail. Climb sharply to a cutline where you bear left.

At an intersection with a second cutline, turn right onto the cutline and follow it to the 12 Level Road that leads up to the twelfth level in the mine from Nordegg. If you had followed the road you would have added a full kilometre to your hike. Walk along this wide, hard-packed gravel road to reach two of the Brazeau Collieries' mine sites. The first and largest is an open pit where coal that lay close to the surface was surface mined. Spend a little time exploring this open pit mine. A viewpoint overlooking the workings can be gained from an old roadway on your right at the lower end of the mine. The workings

are not a pretty sight because open pit mining has changed the profiles of the mountainsides. In open pit mining, all vegetation is first stripped and then fleets of trucks and shovels move in to dig out and remove the coal. Today, abandoned open pits have to meet reclamation standards, but in the 1950s when the Nordegg mine closed there were no regulations in place to enforce the contouring and seeding of old open pit mines. Neither of the two sites that you visit along 12 Level Road has been reclaimed. Nature, though, has a way of reclaiming what is her own. On the bench below the viewpoint you can see where poplars have taken root.

Continue walking up 12 Level Road to the second mine. This mine appears much smaller than the first. Brazeau Collieries began an open pit mine here, but soon abandoned this strategy when the coal seams plunged deep into the mountainside. Unwilling to abandon what was a good seam, Brazeau switched its operations from an open pit mine to a traditional underground mine. To access the best view of these workings walk up the road 400 m to the top of the mine. An old road on the left takes you along the lip of the open pit for approximately 100 m where it connects with a cutline.

Return to the road and continue climbing to a fork. The right-hand fork leads up to an AGT tower where there are no views, so keep to the left. Energetic souls have dug a series of trenches along this older road to discourage vehicular traffic. Continue walking on this road past two cutlines and two side trails. At a junction with an old grassy road on your left (it leads to the Brazeau Lookout) continue straight ahead and downhill past two more cutlines to a crossroads. Continue straight ahead ignoring the roads to the left and right. The main road slopes downhill.

Now you begin to gain a little elevation. At a fork, bear left and push uphill 100 m to another fork where you turn right. Just beyond a large meadow on the right you climb a low ridge where you can catch sneak views of the First Ranges. Within the next few hundred metres there are three more junctions; bear right at each of them. Finally, a short, steep pull brings you to a cutline

near the top of the hill. To catch a beautiful vista of the Rockies jaunt to the right along the cutline for 20 m to a viewpoint. Below, the dense carpet of evergreens is broken by the Forestry Trunk Road as it snakes its way south, while the snowcaps along the national park boundary march along the horizon. To view the less rugged slopes of the Brazeau Range, return to the road, cross it staying on the cutline. Another 20 m brings you to another viewpoint. In midsummer, the hillside is sprinkled with colourful Indian paint brushes, wild strawberries, yarrow, showy locoweed and yellow hedysarum.

It's only a short scamper up the road to the top of the hill. With a 360 degree sweep that takes in Shunda and Coliseum mountains on your left and the jagged peaks of the Rockies on your right, you can understand why surveyors chose this hilltop to base their surveys in this part of the Brazeau Range. The brass benchmark can be found at the base of the surveyor's stake.

Return the way you came.

Fine coal slack tailings are all that remain of this large open pit mine.

HISTORICAL FOOTNOTES

Brazeau Collieries

Today the Brazeau Collieries mine site is quiet except for visitors who can take daily guided tours.

The Nordegg coal mines, incorporated in 1910, were owned and operated by Brazeau Collieries Ltd. Its President was Sir William MacKenzie, who represented the Canadian Northern Railway. Martin Nordegg, representing the German development company, was the Vice-President.

The German company was responsible for supplying coal, while the railway was to buy it. Mine development began in 1911. By the time the CNR line reached Nordegg in 1913, 136,000 tonnes of mined coal awaited shipment. Shipments began at a rate of 450-545 tonnes of coal daily, and by 1915 the Brazeau Collieries was the second most important producer in Alberta.

The mine was developed originally to supply coal to the Canadian Northern Railway. Production depended upon the railway's requirements and these varied considerably. The main business of the railway was to haul grain to the lakehead. In the spring when crop movement started, demand for coal was heavy, but slackened as the grain movement slowed. Production peaked during the early 1920s, but during the Depression employment declined to 250 men and production to 150,000 tonnes annually.

During World War II, production increased, but by 1942, production figures began to drop as the railway began to convert to diesel-powered locomotives. Between 1949 and 1954, coal production dropped by one-third. For most of 1950-1951 production ceased due to a fire that destroyed the briquet plant. Financed by the province of Alberta, a new $2 million plant was built. Rising transportation costs, and conversion of the railways to alternate energy resources eventually resulted in 1954 in the lay off of 221 men, and the cessation of mining operations a year later. Since the province was not repaid its loan, it was named the receiver of the plant and town.

7 Coliseum Mountain – map p. 37

Duration ~ full day
Distance ~ 17 km
Degree of Difficulty ~ steady climb followed by an easy stroll
Maximum Elevation ~ 2,040 m
Elevation Gain ~ 680 m
Map ~ 83 C/8 Nordegg; 83 C/9 Wapiabi Creek

One of the most popular day hikes in the Nordegg area, Coliseum Mountain provides significant elevation gain and a grand 360 degree panorama that accompanies you the entire length of its spine along the top of the "coliseum." At the lookout, there is a pile of stone rubble—all that remains of the first mountain fire lookout in Alberta.

~

Access ~ Park your vehicle at the Coliseum Trail Staging Area parking lot. The parking lot is reached from the Upper Shunda Recreation Area road located one km west of Nordegg on Highway #11. Follow the Upper Shunda road approximately one km and take the first turn-off to the right. There is a fork in the road 500 m past the turn-off. Keep on the main road by going straight ahead. Within metres you will arrive at the Coliseum Trail parking lot.

0.0 trailhead
0.2 junction
1.3 junction
1.5 braid
3.4 rocky slope
3.9 meadow and campsite
6.2 junction
8.5 Coliseum Mountain lookout
17.0 trailhead

The "cap" of Coliseum Mountain from the ridge.

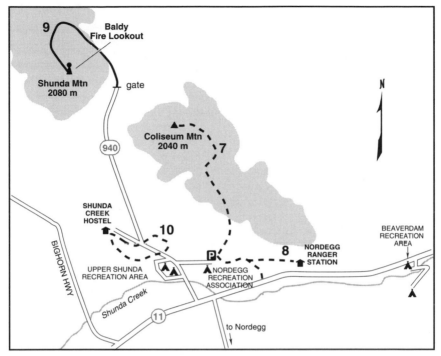

The trail begins innocently enough as a wide slash through the spruce and pine forest. Within a short distance of the parking lot there is a junction with two other trails. Keep to the left. The trail to the right leads to the Nordegg Recreation Association camping area and the trail straight ahead goes to the Nordegg Ranger Station. From this junction, begin your slow climb upwards along what is a wide, well-defined trail. The trail climbs relentlessly offering occasional glimpses of the mountains of the Brazeau Range, but for the first several kilometres you will be enshrouded in the cool shadows of a spruce forest. Nevertheless, on a warm day, this part of the hike can be difficult and you can easily quaff a full litre of water. If you forgot to fill your canteen, the only water along this trail can be found near the second junction. Here, a narrow foot-path to the right leads 50 m to a stream. Return to the main trail and continue to climb.

Coliseum's popularity is such that you can expect to meet other hikers as well as mountain bikers, equestrians and quads. Evidence of this trail's heavy use becomes clear when you reach a braid. From here, the trail switches 11 times up this, the steepest section. Those people impatient with this gradual ascent have cut a broad path straight up the hillside, bisecting the switchbacks. The folly of this can be seen in the erosion that is scarring the mountainside.

Finally, you break out of the forest giving you, for the first time, a close-up view of the rocky cliffs above and to your right. Within several hundred metres you reach a welcome meadow near the top of the south end of the mountain. Several campsites dot the meadow. Here there is

37

also a fork. The trail to the right leads to the highest point on Coliseum Mountain. The trail to the left leads to a rocky cliff and scree slope that you must cross to gain access to the meadows on the upper spine. Once across the scree the trail traverses an undulating meadow interspersed with spruce copses. Terrific views on either side of the trail assure you that the climb was worth it. You soon realize, too, that the "cap" is a long way away. It's a grand walk across the meadows around the curving ridge of the "coliseum" to the remains of a 1920s fire lookout that used to perch on top of the "cap" on the extreme north end of the mountain. Forestry Rangers discovered the view from Coliseum as early as 1914 when they first climbed this imposing mountain, but it wasn't until 1925 that a fire lookout, the first in the province, was built on Coliseum Mountain.

There is very little left of the lookout, which at the time it was built, "set a new standard of efficiency and economy of construction." Unfortunately, no description of this mountain lookout survives. Some people in Nordegg remember climbing up Coliseum to deliver mail to the Ranger stationed in the lookout. Their reward for the long climb up was to take an exhilarating shortcut down from the "cap" through the scree and rock. Today, a crumbling cement foundation and a tangle of old telephone wires are all that remain to tell the story of the first mountain fire lookout in the province.

After enjoying the views and a rest, return the way you came.

WHAT'S IN A NAME?

Coliseum Mountain

Dominating the skyline by Nordegg is the 2,040 m-high Coliseum Mountain. The "coliseum" proper is the cirque on the west side of the ridge with its attendant tower or "cap" to the north. The best spot to see these descriptive features are along Highway #11 west of the Forestry Trunk Road.

Martin Nordegg claimed that he climbed the mountain in 1913. The first map showing Coliseum may be Sir James Hector's enlarged sketch of the route taken by the Palliser expedition in 1858. The map shows an unnamed mountain with a curving ridge and a peak at the end on the north side of Shunda Creek.

The Stoney name for this mountain is just as descriptive. They call it Yahareskin: the Mountain with the Cap On.

Coliseum Mountain from Highway #11.

HISTORICAL FOOTNOTES

The Life of a Forest Ranger

Trailing his pack horses, this Ranger was on the trail for weeks at a time. Courtesy of the Department of Environmental Protection.

Loneliness, fear of bear attacks and hostile poachers, rivers in flood, and at times, raging forest fires were all part of a day's work of a Forest Ranger. The job was anything but glamorous. While their primary function was fire control, Rangers also cruised timber, checked on logging operations, built bridges and stopover cabins, cut fireguards to protect settlements and constructed trails.

And for their trouble, they received wages varying from $3.00 a day in 1903 to $75.00 in 1911.

Until the 1950s, Forest Rangers patrolled their territories on horseback. Although they travelled as lightly as possible, Rangers found that they still required several packhorses to carry their axes, climbing spurs, binoculars, food, tent, bedroll, extra clothing and radio equipment. When forestry roads and helicopters made the horse redundant in the 1950s, it was with some sadness that the Rangers said goodbye to their trusty companions. "Things had to progress, but it was sad to see," said one old-time Ranger.

Communication between the Ranger and the Ranger Station was, of course, critical. The first form of communication was the "treeline telephone system," so-called because the Rangers had to string a base wire telephone line from tree to tree through insulators. Since cabins were about 24 km apart, each Ranger had hundreds of kilometres of telephone line to keep in repair. The first radio system received mixed reviews from the Rangers out on patrol. On one hand, fires could be reported to the forestry station in Nordegg immediately upon detection. On the other hand, the short wave radios weighed 80 pounds and were awkward to pack on a horse. These early radios could only transmit, so the Ranger had no way of knowing whether the Ranger Station had received his message. Later, when two-way radios were introduced, the Rangers had to unpack the equipment three times a day to report at prearranged times. At forestry lookouts such as that on Coliseum, communication between the lookout and the Ranger Station was by telephone. When FM radiotelephones were installed in 1953 the need for telephone lines was eclipsed and the lines were cut.

8 Nordegg Ranger Station Walk – map p. 41

Duration ~ half day
Distance ~ 6.6 km
Level of Difficulty ~ easy stroll with some light bushwhacking
Maximum Elevation ~ 1,380 m
Elevation Gain ~ 40 m
Map ~ 83 C/8 Nordegg

This hike is ideal for families or for those who want to stretch their legs on a warm day without getting too hot. The trail through the cool forest is an appropriate introduction to the Nordegg Ranger Station and the important work of the Forest Rangers. On weekdays at the Station, you may purchase maps and ask questions about the area. From here, the trail leads to Shunda Creek and its beaver dams where you can enjoy a picnic lunch.

~

From the Coliseum Trail Staging Area sign, head east along a broad trail that doubles as a bridle path. A quick jaunt brings you to a major intersection. The trail on your right leads to the group campground of the Nordegg Recreation Association; the trail to the left leads up Coliseum Mountain. Continue straight ahead to enter a cool, mixed forest of spruce and poplar. If you are hiking here in late spring or early summer, wild roses sprinkle the borders of the pathway. At a fork, keep to the left to continue straight ahead; the trail on the right leads down to Highway #11. From the fork, climb slowly as the trail winds its way around the south flank of Coliseum Mountain. Then you dip gently through deep forest, pass a junction on your right and come out on the backside of the Alberta Transportation gravel yard. Released from the darkness of the forest, wildflowers such as Indian paintbrushes, daisies and purple clover clamber for the sun's attention. You immediately jump across a small stream that is your only source of water on this part of the hike. The trail reenters the forest. A 90 degree turn to the north some 300 m beyond the gravel yard is short-lived, for within 30 m the trail again jogs to the east. Suddenly, you arrive at the Nordegg Ranger Station.

Access ~ Park your vehicle at the Coliseum Trail Staging Area parking lot. The parking lot is reached from the Upper Shunda Recreation Area road located one km west of Nordegg on Highway #11. Follow the Upper Shunda road approximately one km and take the first turn-off to the right. There is a fork in the road 500 m past the turn-off. Keep on the main road by going straight ahead. Within metres you will arrive at the Coliseum Trail parking lot.

0.0	trailhead
0.2	intersection
0.9	junction
1.3	junction and Alberta Transportation yard
2.3	houses behind the Nordegg Ranger Station
2.5	Nordegg Ranger Station
2.7	Highway #11
3.0	turn-off to Shunda Creek
3.2	campsite
3.3	meadow
4.7	stream
4.9	Alberta Transportation yard
5.3	main path
6.6	trailhead

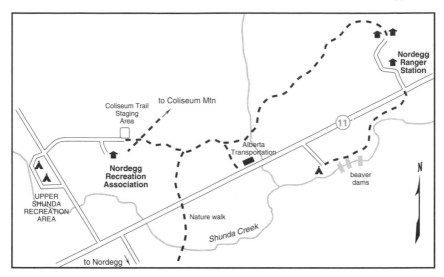

You actually come out between two of the upper houses in the Ranger Station complex. Follow the road down to the station. During regular office hours, you may purchase maps and get information from the station staff. Continue to Highway #11. Cross the highway, turn right and head west along the highway right-of-way for 100 m. Here, the right-of-way narrows due to a shallow ravine. On the west side of the ravine turn away from the highway and bushwhack for 40 m down to Shunda Creek. Turn right in the mossy underfooting and follow a well-trodden trail upstream past a series of beaver dams. Within a short distance you come upon the informal campsites of keen fishermen. This fishermen's delight makes an excellent resting spot before continuing your loop back to your vehicle.

Follow the old road as it leaves Shunda Creek and heads back to Highway #11. Before reaching the highway it swings sharply to the left and westward before disappearing in the grass. Continue westward. At a small stream, which corresponds to the stream at 1.8 km, cross the highway and walk past the entrance to the Alberta Transportation yard. At the edge of the cut grass on the west side of the yard entrance there is a low rise. Go up the rise and follow a game trail that parallels the three-string chain link fence. The game trail leads past the gravel yard where it will then swing slightly to the left to intersect with the main trail. This junction corresponds with 1.3 km. Bear left along the main pathway and return to your trailhead.

HISTORICAL FOOTNOTES

The Alberta Forestry Service

Fire! The very word caused early homesteaders and cattlemen to blanch. So, in 1882 and 1883 the federal government established timber agents in Edmonton and Calgary respectively. After the formation of the province of Alberta in 1905, the federal government retained control over the province's natural resources, including its forests.

The Dominion Forestry Branch fought for and gradually won expenditures for qualified stable staff, lookouts, trails, cabins and tool caches. This growth was the result of the Forest Reserve and Parks Act that set aside 7,400,000 hectares for the Rocky Mountains Forest Reserve. Ranger districts were set up in the reserve with each having a Forest Ranger who lived in and patrolled a district. Later, the Reserve was divided into five administrative districts called Forests. The Clearwater Forest with its headquarters in Rocky Mountain House was responsible for more than 6,000,000 hectares of foothills and mountain forests. A Ranger Station was built at Shunda in 1916. The present station at Nordegg was constructed in 1963.

On October 1, 1930 responsibility for all natural resources was transferred from Ottawa to the province of Alberta, which then set up the Alberta Forest Service (AFS). In the late 1940s the joint federal and provincial Eastern Rockies Forest Conservation Board was established for the three Forests, Crowsnest, Bow River and Clearwater. There was now a new emphasis on reforestation, training of initial attack crews and a general upgrading of communication equipment. Aircraft patrol was reinstituted in 1950 and a FM radio/telephone system was installed at all mountain lookouts and fire towers. In 1951 the AFS started a Forestry Training School at Kananaskis to provide a 12-week intensive training for its ranger staff. Its success led to opening a new Forest Technology School in Hinton in 1960. One of the first new courses was the training of Indians and Metis as fire fighters. With a recent appreciation for the economic opportunities offered by the timber reserves, the work done by the AFS has been given a high profile.

Nordegg Ranger Station, no date. Department of Environmental Protection, #10610.

9 Baldy Fire Lookout – map p. 37

Duration ~ half day
Distance ~ 8 km
Level of Difficulty ~ steady climb along a fire road
Maximum Elevation ~ 2,080 m
Elevation Gain ~ 460 m
Map ~ 83 C/8 Nordegg; 83 C/9 Wapiabi Creek

A 360 degree panorama that takes in both the forest-carpeted foothills and the snowcaps of the Rocky Mountains is your reward for this short, steep walk up a fire road. As well, a visit with the lookout person is a bonus to this pleasant half-day hike.

~

From the gate, walk up the steep road, as it switches through old-growth spruce forest dripping with old man's beard. As you climb, better and better views of the foothills and the large area that this fire lookout oversees unfold before you. Sprinkled along open slopes and cuts are hairy golden asters, the dainty white draba and the showy purple fleabane.

At 1.8 km from the trailhead, the road swings left along the edge of Shunda Mountain, giving you an unobstructed view below of the chequerboard of block timber cuts. Past here, the road

Access ~ Turn north off Highway #11 onto the Upper Shunda Recreation Area road located 300 m west of Nordegg. Drive 2.2 km to a fork. Take the right fork and drive 4.4 km to another fork. Here, bear left and continue for 1.2 km to the Baldy Fire Lookout gate.

0.0	trailhead
2.5	junction
4.0	Baldy Fire lookout
8.0	trailhead

Friendly marmots at the fire lookout are interested in what you bring for lunch.

flattens a little for several hundred metres. At a fork in the road, turn left. Fifty m later you come upon a rainfall collection station in the middle of a grassy meadow. Return to the main road and continue to climb. Finally, the road breaks out of the spruce forest and onto the slope immediately below the summit of Shunda Mountain. Cooling breezes are a welcome relief on a hot, sunny day. From here, the road swings to the right around the summit before switching to the top. Views to the west as far as Abraham Lake, the Front and Siffleur Ranges and the magnificent glacier on Mount Loudon inspire you to continue to the top.

The easy accessibility of the Baldy Lookout has made it a popular destination for hikers, quad riders and mountain bikers. More than 1,000 people visit this lookout each season. Many lookout personnel spend their spare time sketching, writing or engaged in arts and crafts. A possible purchase from the lookout person at Baldy will complete your pleasant visit. Before leaving, do not forget to ask to sign the guest book.

Baldy Lookout takes its name from the local unofficial descriptive name for the mountain. Its official name is taken from Shunda Creek below.

The bald grassy summit of Shunda Mountain is worth a stroll. In early summer, the hilltop is literally a carpet of dainty, vibrant blue forget-me-nots. The sweeping panorama will entice you to linger awhile before returning to the trailhead the way you came.

HISTORICAL FOOTNOTES

Fire Detection

The Alberta Forest Service (AFS) prides itself on its policy to anticipate fires rather than just react to them. Lightning strikes account for approximately half of the fires that break out in Alberta's Green Zone. People cause most of the other half of the 1,000 fires that occur annually in the province.

Fire detection at mountain lookouts is done manually. A heavy brass protractor, called a fire finder, gives the coordinants of a fire. These coordinants are telephoned to the closest Ranger Station. Most mountain lookouts also have a rifle scope mounted on top of the fire finder for the lookout personnel to better differentiate between smoke, dust and ground fog. You will also find a good pair of binoculars at any lookout.

The AFS believes in an aggressive initial attack on a fire to prevent it spreading. When a fire does break out, the AFS determines not only its location, but its size and behaviour. Most fires are attacked immediately by a five-member initial attack crew. Water bombers are also available for first strikes to stop or slow the fire until the crew arrives. If a fire escapes, an assessment is made of the values at risk. In remote areas the fire may be allowed to play out its traditional role in the forest ecosystem. In other areas, such as Nordegg, a crew of 25 men is initially placed on standby near the scene of the fire. A Level 5 escaped fire calls for an all-out effort, which will see bulldozers, helicopters, water bombers and hundreds of specially-trained men, many of whom are natives, thrown against the inferno. Fire detection is not the only responsibility of lookout personnel. They also report twice a day to the closest Ranger Station local weather conditions and other meteorological data.

Baldy Lookout replaced the fire lookout on Coliseum Mountain in the 1960s.

10 The Hostel Hike – map p. 45

Duration ~ one hour
Distance ~ 3.4 km
Level of Difficulty ~ easy stroll with optional bushwhacking
Maximum Elevation ~ 1,350 m
Elevation Gain ~ 10 m
Map ~ 83 C/8 Nordegg

For those staying at the Shunda Creek Hostel or at the nearby Upper Shunda Recreation Area campground, this short walk makes a pleasant early-morning or after-dinner constitutional.

~

From your vehicle there is a broad swath through the long grass heading south toward Nordegg. Follow it through the willows to a fork. Keep to the left to begin your circle loop. This is a pretty walk through the swamps for which Shunda Creek was, and still is, known. When you come to a T-junction you can swing to the right if you want to go to a campground on a dry island beside Shunda Creek. To continue along the hike bear to the left and head toward the spruce trees. Your path becomes an old road that passes through open

Access ~ Park your vehicle in the meadow just below the Shunda Creek Hostel parking lot. To get to the Hostel, turn north off Highway #11 onto the Upper Shunda Recreation Area road 300 m west of Nordegg. Drive 2.2 km to a fork. Take the left fork and continue on the main gravel road for one km. At an intersection turn left and go 150 m down to the Hostel and your trailhead.

0.0	trailhead
0.2	fork
0.3	T-junction
1.2	Upper Shunda Recreation Area road
1.3	junction
1.5	junction
1.6	junction
2.4	Baldy Lookout fire road
3.4	trailhead

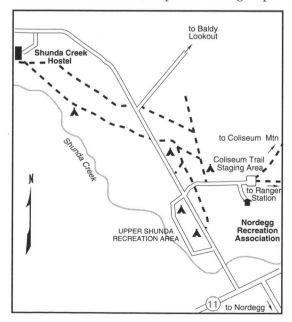

pine and spruce forest en route to the Upper Shunda Recreation Area road. When you reach the road, turn right and walk approximately 30 m to a trail on the other side of the road.

The trail plunges into the forest. Within 100 m there is a junction with a footpath on the right. Keep to the left and continue along what is now an ATV track. There are several braids in the track that soon all rejoin. The track climbs a little, swinging toward Shunda Mountain as you begin the back side of the loop. At another junction, turn left onto a cutline; the trail to the right goes to an informal campsite and beyond that to the Coliseum Trail Staging Area access road. Continue along the cutline approximately 100 m and take a foot-path on your left. This well-used blazed trail takes you into an old-growth forest area where old man's beard drips from the branches of the spruce trees. When you encounter a main gravel road (the Baldy Lookout access road) turn left and within 20 m you arrive at the Upper Shunda Recreation Area road.

To regain the trailhead you can turn right onto the road and walk back to the Shunda Creek Hostel. If you are feeling adventurous and want to avoid the hard-packed road, cross the road and bushwhack to the bottom of the slope. Continue bushwhacking until you reach a marshy meadow. Swing to the right, keeping the marsh on your left until you can see the Hostel and your vehicle.

HISTORICAL FOOTNOTES

Big Fish Trail

The Big Fish Trail is the Stoney name for the major route they followed when visiting relatives west of Edmonton and trading with northern Alberta Indians. This was from the Nordegg area north toward the Blackstone River, then on to the Athabasca. This may also be the route along which, beginning around 1820, the Stoneys began to filter south from the Athabasca region to the upper North Saskatchewan.

The southern terminus of the Big Fish Trail is near Nordegg where it intersects the Brazeau bypass. The bypass through Shunda Gap was part of the east-west trail used by Indians, fur traders and explorers to go around The Gap when travelling up the North Saskatchewan. The old bypass route follows the north side of the southwest fork of Shunda Creek to near the Alberta Forest Service houses west of Nordegg, then on toward Shunda Lake.

Along a portion of the Big Fish Trail a number of historic Stoney campsites have been found. One of these is located at the Upper Shunda Creek Recreation Area. The general route of the trail from this campsite is said to be west to the forestry trunk road, then north along the road up Shunda Creek, down Lookout Creek and on to the Blackstone.

Prehistoric sites of an unknown age coincide with two of the historic Stoney hunting camps. They probably represent fall-spring base hunting camps for wood bison and elk in the Shunda basin, and bighorn sheep and mountain goats on the Brazeau Range. One of the sites may have also been a favoured spot for fishing in Shunda Creek.

WHAT'S IN A NAME?

Shunda Creek

Previous Names ~ Mire Creek ~ Miry Creek ~ Jaco's Brook ~ North Brook Stoney Names ~ Sinda Waptan (Mire Creek) ~ Big Fish Creek ~ Fishing Creek

Shunda Creek is named after the swamps that characterize the stream's upper reaches near Nordegg. Shunda is a corruption of the Stoney "Sinda," which means mire, muskeg or swamp.

David Thompson and Alexander Henry, in approximately 1810, called the stream Jaco's Brook. Jaco was a nickname for Jacques. Jacques or Jaco might have been Jacques Cardinal, the horse keeper at Rocky Mountain House fur trade post. One of his duties was to take the horses to the Kootenay Plains in preparation for the fur brigades crossing Howse Pass, so he would have been familiar with the route around the Brazeau Range via the creek. Or Jaco might refer to Jaco Finlay who, in 1806, blazed the trail for David Thompson to cross the Rocky Mountains.

North Brook was another name David Thompson called this creek. North being the direction from which the stream enters the North Saskatchewan River.

In 1858 Sir James Hector of the Palliser Expedition recorded Mire Creek on his map. He also called the stream Miry Creek. On September 28, 1858, he recorded crossing Miry Creek by way of "a rude Indian bridge." Locals in the Nordegg area still perpetuate the latter name.

Despite these earlier names, the most common name until 1912 was Mire Creek,

when the name was changed officially to Shunda Creek. A 1914 topographical map shows both Shunda and Mire Creek, with Mire Creek running from Coliseum Mountain to the North Saskatchewan River and Shunda Creek as a tributary that joins Mire Creek just below Nordegg.

The stream has always been a popular fishing area. Hence two other Stoney names, Big Fish and Fishing Creek.

Shunda Creek. Courtesy of Alfred Falk

47

Shunda Creek Hostel

The Shunda Creek Hostel near Nordegg. Inset: Building the hostel in the early 1980s. Courtesy of Alfred Falk.

The Shunda Creek Hostel is the result of almost 40 years hostelling activity in the area. Their original purpose was to provide comfortable, primitive and supervised shelters attracting youth from around the world, thereby providing a focus for international communication. In Canada, the first Youth Hostel was built in 1933 at Bragg Creek near Calgary.

As the organization grew, regional districts were established. In 1960 during a camping trip on the Kootenay Plains, an agreement was reached with hostellers from the Mountain Region, based in Calgary, to establish a North West Region based in Edmonton. It was this Edmonton group that established the first hostel near Nordegg. A miner's cabin from Nordegg was moved close to the site of the current hostel. In the mid-1960s, this cabin was named the Luke Condron Memorial Hostel. Condron, who had died at an early age of cancer, was a very active association member and instrumental in establishing the Nordegg facility.

The miner's cabin apparently made a poor hostel, so the association began searching for a replacement. They purchased the Upper Saskatchewan Ranger Station building located on the Abraham Flats. However, because of the prohibitive cost, they did not move it to Nordegg, so it remained abandoned by the shores of Abraham Lake until about 1977 when Alberta Forestry burned it down.

The present log building was built with contract and volunteer labour to replace the Condron Hostel. Called the Shunda Creek Hostel, it opened to hikers, bikers and world travellers in the mid-1980s.

11 Fish Lake Loop – map p. 54

Duration ~ two hours
Distance ~ 4.7 km
Level of Difficulty ~ easy stroll
Maximum Elevation ~ 1,370 m
Elevation Gain ~ 10 m
Map ~ 83 C/8 Nordegg

When the sunlight sparkles and dances off the blue waters of Shunda Lake, otherwise known as Fish Lake, there can be nothing more pleasant than strolling along the lake's shoreline. If you are taking this walk in the evening, you can watch the fish jump and the loons dive for their supper.

~

From the trailhead, bear to the right toward the cookhouse and cross the small wooden bridge to begin your loop around the lake. Fishermen trying their luck from the shore or from boats confirm why this body of water is known locally as Fish Lake. Within a few metres there is a fork in the trail. Keep to the left. The path to the right is the end of the Fish Lake Resource Management Trail loop. A half a kilometre later you come to another fork. Again, keep to the left to continue along the lake's edge. The trail to the right is the beginning of the aforementioned loop.

This walk is very popular and as a consequence is well defined the entire way, even after it leaves the immediate lakeshore and dips a little into the forest. Here, the trail swings sharply away from the water as it skirts the marshy entrance to the lake. Cross a cutline at the top of the lake. The trail begins to lead into the forest but you soon come to a fork. To complete the loop, bear a sharp left and recross the cutline. The trail to the right leads either to Goldeye Lake or Black Canyon Creek.

You are now on the back side of the loop. This part of the trail can be wet and some parts of the path have a boardwalk across the wetter sections. You finally leave the forest behind and arrive at a wide slash that is a firebreak around Frontier Lodge. At the far side of the firebreak there is a fork with a sign for the Lake Loop trail and another for Frontier Lodge. Bear left and go down the slope toward the lake and a road. When you reach the

Access ~ Turn south off Highway #11 at the Fish Lake Recreation Area sign located four km west of Nordegg. Follow the Fish Lake road for one km to a junction. Turn right and drive 200 m down the gravel road and park right of the boat launch at the Recreation Area parking lot.

0.0	trailhead
0.1	bridge
0.2	junction
0.7	junction
1.8	cutline
1.9	fork
2.0	cutline
2.5	boardwalk
2.6	firebreak
2.7	junction
2.8	road
3.3	T-junction
3.4	T-junction
3.5	firebreak
3.8	campground road
4.4	bridge
4.6	boat launch and dock
4.7	trailhead

A fisherman continues to try his luck even as the sun sets. Courtesy of Chris Hanstock.

road swing right onto it. A number of footpaths from Frontier Lodge to the lake cross the road. Ignore them and stay on the road as far as a T-junction and a sign for the Lake Loop. Turn left toward the lake. At the lake's edge, there is another T-junction. Bear to the right onto a footpath. You recross the Frontier Lodge firebreak before you come out onto the Fish Lake Recreation Area campground. Campsite #19 is on your right. Bear left along the campsite road for 15 m and find a footpath that leads to the right along the lakeshore. Near the end of the loop, cross a small bridge. Cut across the parking area to reconnect with the lakeshore trail near campsite #6. Continue past the boat launch and dock back to your vehicle.

WHAT'S IN A NAME?

Shunda Lake

Previous Names ~ Fish Lake

Shunda Lake is named after Shunda Creek. The lake is one of the sources of the creek.

The colloquial name "Fish Lake" is still in some local use. This name has never been made official because the name Fish Lake had already been claimed by a lake near Hardisty. Nevertheless, Alberta Forestry perpetuates the local name in its designation of the Fish Lake Recreation Area.

For years the swamps, lakes and streams in the upper Shunda area were a source of some confusion to travellers and geographers. A 1914 topographic map shows Shunda Creek connecting two nonexistent lakes just west of Nordegg with what appears to be present day Shunda Lake, which in turn, is shown to have a nonexistent connection with Goldeye Lake to the northwest.

The area has been popular with campers for years. Fifty years ago during the summers, many young single miners, rather than continuing to pay for their accommodation in Nordegg, pitched their tents at Fish Lake.

12 Shunda-Goldeye Connector – map p. 54

This is a 4.5 km-long connecting trail between Shunda and Goldeye Lakes. The nine-km round trip is an easy stroll.

~

At the 1.9 km junction on the Fish Lake Loop, bear right and continue into the forest. Taking a sharp left at this point continues the Fish Lake Loop. You quickly pass two cutlines before coming to a small meadow. Continue forward and slightly to the right through the meadow. The trail out the left side of the meadow goes to Black Canyon Creek. The trail leaves the forest at a power line right-of-way near power pole #67. Bear right along the right-of-way and continue past a cutline to a junction. Turn right, cross Highway #11 and continue to follow the right-of-way until you reach the Goldeye Lake Recreation Area road. Turn left and follow the road to the Recreation Area sign. Behind the sign is a footpath that leads to campsite #31. Follow the road out of the campsite area to the main Recreation Area road. Find the footpath across the road and follow it down to the Recreation Area parking lot beside Goldeye Lake.

Access ~ The connecting trail begins at the 1.9 km junction on the Fish Lake Loop and ends at the Goldeye Lake Recreation Area parking lot.

1.9	junction Fish Lake Loop
2.2	meadow and junction
3.1	power line right-of-way
3.2	cutline
3.7	junction
3.8	Highway #11
3.9	road to Goldeye Lake Recreation Area
4.2	Recreation Area sign and campsite #31
4.3	footpath
4.5	Goldeye Lake Recreation Area parking lot

HISTORICAL FOOTNOTES

Frontier Lodge

Frontier Lodge is a Christian wilderness camp first conceived by Rev. Louis Peskett of the Youth for Christ movement in the 1960s. Originally built as a youth camp, Frontier Lodge now offers a variety of programmes to anyone interested in whitewater canoeing, rock climbing and rappelling, mountain cycling and touring, day hiking, backpacking, cross-country skiing, ice climbing and snow camping. If you are female and want to test your skills and endurance in several areas, you may be interested in the "Women Of Steel" course. For five days you can climb and rappel, mountain bike, canoe and finally complete a two-day backpack.

The Lodge hosts a fat tire festival every July known as the Black Mountain Challenge, which sees cyclists pitting themselves against time and a variety of trail conditions.

The entrance to Frontier Lodge.

13 Fish Lake Resource Management Trail – map p. 54

Duration ~ one hour
Distance ~ 2.2 km
Level of Difficulty ~ easy stroll
Maximum Elevation ~ 1,380 m
Elevation Gain ~ 20 m
Map ~ 83 C/8 Nordegg

Interested in seeing a stand of 275 year-old trees? Or learning about the mammals and birds that inhabit the forest? This short hike will answer many questions that you may have. The kids, too, will enjoy this educational walk. Just pick up an Alberta Forestry brochure at the dispenser at the beginning of the trail.

~

From the trailhead bear to the right toward the cookhouse, then cross the small wooden bridge at the lake's outlet. Within a few metres there is a fork in the pathway. Keep to the left. This is the beginning of the Fish Lake Resource Management Trail. The path to the right is the end of the Fish

Access ~ Turn south off Highway #11 at the Fish Lake Recreation Area sign located four km west of Nordegg. Follow the Fish Lake road for one km to a junction. Turn right and drive 200 m down the gravel road and park right of the boat launch at the Recreation Area parking lot.

0.0	trailhead
0.1	bridge
0.2	junction
0.7	junction
1.5	swamp
1.8	viewpoint
2.0	junction
2.2	trailhead

There is a pleasant stroll along the lakeshore at the beginning of the hike.

Lake Resource Management Trail loop. Pick up a brochure at the self-serve station to the right of the path. The brochure provides a self-guiding tour of the natural resources in the area and some of the concepts of their management. The information in the brochure corresponds to numbered posts, or stations, erected along the 1.8-km route.

The wide path skirts the edge of Fish Lake for 500 m to a fork in the trail. The several stations along this part of the hike provide information about the trail and the Fish Lake campground: the trail was built in the mid-1980s by inmate labour from the minimum security camp at Nordegg, while most of the campground was built by the Alberta Forest Service in the 1950s. The good rainbow trout fishing was popular even then!

At the fork, swing to the right away from the lake. The path winds up a low ridge past deadfall, known as snags, and through old-growth forest of white spruce. Along this trail, wildflowers grow in profusion although some, like the sweet-scented twin flower, are so small that you have to keep a sharp eye on the forest floor for them. Pass through a small meadow and an old 1930s forest fire area before coming to a swamp where there is a change in the vegetation. White spruce dominated the ridge above, but black spruce, willows and sedges prefer the water-soaked soil of the swamp. A short distance past the swamp there is an opportunity to see the majestic blue heron fishing for trout in the pond below your viewpoint.

The trail begins to descend sharply past a 1975 weir to regulate the water level in Fish Lake, and then, finally back to the beginning of the Fish Lake Resource Management Trail. Turn left to return to your vehicle.

HISTORICAL FOOTNOTES

Nordegg Correctional Institute

As you hike along the groomed trails or burn the firewood at one of the campsites, spare a thought for the inmates at the Nordegg Correctional Institute. It is they who work on these outdoor recreational facilities.

The Institute was established in 1963 as a minimum security jail and work camp. There are no rehabilitation programmes. Rather, it is felt that work has a rehabilitative effect. Tasks include fire-fighting, woodcutting and hauling for campsites, highway cleanup, ditch clearing and campground and trail maintenance and development. Past projects at Fish Lake include the Resource Management Trail and the Recreation Area campgrounds.

The inmates are first screened at the Calgary Correctional Centre before being selected for Nordegg. Those who are chosen can be trusted to work under no or minimal supervision. They work from 7:30-4:30 pm, Monday to Friday. They are paid a small salary. They may be allowed to go home or take backcountry excursions on weekends.

14 Black Canyon Creek – map p. 54

Duration ~ full day
Distance ~ 18.4 km
Level of Difficulty ~ long walk with some steep slopes
Maximum Elevation ~ 1,410 m
Elevation Gain ~ 50 m
Map ~ 83 C/8 Nordegg

This rather long day hike leads through old-growth forest and past swamps where blue herons can be seen at two viewpoints. The first viewpoint is from a surveyor's benchmark overlooking the North Saskatchewan River valley; the second overlooks the gorge of Black Canyon Creek.

~

From the trailhead, bear to the right toward the cookhouse and cross the small wooden bridge.

Access ~ Turn south off Highway #11 at the Fish Lake Recreation Area sign located four km west of Nordegg. Follow the Fish Lake road for one km to a junction. Turn right and drive 200 m down the gravel road and park right of the boat launch at the Recreation Area parking lot.

0.0	trailhead
0.1	bridge
0.2	junction
0.7	junction
1.8	cutline
1.9	fork
2.2	meadow
4.2	cutline and junction
4.6	surveyor's benchmark
5.9	stream
7.2	junction
7.5	cutline
7.7	wagon road
7.9	stream and Black Canyon Creek crossings
9.3	cutline
9.6	junction, survey benchmark and viewpoint
9.7	wagon road
10.0	cutline
10.8	Black Canyon Creek and wagon road
10.9	cutline
11.1	cutline
11.2	Black Canyon and viewpoint
11.4	cutline
11.5	junction

(continued)

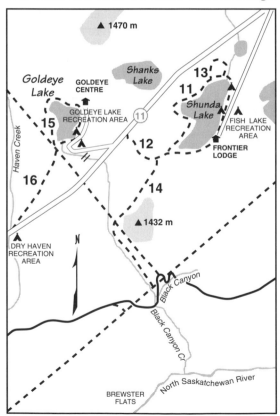

13.9 trail leaves to left of
      cutline and drops
      down slope
14.1 cutline
14.2 junction
18.4 trailhead

*Looking toward Black
Canyon Creek gorge.*

Follow the main trail beside the lake and ignore the two side trails that come in from the right. These are the Fish Lake Resource Management Trail loop. Cross a cutline past the marshy top end of the lake before coming to a fork. Bear right. The trail to the sharp left continues the Fish Lake Loop.

The well-defined trail leads to a small meadow. As you enter the meadow, look sharply for a secondary trail that leads to the left. Turn onto this trail; if you continue on the main path you will end up at Goldeye Lake. It is a good, definite footpath that is shared with mountain bikers and horses. It leads slowly upward through spruce trees where old man's beard hangs from the limbs like so many cobwebs. Delicate feather mosses cover the forest floor where the deep shade helps their leaves retain precious moisture. Where the path crosses a cutline bear left along the cutline for about 20 m. Keep a sharp eye for a junction with a trail. Bear right along the trail as it heads toward Black Canyon Creek. Swing to the left before reaching a small stream. Do not cross it. At a surveyor's benchmark keep to the right. You are now out of the forest and walking through an open meadow where there are views to the west. You soon come upon a series of beaver dams on your right. It's a pretty walk as the trail leads between two low spruce-covered ridges. Anywhere along this section of the hike makes a good resting spot. The meadows here are a cover of cinquefoil, old man's whiskers, yarrow, the blue harebell and sweetvetch.

After a short rest, continue along the path above Black Canyon Creek. There are open slopes with tiger lilies, goldenrod and purple asters that make for a pleasant walk. Cross a shallow stream. The beaver dams and swamps are now behind you as you begin a bit of a trudge through the bush. But you soon break out onto an open hillside where you can see the creek below and to your right. The trail comes to a junction. Bear right. The trail to the left simply disappears in the open area above. At a cutline, bear right and go down toward the creek and then to the left to an old wagon road. Bear right along the road and within 200 m cross a small stream. Within metres you must finally cross Black Canyon Creek. Once across, continue along the old road as it swings up and westward, leaving Black Canyon Creek far behind. As you puff your way to the top of a hill there is a cutline that offers good sneak previews of The Gap and the mountains to the south and west. Turn left onto the cutline and follow it down to an intersection with another cutline. The view here is great, but turn right onto the cutline, finding a game trail. Follow it for 50 m or so, then climb up the open slope where there is a surveyor's benchmark.

HISTORICAL FOOTNOTES

Brazeau Bypass

On the drive west along the highway, the route near Saunders swings northwest, going around the Brazeau Range. This bypass route has no name, yet travellers have gone around the Brazeau, rather than through The Gap, for at least 150 years.

The Gap is where the North Saskatchewan River cuts through the Brazeau Range. Fur traders followed the river only as far as the mouth of Shunda Creek. From there, according to Jean Findley's 1806 drawing, the earliest map of the region, they took "a track cut thru thick woods" along Shunda Creek before returning to the North Saskatchewan. Why? Alexander Henry in 1811 explains: "It being nearly impossible for horses to proceed further along the main river. The banks here [The Gap] begin to close in on the river on both sides, presenting faces of perpendicular rocks, much higher than those below [downstream], and covered with immense piles of wind-fallen wood. The surface is also intersected by deep valleys."

The location of the eastern portion of the bypass route along Shunda Creek has always been clear to historians. The western end in Alexander Henry's day was not. One possibility is along Black Canyon Creek. Almost 50 years later we know that the land track rejoined the North Saskatchewan at the mouth of the Bighorn River. In 1858, Sir James Hector of the Palliser Expedition camped near the mouth of the Bighorn. From there he headed northeast away from the North Saskatchewan, found Shunda Creek, and followed it back down to the North Saskatchewan. It was, according to Hector, a well-established trail.

The old trail has largely disappeared. In some places it is overgrown; in others, it is overbuilt as the horse trail became a wagon track, which then became a gravel road, and finally a modern highway. But there is one spot where you can still see the old wagon track—at the Upper Shunda Recreation Area campground. There you can still see the granddaddy of the David Thompson Highway as you walk among the trees between the campsites and Shunda Creek.

It's been a few hours since you left the trailhead, so why not take advantage of the tree stumps and sit awhile enjoying the view and munching a snack? Wildflowers that prefer full sun and open slopes, such as the nodding harebell, pussytoes, brown-eyed susans and sweetvetch, can be found in profusion. Perched as you are on a hillside overlooking the western approach to The Gap, you can identify a number of landmarks along the David Thompson Highway: Mount Michener with Phoebe's Teat, Windy Point Ridge and the glacier on Mount Wilson. In the autumn, the carpet below is a patchwork of the dark green spruce and the gold and orange of the poplar trees.

After resting, walk down the slope back to the game trail. Turn right and follow it to the old wagon road. Bear right again, continuing uphill as far as the junction with the cutline that was first encountered at 10.9 km. For a shortcut back to Black Canyon Creek, turn left onto the cutline. When the bottom of the slope is reached, cross Black Canyon Creek and find the old wagon road. Once at the wagon road turn left onto it and climb the slope. You quickly cross the cutline, swing back, then cross it again. The road now climbs steeply. At a 90 degree turn in the road, look back for views of The Gap and Blister Falls on the south side of the North Saskatchewan River. For the best photo opportunity of Black Canyon Creek gorge turn onto a trail that leads to the edge of the gorge. Interestingly, the gorge is not on the creek, but rather on a tributary of Black Canyon Creek.

Return to the road and climb to the cutline where you turn right. Within 100 m you come upon another cutline. Swing left onto this

FLORAFACTS

Harebell

Harebell. Courtesy of Julie Hrapko.

Scientific Name ~ *Campanula rotundifolia*, Other Names ~ Bluebell Stoney Name ~ Nabeopostabin
Translated from the Stoney, Nabeopostabin means "shaped like a thimble," a good description for this blue flower that can be found in sun-drenched meadows or on stony scree slopes.

Crees as well as Stoneys used the whole plant to make a tea to treat a variety of ailments, but it was the root of the plant that was most useful. Crushed, it was used on cuts and swellings. Nursing mothers chewed the roots to increase lactation.

second cutline. For the next three km the cutline slashes its way down to the Black Canyon Creek trail. En route, your march is hindered by swampy patches that force you into the forest, first to loop around to the left, then around to the right. Cross a small stream. Another cutline crosses the path. Ignore it. Continue walking along the cutline until you come to a steep slope. Bear left on a trail off the cutline down the slope, then rejoin the cutline. Shortly beyond here is the junction that corresponds with 4.2 km. Bear to the right onto the trail back to the small meadow, Shunda Lake and, finally, to the trailhead.

15 Goldeye Lake – map p. 54

Duration ~ two hours
Distance ~ 4.5 km
Degree of Difficulty ~ easy stroll
Maximum Elevation ~ 1,370 m
Elevation Gain ~ 10 m
Map ~ 83 C/8 Nordegg

A relaxing stroll around this fisherman's delight leads past the Goldeye Centre and down a small gorge before you return to your vehicle.

~

Find the groomed and gravelled path at the northeast corner of the parking area. Within a few metres there is a braid in the trail. Keep to the right; the left-hand braid leads down to the lake and then circles back to the parking lot. This first part of the walk goes through the cool spruce forest. In late spring, watch for the delicate magenta-speckled flowers of the round-leaved orchid and that of the graceful sparrow's egg or Franklin's lady's slipper orchids that grow profusely in the dank undergrowth. Resist the temptation to pick these exquisite flowers. Not only will they wilt quickly, but in the case of the sparrow's egg orchid, the plant will die.

Where the trail breaks out onto the warm south-facing slope just above the lake, cross a wide cut in the forest that is the fireguard around Goldeye Centre. Just beyond here is the dock and pumphouse of the Centre. On a sunny, warm day it is hard not to spend some time on the dock soaking up a few rays before continuing your walk. If you wish to look around the Goldeye Centre simply climb the stairs. From the dock, this pretty jaunt leads past fishermen trying their luck near the marshy edges of the lake. Shortly, there is a junction in the trail. Continue along the main path to the left; the trail to the right is a cross-country ski trail. The marsh at the north end of the lake might have posed a dilemma from this point, but for a 100-m boardwalk. One of the many flowers found in this area is butterwort. This attractive purple flower is one of the few carnivorous plants that you can find in the mountains. The leaves of the plant ooze a sticky substance in

Access ~ Turn north off Highway #11 at the Goldeye Centre sign located eight km west of Nordegg. Bear left at a fork in the road 100 m from the highway and continue for another 700 m to the next junction. Here, keep to the right along the main road for another 100 m and another fork. At this junction, bear left. The parking lot of the Goldeye Lake Recreation Area is 200 m away.

0.0	trailhead and junction
0.1	footbridge
0.4	Goldeye Centre dock and pumphouse
0.6	junction
0.7	boardwalk
1.1	junction
1.5	junction
1.7	junction
2.0	bridge over Black Canyon Creek and junction
2.6	waterfall
3.1	Highway #11
4.2	Goldeye Lake trail and second bridge
4.5	trailhead

Goldeye Lake from the Goldeye Centre's dock.

which small insects become trapped. The insects are then digested to give the plant the nutrients it does not otherwise obtain from the boggy soil. This area near Goldeye Lake is a pro-vincially-significant environmental area. There are coniferous and mixed-wood forests and numerous spring-fed fens, swamps and lakes. A number of rare and uncommon plants grow here, such as Parry's sedge and Greenland primrose.

Once past the boardwalk, the path reenters the spruce forest. Keep to the left where the trail branches. In several places, you may see where Forestry workers accidentally dumped several shovelfuls of gravel at the edge of the lake. More interesting and numerous are what, at first, appear to be trails joining from the right. But look again. These "paths" cross the trail and go into the lake. These are trails made by beaver in search of poplar and other deciduous trees for food. At the next two forks, again keep to the left to remain as close to the lake as possible. Evidence of just how busy the local beaver population has been becomes clear at the bridge that crosses the lake's outlet. A large beaver dam parallel to the bridge has helped maintain high lake levels.

Just across the bridge turn onto a footpath leading to the right as it follows Black Canyon Creek down-stream. As the creek cuts its course through the rock, you suddenly find yourself on an embankment some 10 m above the stream. Emerging from the spruce forest onto a sunny slope, you can see below a delightful little waterfall marking the beginning of a small gorge that stretches to the high-way. Lodgepole pine fringes the sides of the deepening gorge as you work your way downstream. The gorge and your short detour end at the highway.

Returning to Goldeye Lake, bear right at the junction with the main trail. A second bridge and campsites above and to your right are indicators that the parking lot and your vehicle are but a short distance away.

16 Dry Haven-Goldeye Lake Connector – map p. 54

This is a 2.4 km-long connecting trail between Goldeye Lake and Dry Haven Recreation Area campground. The 4.8-km round trip is an easy stroll.

~

From the Dry Haven turn-off, cross the highway and turn right. Walk up the road for 300 m where you will come to a gravel turn-off on the left. Bear left here, then bear right at the junction above the abandoned British Army Training Unit, Suffield site. A cutline and trail will come into view on the right. Follow the cutline until it intersects with another cutline. Turn left and find a trail on the right after 100 m. Bear right onto this trail and follow it to a junction beside Goldeye Lake. Bear right. At a junction just past Black Canyon Creek, bear left to reach the Goldeye Lake parking lot.

Access ~ The connecting trail begins at the Dry Haven Recreation Area campground and ends at the Goldeye Lake Recreation Area parking lot.

0.0	Highway #11
0.3	gravel turn-off
0.4	junction
0.4	BATUS site
0.7	cutline
1.5	cutline
1.6	junction
1.8	junction
2.0	Black Canyon Creek bridge
2.0	junction
2.4	Goldeye Lake Recreation Area parking lot

HISTORICAL FOOTNOTES

Goldeye Lake

Goldeye, a popular silver-coloured sport fish, was stocked in this lake in the 1940s, thereby lending its name to these waters. Today, goldeye cannot be found in this lake; indeed, it is only found in the North Saskatchewan River downstream of Rocky Mountain House. However, the lake is stocked with rainbow trout. Fishermen are restricted to electric motors.

Another name for Goldeye Lake, still in some local use, is Pine Tree Lake.

During the 1980s, researchers with the Archaeological Survey of Alberta conducted palynological research at a number of sites along the eastern slopes, including Goldeye Lake. They drew core samples from the bottom of the lake to study the pollen trapped in the mud. By studying the ancient pollen, the research-

ers learned what plants grew in the area, and therefore, what the climate was like thousands of years ago. Because the site at Goldeye Lake was part of the ice-free corridor during glacial times, the climatic record here is longer than in most other parts of Alberta.

What the record showed was that about 13,000 years ago the area around Goldeye Lake was tundra. There were no trees. The dominant pollens were willow, sage, grass and sedge. At about this time the climate slowly began to moderate. Trees including aspen, spruce, birch and pine began to make their appearance. By about 10,000 years ago the tundra had disappeared and the vegetation that is seen today around Goldeye Lake was established.

Bighorn Country

Bighorn Country stretches from the Bighorn River south to just past Windy Point on Abraham Lake. This area offers beautiful waterfalls, stunning gorges and open ridges where you have a better-than-normal opportunity to see some of the wildlife that inhabits these forested hills and rocky ridges. The Bighorn Dam and its reservoir, Abraham Lake, dominate your views along the highway, while mountain meadows and open slopes await those who venture further afield.

Two ecoregions, the boreal uplands of the foothills and the montane ecoregion of the North Saskatchewan River valley, introduce you to a wide variety of flora, fauna and geological features. The rolling hills of the boreal uplands support white-tail deer, black bear and moose. Mule deer and elk favour open slopes and meadows, while bighorn sheep prefer the rocky ledges of gorges and the higher ridges. There are numerous streams that cut through the valleys where you can find small, but nevertheless, very photogenic waterfalls. Wide, U-shaped valleys are proof of the past presence of glaciers that held the land in its icy grip, off and on, for perhaps more than 1.5 million years.

Windy Point marks the boundary between the two ecoregions and between the foothills and the Front Ranges. When you look across the reservoir from Windy Point you see evidence of the effect that the McConnell Thrust, one of the great thrust faults of the Rocky Mountains, had on the local physiography.

The physical feature, though, that dominates this and other areas of the

Although the lower reaches of Allstones Creek have been flooded by Abraham Lake, the tilted and folded rock is still clearly discernible at Allstones Cove.

David Thompson corridor is Abraham Lake, a man-made reservoir behind the Bighorn Dam. When full, the reservoir stretches 32 km back along the North Saskatchewan River valley and has a maximum width of more than three km. It has a surface area of more than 32,000 hectares, a sizeable body of water in Alberta. If you are here in the spring and early summer, the reservoir will be low and what captures your attention are the barren, sterile terraces encircling the lake. In late summer and autumn as the reservoir fills, "the magnificent view from Windy Point is likely to become even more exciting when looking over the man-made lake at full supply," as a report on the recreational potential of the reservoir stated in 1970. You can visit the Bighorn Damsite Information Centre daily from the May long weekend until Labour Day. It is located 5.6 km south of Highway #11 on the dam site road 23 km west of Nordegg or 60 km east of the Banff National Park boundary.

A dam built close to the confluence of Tershishner Creek and the North Saskatchewan had received Calgary Power's consideration as early as 1953, but due to the particularly thick overburden of gravel, stones and boulders, Calgary Power decided to abandon the idea in favour of developing the hydroelectric potential of the Brazeau River further north. By 1965, though, Calgary Power was taking a second look at the Bighorn site and in 1967 presented its first cost estimates to the provincial government. The two parties signed an agreement on the construction of the dam and reservoir in early 1969. Calgary Power boasted that the dam would generate 108,000 kilowatts of hydro and that the reservoir would provide numerous recreational op-

---

HISTORICAL FOOTNOTES

Joby Chungo

A. P. Coleman called him "that born explorer." The Stoney called him "trailmaker." He was the man who blazed many of the trails later followed by the famous guides and travellers in the Canadian Rockies. Coleman wrote that whenever his group picked up a new trail, their Indian guide would say in Cree: "Joby Chungo" or Joby's trail. If it was a new trail far away from the usual Stoney haunts, then Joby must have been there.

Joby was Job Beaver, a Stoney Indian from Morley who every summer would pack his family and head into the mountains to hunt. Whereas other family groups would limit their expeditions to the same region year after year, Job Beaver ranged throughout the Rockies. Job Pass, Job Creek and Job Lake are named after him. His usual routine was to head for the Kootenay Plains, then pick any number of routes on a wide-ranging hunting expedition. One trip around 1890 later triggered a more famous expedition. That year Job Beaver had gone via the Bighorn and Brazeau Rivers to hunt by a lake called Chaba Imne. With Job was his 14 year-old son, Samson. Samson, in 1907, drew a map of Job's route to Chaba Imne, today called Maligne Lake, for Mary Schäffer.

Job had another son, older than Samson, named John. John rarely smiled and had a face, according to Coleman, "cynical enough for Mephistopheles." Coleman wrote that neither he nor his companions loved John. But John's father, Job, loved him and here lies a tragic story. John died of consumption (another account says drowning) during the winter of 1893-1894. Job, heartbroken and inconsolable in his grief, committed suicide.

portunities. The provincial government of the day declared that the dam would provide flood control for the towns and cities downstream. At first, little thought was given to environmental or the residents' concerns. The government gave barely two weeks notice for its public hearings, not enough time for most parties to gather their forces. The St. Albert Fish and Game Association, which looked upon the David Thompson corridor as "a hunter's and outdoor sportsman's paradise," was primarily concerned with the loss of nearly 2,500 hectares of winter grazing range for sheep and elk. The association also pointed out that the fluctuating water levels and seasonal flooding of rivers and streams would place fish populations in jeopardy. When asked at the hearings whether these concerns arose from socialist sympathies, the petitioner said no. To which a member of the committee conducting the hearings said "Good. Glad to hear it." This did not stop the committee from tearing apart point by point the fish and game association's arguments.

Not as easily dismissed were the Stoneys at the Bighorn Reserve. The Reserve itself was downstream of the dam and would not be affected by the flooding upstream. However, the Stoneys were affected. Their winter hunting and grazing lands were about to be destroyed and six trap lines flooded. And above all, some 24 graves were to be flooded. "The white man, he is proud of his history, he writes of it in books, he saves old buildings and he makes special

places to save his history to remind him of his culture. The Indian, too, has things in his history and his culture which he wants to save," the Stoneys asserted in their brief. In the end, the government agreed to remove most of the graves and reinterred them at Two O'Clock Creek.

In the early 1960s, the Central Alberta Chambers of Commerce lobbied for the creation of a provincial park from Nordegg to the Banff Park boundary. This hope was dashed by the construction of the Bighorn Dam. Abraham Lake, which was thought at first to offer unlimited recreational opportunities, was recognized in the 1970 report as being far too dangerous. It is a long and relatively shallow lake. Lying in the North Saskatchewan River valley it is subjected to the strong southwesterlies that blow from the mountains on most days. You only have to stand at Windy Point on one of these days and watch the white caps on Abraham Lake to appreciate why signs are posted warning swimmers and boaters of danger. The 1970 report concluded that the establishment of a provincial park would be "an error."

Eighteen km of recently-constructed highway between Tershish–ner Creek and the Kootenay Plains were flooded. As early as 1966-1967 surveys were conducted to relocate this stretch of highway on higher ground. Today, most of the old highway has disappeared under the waters of Abraham Lake. At the north end of Windy Point, though, a part of the old highway can be seen cutting between an "island" and the shore.

17 Crescent Falls & Bighorn Canyon – map p. 65

Duration ~ half day
Distance ~ 6.2 km
Level of Difficulty ~ easy walk followed by a short, steep scramble
Maximum Elevation ~ 1,440 m
Elevation Gain ~ 80 m
Map ~ 83 C/8 Nordegg

Judging by the traffic on the road and at the falls themselves, Crescent Falls is certainly one of the more popular attractions of the area. Nearly as popular is this short, easy walk along the Bighorn Canyon from the viewpoint to the falls and back. This is a hike that the whole family can enjoy.

~

Access ~ Park your vehicle at the Bighorn Canyon parking area and viewpoint four km up the Crescent Falls road. The Crescent Falls road turn-off is 18 km west of Nordegg, or 65 km east of the Banff National Park boundary on Highway #11.

0.0	trailhead
1.5	view of first set of waterfalls and cutline
1.8	intersection with old road
2.0	bog and stream
2.3	junction
2.4	bog and stream
2.5	view of Crescent Falls
2.8	bog and stream
2.9	junction with "Lower Falls" trail
3.0	upper falls and campground
3.1	junction with "Lower Falls" trail
3.9	"Lower Falls" trail sign after side trips to upper and lower falls
5.0	intersection with old road
5.1	fork
5.2	cutline
5.3	cutline
5.7	fork
5.8	Crescent Falls road
6.2	trailhead

For five km the Bighorn River twists its way through the spectacular Bighorn Canyon.

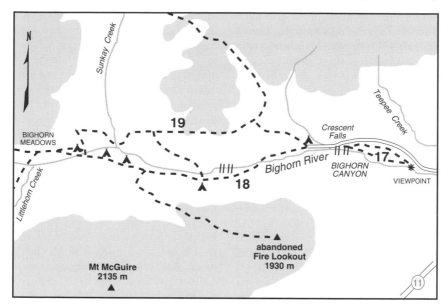

The view of the Bighorn gorge from the car park entices many visitors to climb over the guard rail to walk along the edge of the cliffs—witness the number of trails that lead both up and downstream. You, of course, want to walk upstream to reach Crescent Falls, so turn right onto the trail. The view of the Bighorn River as it plunges through its spectacular gorge makes the jaunt along the canyon's edge quite exciting. Soon, though, the trail enters the forest to cut off a number of the bends that the river takes in its journey to the North Saskatchewan River. It's a full kilometre before you emerge from the forest to a viewpoint of four small waterfalls. These are not the Crescent Falls, but a smaller set of waterfalls downstream from the main attractions. Shortly beyond the viewpoint the trail crosses a narrow cutline.

Within 300 m the trail swings left onto an old road for 20 m before swinging left again into the forest and away from the road. Another 200 m brings you to a wet, boggy area where you must pick your way along the driest of the braids in the trail. This is the most tedious part of the hike. Thankfully, the springs only disrupt your walk for 100 m or so. At a fork in the trail, keep right and continue past another boggy area before coming to a tantalizing view upstream of the two dramatic waterfalls that are your destination. Each waterfall has a punch bowl at its base for that perfect snapshot or video footage. There are several secondary footpaths leading to the left, but ignore them and continue to an intersection with the "Lower Falls" trail. For now, continue straight ahead to stay on the main trail. The fact that you are very close to the Crescent Falls parking lot is obvious since at this point the trail becomes a broad pathway. Continue straight ahead to a chain link fence that protects the too-eager hiker from the sharp drop into the punch bowl at the base of the upper falls. A seating bench just to the right of the path has a plaque dedicated to James "Jimmy" Hammond. Hammond was an avid outdoorsman who enjoyed the Crescent Falls area. After he died his family installed the plaque in his memory.

Now that you are here you may want to explore. The view from the flat rocks jutting out over the Bighorn River at the lip of the escarpment is difficult to ignore and we suspect many a hiker has enjoyed a pleasant rest here. A campground, picnic area and washrooms are found across the creek just upstream of the upper waterfall. Short side trips to the base of both the upper and lower falls are also worthwhile. To reach the access for both waterfalls, retrace your steps downstream to the "Lower Falls" sign. Turn right onto this trail and follow it 30 m to a junction. To view the upper waterfall at its base, bear to the right and go down the slope along the good pathway. The flat rocks at the edge of the punch bowl at the base of the falls makes another excellent place to munch a lunch, sketch or try your hand at some innovative photography. Return to the junction at the top of the slope. If you want to go to the base of the lower waterfall take the right-hand fork. Of the two side trips, this one is more difficult. Your footpath skirts the canyon's edge for 200 m to a scree slope. Skid your way down through the wolf willows approximately 100 m to the river. The base of the lower waterfall is to your right. From here there is an excellent view down the canyon.

To return to the main trail and your vehicle, return to the "Lower Falls" sign, then follow the main trail to the junction with the old road at the 1.8-km mark. Follow the road past the junction on the right, which is the trail you took coming from the trailhead. There is a fork in the road after a short distance. Keep to the right, or straight ahead. The left-hand fork goes up the slope 100 m where it intersects with the main Crescent Falls road. Continue along the old road past two cutlines. The second cutline corresponds to the one at 1.5 km at the beginning of the hike. Your trot through the forest next brings you to another fork. Bear right. About 100 m later intersect with the Crescent Falls road. Bear right and follow the footpath that parallels the road back to the car park and your vehicle.

WHAT'S IN A NAME?

Crescent Falls

Previous Names ~ Bighorn Falls

The two waterfalls at the top of the Bighorn Canyon are known as the Crescent Falls. The name describes the shape of the cliff over which the two 30-m waterfalls drop.

The first recorded mention of the waterfalls is attributed to A. P. Coleman, a professor of geology at the University of Toronto. In 1892, he and his party were travelling from the Kootenay Plains to the upper Brazeau River. After following a muddy trail from the mouth of the Tershishner River to the Bighorn River they "came upon a beautiful waterfall leaping into an amphitheatre, far better scenery than we had been used to in the foot-hills." Coleman did not designate any name to the waterfalls. The original name, Bighorn Falls, goes back at least to 1900. It was first recorded by Martin Nordegg who visited the falls many times, either for recreation or while prospecting for coal. The waterfalls during this time were named, obviously, after the Bighorn River on which they are located. This name is still in some local use.

The flat rocks beneath the upper waterfall invite a picnic lunch.

18 Upper Bighorn Falls – map p. 65

Duration ~ half day
Distance ~ 8 km
Level of Difficulty ~ steady walk with two river crossings
Maximum Elevation ~ 1,460 m
Elevation Gain ~ 30 m
Map ~ 83 C/8 Nordegg

Although the Crescent Falls are the largest and the most photogenic waterfalls, they are not the only ones on the Bighorn River. Two very pretty waterfalls upstream of Crescent Falls are the reward for getting your feet wet crossing the Bighorn River.

~

At the parking area there are two trailheads. Follow the wide trail that leaves the west side of the parking area. The trail on the north side and marked by the equestrian trail sign leads to the Bighorn Meadows. As you approach the Bighorn pretty views up the valley come into sight. The

Access ~ The Crescent Falls road is located 18 km west of Nordegg, or 65 km east of the Banff National Park boundary on Highway #11. Drive up the Crescent Falls road past the upper equestrian staging area, and down the hill past the falls and through a shallow ford. Continue past the campgrounds for another 800 m to a small parking area marked by an equestrian trail sign.

0.0	trailhead
1.4	Bighorn River
3.7	braid
3.8	junction and first waterfall
3.9	end of braid
4.0	second waterfall
8.0	trailhead

The second waterfall as seen from the viewpoint.

trail keeps to the right of the river and skirts its banks as you walk upstream. An easy lope brings you to a ford across the Bighorn River. The river here is wide and, therefore, relatively shallow so the crossing is easy and not dangerous. However, you should be cautious during spring runoff or after a heavy rain when the river is swollen. Just below the ford, the river makes a sharp turn and drops through a series of rapids and a small gorge. This is a favourite spot for fly fishermen, who can be seen casting for recently-stocked cutthroat trout.

Once across, the trail continues its slow ascent, climbing beside small cascades and rapids in the river. Keep a sharp eye for a fork or braid in the trail at the 3.7-km mark. It is here that you bear right off the main trail and head into the open forest. Within 100 m there is a junction. Swing to the right. A 30 m jaunt brings you to a viewpoint above the first of the upper Bighorn waterfalls. Squeezing through a narrow gap in the rock, the river drops some three m into a quiet pool before it races through a small gorge on its way downstream. You can get a better view of the waterfalls if you follow the river's embankment to the right and find an easy way down to the rocks at water level. This attractive spot is frequented by hikers catching a few rays and fishermen angling for elusive trout.

Return to the junction. Turn right and follow the path to the intersection with the main trail at 3.9 km. At the main trail turn right and follow it upstream for 100 m. Another secondary path leading off to the right will take you to a viewpoint high above the second waterfall.

Return the way you came along the main trail.

HISTORICAL FOOTNOTES

Bighorn Coal Basin

Coal deposits along the Bighorn River were discovered in 1906 by D. B. Dowling of the Geological Survey of Canada. Analysis of his samples found that the coal was suitable as steam coal. This was an important discovery, since at the time the only known deposits of steam coal in western Canada were at Crowsnest Pass, Canmore and Vancouver Island.

Dowling's report caught the attention of Martin Nordegg who at the time was investigating investment opportunities in Canada. In 1907, Martin Nordegg visited the Bighorn River and had a short tunnel dug to determine the extent of the deposits. Six workable seams varying in thickness from one to four metres were located. Dowling, who accompanied Nordegg on the trip, estimated that the deposit held over 1.4 billion tonnes of commercially exploitable coal.

It was because of the commercial promise of the Bighorn Coal Basin that Nordegg was able to form a partnership with the Canadian Northern Railway and raise the necessary capital. Yet the Bighorn basin was never exploited. In 1910, Nordegg discovered coal east of the Bighorn at present-day Nordegg. This discovery saved Nordegg and his investors approximately $2 million in development costs since about 50 km less rail line needed to be built.

19 Bighorn Meadows – map p. 65

Duration ~ full day
Distance ~ 18.3 km
Level of Difficulty ~ steady walk with two wide stream crossings
Maximum Elevation ~ 1,700 m
Elevation Gain ~ 270 m
Map ~ 83 C/8 Nordegg

This long, but relatively easy and straightforward hike offers moderate elevation gain to a broad subalpine meadow along the Bighorn River. Two picturesque waterfalls add interest to the return loop.

~

From the trailhead choose the wide, well-gravelled path on the north side of the parking area by the equestrian trail sign. Almost immediately it begins to climb steeply through white spruce and lodgepole pine. When you reach the top of the rise you realize that you have merely completed the first of several steps that take you up to Sunkay Creek. From this vantage point you can see straight ahead where the trail climbs up the next ridge. At a junction bear to the right off the cutline onto the main trail. The trail now winds down and

Access ~ The trailhead is accessed from the overflow campground at Crescent Falls. The Crescent Falls road is located 18 km west of Nordegg, or 65 km east of the Banff National Park boundary on Highway #11. Drive up the Crescent Falls road past the upper equestrian staging area, down the hill past the falls and through a shallow ford. Continue past the main campground 800 m to a small parking area marked by an equestrian trail sign.

Bighorn Meadows.

around before coming to a T-junction. Keep to the left. The trail continues to wind around a boggy area before switching up the hill to a junction with a path on the right. Remain on the main trail; the path is a shortcut to a cutline. When the trail reaches the cutline, turn right onto it. Ignore a junction with a small path on the left—it leads to a cut block—and continue along the cutline trail. There is an easy stream crossing before the road once again rises steeply in a series of steps to the highest point on this hike at 1,700 m.

For the past five km you have been climbing through forest with no views to inspire you. Now, though, tantalizing peeks of the Bighorn valley and Mount McGuire are yours. These disappear, briefly, as you descend steeply past an ATV track on the left. At the next junction with an ATV track bear left onto it as it goes around some cliffs and down a steep, but short incline. The trail appears to end abruptly on the embankment just above the confluence of Sunkay Creek and the Bighorn River, but turn right and follow the Sunkay upstream to a ford. The Sunkay is not a very wide stream so your crossing should be easy, if cold!

Once across, the trail does not dip down to the Bighorn, but continues along the top of the embankment. Before continuing, though, a delightful diversion is to scramble down the sand and gravel embankment and walk back to Sunkay Creek where it tumbles through a narrow gap in the rocks down to the Bighorn River. The waterfall and the pool at its base have enticed more than one hiker to take a quick skinny dip, especially on a hot day, before continuing along the trail.

Pleasant views of the Bighorn valley now accompany you. The trail braids for some 400 m, but keep to the right along the main trail as it swings away from the Bighorn River and climbs a ridge overlooking the Sunkay valley. At another junction bear to the left onto the cutline and begin a slow ascent, then descent, to the Bighorn Meadows.

Bighorn Meadows is the local unofficial name for the wide, long stretch of willow shrubs and grassland that extends on both sides of the Bighorn River. For the next three km you can enjoy the open views of the Bighorn River valley and Mount McGuire. So, drop to the meadow. At the base of the hill turn a hard left and walk along the base of

0.0	trailhead
1.3	junction
1.9	T-junction
2.7	junction
2.8	cutline
4.0	junction
5.3	viewpoint
6.1	junction
6.7	junction
6.9	Sunkay Creek
7.0	braid
7.4	end of braid
8.0	junction
9.1	Bighorn Meadows
10.0	Bighorn River
11.2	meadow and horse camp
11.7	horse camp
12.0	stream crossing
12.1	junction
12.2	horse camp and junction
13.5	junction
14.3	second waterfall on upper Bighorn River
14.4	braid
14.5	junction
14.6	end of braid
16.9	Bighorn River
18.3	trailhead

Looking up the Bighorn valley.

the hill for 50 m before striking out across the meadows toward the Bighorn River. Find an old grassy east-west track where you turn left. The trail goes past a campsite and down to the river. Fording streams and rivers is always fun, and crossing the 30 m-wide Bighorn River is no exception. No matter how hot the day you emerge on the other side refreshed!

If you look upstream about 50 m, you notice another ford. This is the upstream route of the trail you are now on. Alberta Forestry has named this the Bighorn/Littlehorn Circuit Trail. It takes you to the upper reaches of the Bighorn and Littlehorn Rivers.

With dry footwear back on, turn left and go downstream along the trail past two smaller trails that join from the right. The trail begins to swing away from the river and through a small meadow. Within a short distance, you come onto a wide meadow that stretches downstream between the river on your left and Mount McGuire on your right. Looking downstream past Mount McGuire, you can see an old road that leads up to a now-abandoned fire tower.

WHAT'S IN A NAME?

Sunkay Creek

Stoney Name ~ Sunkay Waptan (Wild Horse Creek)

Sunkay Creek takes its name from the wild horse herds that once ranged along this stream and the Bighorn River. Sunkay is Stoney for wild horse. The creek was officially named in 1932.

During the 1930s and 1940s, the number of wild horses along the upper Bighorn, Ram and North Saskatchewan Rivers rose to their all-time high. Citing the need for ecological control and the preparation of the region for commercial grazing leases, Alberta Forestry conducted an extermination campaign in the 1930s. Horse carcasses were often laced with poison to kill wolves. Animals owned by the Stoney Indians were also destroyed and Alberta Forestry was accused of waging a campaign of harassment against the Indians.

The Stoneys depended upon the wild horses both to replenish their own stock and as a source of income. The Stoneys would catch the horses and sell them to dealers in Nordegg who, in turn, sold the animals to be processed as pet food. One Stoney, Chief Walking Eagle, was outraged and stopped participating in their hunt when he learned how the wild horses were disposed of: "Horses are the Indians' friends and too good for fox and dog meat," he said.

The active campaign to exterminate the wild horse herds ended in the early 1960s when the commercial focus of the region changed to tourism. Several herds remain. There is one near Nordegg and another along the upper Ram River.

Sunkay Creek disgorges over a three metre-high cliff close to its confluence with the Bighorn River.

20 The Sasquatch Track – map p. 75

Duration ~ half day
Distance ~ 5.4 km
Level of Difficulty ~ easy stroll
Maximum Elevation ~ 1,320 m
Elevation Gain ~ 90 m
Map ~ 83 C/8 Nordegg

Access ~ Park your vehicle at the Bighorn Damsite Information Centre parking lot 5.6 km south of Highway #11. The Information Centre turn-off is 23 km west of Nordegg, or 60 km east of the Banff National Park boundary.

From an easy trail along the top of a ridge you can reenact the movements of a curious sasquatch that, in 1969, calmly watched workers building the Bighorn Dam. The trail then leads down to the North Saskatchewan River just below the damsite and back to its Information Centre.

~

Walk back up the hill from the Information Centre parking lot. At the top of the hill near the intersection, cross to the northeast side of the gravel road. A footpath to the right goes straight up the open slope of the ridge that overlooks the Bighorn Dam and the Information Centre. Scramble up the slope and follow the ridge. There is no continuous footpath here so work your way along the edge of the cliffs keeping the valley floor in sight. Soon, your faint track along the edge of the ridge joins an old road that immediately swings to the left away from the pretty views. Ignore the road and continue your stroll along the cliffs above some fascinating hoodoo-like formations. A game trail joins from the left. If you follow it you intersect with the old road at 1.6 km. But hug the cliff's edge for its scenic views instead. Drop one m when approaching the junction with the road and main trail. From the junction continue along the edge of the cliffs. It was somewhere along this part of the trail that a sasquatch stood for nearly an hour watching the activity at the damsite below, no doubt wondering what its world was coming to.

As you wend your way along the cliff's edge, pass through a grove of trees before breaking out onto a broad, open meadow sprinkled with yellow snapdragons, better known as butter-and-eggs. It is an easy lope down the grassy ridge to its end, where there is a surveyor's stake. Across the North Saskatchewan there are more hoodoos carved from the river's cliffs. Below is a levee in the river,

0.0	trailhead
1.0	intersection
1.2	crest of slope
1.3	road cut
1.4	game trail
1.6	junction
2.8	survey marker
3.1	meadow
3.4	North Saskatchewan River
3.8	gravel road and levee
4.5	junction
4.8	gate
5.1	T-junction
5.4	Bighorn Dam Information Centre

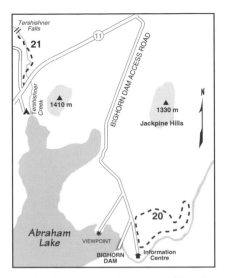

ravine to the right of the meadow. Follow it as it angles to the right before descending down the ridge to the North Saskatchewan River. Find a bridle path that skirts the edge of the river. Turn right onto it and follow it as it passes through wolf willows. The path soon joins a gravel road. Here, you have three choices: bear left onto the levee to follow it one km and then return, or bear right along the main gravel road, or bear a sharp right to follow the base of the cliffs for a better view of the hoodoos. If you decide on the latter, continue some 200 m until you find a road. Follow the road as it swings back to the gravel road of your second choice. Turn right onto the main road and continue to a gate. Continue straight ahead along the road. Several sheds on the right contain core samples. Turn left at the T-junction with the main gravel road to return to your vehicle. Before leaving, a visit to the Bighorn Damsite Information Centre is well worth it, although no mention is made of the dam's famous bigfoot visitor.

and looking down the river valley the distinctive shapes of Shunda and Coliseum Mountains can be seen in the distance.

Turn left to head downstream paralleling the river below. Keep to the left of a grove of spruce trees and find a well-defined track. It leads to a small meadow where it disappears. This can be picked up again in a shallow

The view that the sasquatch enjoyed while watching the construction on the Bighorn Dam.

75

Sasquatch

Put it down to the heat of that hot August day. Or to overwork. Or to an active imagination. Surely five workers at the Bighorn Damsite could not have seen what they reported. But don't repeat that to Harley Peterson and his father Stan, or to the backhoe operator Floyd Engen, or to Guy Heureuse and Dale Boddy. They were there. And they know what they saw.

It was August 23, 1969. Harley Peterson looked up from his job at the pumping station and saw a dark, upright figure on the ridge above him. The others soon noticed it, too. For nearly an hour the five men and the creature watched each other. The creature stood up again, perhaps to get a better view of some machinery moving dirt, before walking along the ridge to finally disappear into the trees.

So, what had the men witnessed? They could neither photograph nor get a better view of the creature since none of them had a camera or binoculars. Neither could they approach it since part of the river flowed between them and the ridge. Later, when they climbed the ridge they could find no physical evidence of its presence. The ground was too hard packed for any footprints and later aerial searches revealed nothing. While it was walking down the ridge the men had made a mental note of its height in relation to the trees behind it. In an attempt to determine the size of the creature, two of the men stayed on the ridge while the other three looked up from below to judge their friends' height against their memory of that of the creature. Imagine their astonishment when they discovered that the creature had to have been at least four or five m in height!

The sighting caused a sensation and was widely reported in provincial newspapers. Earlier sightings by Indians, at Windy Point and along Whiterabbit Creek, were now given credence. Fear of being laughed at had kept Vern Saddleback, Edith Yellowbird, her father, Mark, and another Bighorn dam worker, Alec Shortneck, quiet about their individual sightings earlier that year. Alec had been clearing brush when a creature appeared a scant 55 m in front of him. "I just went on chopping wood ... I thought it best to just go about my business," he said.

Although the five dam workers were too far away to give a detailed description of the creature, their general impressions were consistent with those of hundreds of other sightings throughout the Pacific Northwest. Firstly, the creatures are bipedal and their bodies are covered with hair. The head is apelike with a heavy brow ridge, tiny ears and an extremely short, thick neck. Shoulders are wide and the trunk of the body and the arms are longer than those of a human. Descriptions of adults put them between 2.5-3.5 m tall. There are even reports that they can run up to 100 km/hr! They appear to be solitary, nocturnal creatures that may hibernate during the winter. They do not appear to be acquainted with the use of fire.

Known as Bigfoot in the United States, these creatures are called Sasquatch in Canada. The word is derived from the Salish Indian word "sokqueatl" or "sossq'atl" meaning "wildmen of the woods." Coastal Indian tribes were quite familiar with these half-animal, half-human beasts and their myths are liberally sprinkled with references to a monster-like race that occasionally raided their villages. These references have teased the minds of more than one anthropologist. Some have taken pains to link physical descriptions of the sasquatch to the carved masks and totems of the Pacific coast tribes. Others have tackled the question of genetic evolution, presenting the theory that the sasquatch is a descendent of Gigantopithecus, a line of huge apes that evolved parallel to man, but died out 10 million years ago. Not surprisingly, debates over the existence of the sasquatch have raged back and forth for years.

Do sasquatches exist? Perhaps. And then again, perhaps not.

21 Tershishner Falls – map p. 75

Duration ~ one hour
Distance ~ 2.4 km
Level of Difficulty ~ easy stroll with a short bushwhack
Maximum Elevation ~ 1,400 m
Elevation Gain ~ 50 m
Map ~ 83 C/8 Nordegg

This short, easy hike entails three stream crossings that can be a lot of fun for the family if you wear appropriately old footwear. A four m-high waterfall is the highlight of this hike.

~

Follow the sloping roadside ditch down to Tershishner Creek. At the bottom of the slope there is an old road. Follow the road as it slowly winds its way upstream. In summer, the roadside is a carpet of colour. Indian paint brushes with their splashes of orange and red intermingle with the blue-eyed grasses and clumps of yellow prairie groundsel. Beside you, Tershishner Creek babbles happily on its way to Abraham Lake. The road crosses the creek and continues on the other side. Splash across the

Access ~ Park your vehicle on the west side of Highway #11 beside the gravel road that parallels the south bank of Tershishner Creek. The Creek and road are located 26 km west of Nordegg, or 52 km east of the Banff National Park boundary.

0.0	trailhead
0.1	old road
0.5	Tershishner Creek
0.9	Tershishner Creek
1.0	Tershishner Creek
1.2	Tershishner Falls
2.4	trailhead

WHAT'S IN A NAME?

Tershishner Creek

Previous Name ~ Tetichina Creek
Stoney Name ~ Chasesna Waptan (Burn Creek)

Tershishner is a corruption of the Stoney "Chasesna," which describes an area burnt over by a forest fire. Stoneys camped along Tershishner Creek for a number of years, possibly because of the Bull Trout and Dolly Varden that frequented these waters. Since the flooding of the reservoir, Abraham Lake, the trout population below the waterfalls is unstable and unable to overwinter.

Tetichina is a spelling variation of Tershishner.

Tershishner Falls.

ford and continue along the road. The Tershishner is now on the left, but only for a few hundred metres. The road crosses the creek again. This time there is a log "bridge" to help you avoid wetting your feet in times of high water. In periods of low water, you should be able to skip across from rock to rock. The road ends at a third ford across the creek. This crossing is more difficult, but once again logs thrown across are a boon to those who can walk a balance beam. For the rest, there is no avoiding getting your feet wet this time.

Once on the right bank of the creek look for an orange "17" on a tree. This marks where a game trail leads to the falls. A small gorge comes into view and within a short distance you can see the waterfalls. If you're wearing an old pair of sneakers, why not splash your way up to the base of the falls for a better look? The water is cool and refreshing on a hot day and the current is not strong.

Return the way you came.

HISTORICAL FOOTNOTES

Peter Wesley (1853-1936)

He was described as "a diamond in the rough," an unpolished man driven by indomitable energy, ambition and thrift, but thoroughly trustworthy. His Stoney name was Ta Otha, which means Moosekiller or Provider (of food). A variation to his Stoney name was Ka-o-to-to-a meaning "facing the storm." Most knew him by his English name, Peter Wesley.

It was the combination of willpower and the ability to generate trust that gave Peter Wesley the leadership tools required to play the historical role of Moses. In 1894, he led about 100 people from Morley back to their traditional lands on the Kootenay Plains, where they remained until receiving their own reserve on the Bighorn River in 1947.

Peter Wesley's story begins in 1877 at the signing of Treaty Number Seven. Under this treaty, three Stoney bands were gathered together on a number of reserves near Morley. Life at Morley was difficult as food supplies diminished due to drought, depleted game, hunting regulations and insufficient food rations. During this time Wesley established a reputation as a skillful hunter, supplying meat, including wild game such as deer, sheep, moose and the occasional not-so-wild cow, to the hungry reserve. Then came the crisis.

Hungry families at Morley began to kill their cattle. Under the reserve rules, Indians could not kill their own cattle without permission of the Indian Agent. One Stoney, John Abraham, was jailed two days for this "offence." After Abraham's release, Wesley began the exodus back to the Kootenay Plains. The band that he led was then called the Goodstoney Band. After the trek to the plains, Wesley was elected to the leadership and the band began to be called the Wesley Band.

Photographs of Wesley show a stout, well-built man with a thin moustache and beard. He was the leader of the Wesley Band for about 30 years, dying at the age of 83 at what is now the Bighorn Reserve.

Peter Wesley.

22 Mud Creek – map p. 87

Duration ~ full day
Distance ~ 11 km or 6 km
Level of Difficulty ~ broken terrain, steep scrambles and bushwhack
Maximum Elevation ~ 1,700 m
Elevation Gain ~ 340 m
Map ~ 83 C/8 Nordegg

Access ~ Park your vehicle at Mud Creek located two km north of Allstones Creek on Highway #11, or 29 km west of Nordegg, or 50 km east of the Banff National Park boundary.

There is no trail up Mud Creek so this is a bushwhack the entire way to the top of Allstones Ridge. Despite its rather "plain Jane" name, this valley, with its five waterfalls, is very pretty. The scar on the backside of Allstones Ridge adds a dramatic note to this hike.

~

From the north side of the highway, scramble down the slope to Mud Creek. The north or right-hand side of the creekbed may be easier to walk along, but the terrain is, nevertheless, rough with rocks and some deadfall. So far, this hike does not appear to offer much in the way of scenery, but when rounding the first bend you come upon the first of five waterfalls that are the hallmarks of this hike. This lovely three-tier waterfall cannot be climbed. You must scramble up the south bank of

0.0	trailhead
0.3	first waterfall
0.8	third waterfall
1.0	fourth waterfall
1.1	fifth waterfall
1.2	confluence with stream
3.0	head of Mud Creek valley
	Option #1:
6.0	trailhead
	Option #2:
4.0	notch
5.0	Allstones Ridge
9.0	Allstones Lake trailhead
11.0	Mud Creek trailhead

The scar of the mud slide still dominates the view at the head of the valley.

the creek to bypass the falls. At the top of the slope, a second waterfall comes into view. For those who cannot negotiate the steep scramble around the first waterfall, return downstream keeping on the south side of Mud Creek. Climb the slope where you feel comfortable. For some, this may mean returning most of the way to the highway. Following game trails, climb the slope upstream. The top of the slope directly above the first waterfall hides the view, but cross over to the open slope where you can see both the first and second waterfalls.

You realize that you must stay high to get past the second waterfall, so return to the forest and continue to bushwhack upstream. In late spring, watch for the beautiful calypso orchids that can be found sprinkled liberally on the forest floor. There is a game trail that takes you across the slope above the second waterfall, then down to Mud Creek. As you go up the valley, a third waterfall soon greets you. This time, scramble up the left side of the waterfall. Continue walking up the creekbed. Within a very short distance you come to a double waterfall. Once again, it is an easy scramble up the left side of the falls. The last waterfall is a triple-drop cascade even though that fact is not readily apparent. This waterfall cannot be negotiated and you must scramble up the left slope to traverse around it. Some deadfall has to be crossed but once above the third tier of the waterfall, drop back down to Mud Creek. Unlike the streambed below the waterfall, the streambed above is grassy and more open, making walking much easier.

A short jaunt brings you to a confluence with a tributary stream on the right. Ignore this stream and begin climbing Mud Creek on your left.

Negotiating the creekbed between waterfalls.

You can see the slide area where a wall of mud snapped off mature pines and spruces as though they were matchsticks. Keep on the right side of the stream all the way to the head of the valley. This part of the climb is steeper and rougher due to deadfall, although it is a pretty walk. Numerous springs in the hillsides feed Mud Creek. Despite this, the footing never becomes soggy. Near the head of the valley, the terrain flattens. Raspberries and strawberries grow profusely and if you are here in late summer remember that berries form a large part of a bear's diet, so keep a sharp eye! In spring, blue lugenwort, Indian paint brushes and the tiny white grass of Parnassus lend their colour to the landscape.

Around a lazy bend you can see the head of the valley at the base of Allstones Ridge. Dominating the view is the scar on the backside of the Ridge where rock, scree and dirt sliced off one rainy day in June, 1980. The mud slide that hurled down the valley gave this previously unnamed creek its name.

At this point, there are two options. You can return the way you came as far as the fifth waterfall. From here scramble up the north slope, or the slope on your left. This is the slope opposite to the one climbed en route to the head of the valley. The ridge has no ravines and is open along the edge of the embankment, making for a relatively easy descent to the Mud Creek trailhead.

A longer and more demanding option is to continue up the valley and climb to the notch that lies to the right of Allstones Ridge. When approaching the base of the scar, keep to the right of the lateral moraine. Traverse the south-facing slope as you puff your way up to the notch. Keep to the right of the ravine. The trees that cluster there would make the climb even more difficult. Instead, climb above them, hugging the open slope. The entire hillside is covered with kinnikinnick and low-lying junipers. It's a tough little climb so when you reach the notch at 2,100 m, take a good rest and enjoy the scenery.

To find the Allstones Lake trail that takes you back to Highway #11, girdle Allstones Ridge and find the Allstones Lake hiking trail. So, at the notch, bear left and scramble up the scree slope, traversing above the tree line. Game trails lead the way to a ridge. Continue to traverse the slope of the mountain through a large boulder field. Once past here, scramble up a second ridge above you. From the vantage point at the top of this ridge you can see below the deep aqua-green waters of Allstones Lake. Descend into a small bowl while continuing to work your way around Allstones Ridge. Then, climb through the rock and scree to the open slope just below the top of Allstones Ridge. Turn downhill and 200 m later join the Allstones Lake trail. Bear left onto the trail and follow it down to the highway. Turn left and walk two km back to Mud Creek and your vehicle.

WHAT'S IN A NAME?

Mud Creek

This is a local and unofficial name for a creek that until June 5, 1980 remained nameless. That day, following several weeks of heavy rain, a massive mud slide crashed down the normally dry creekbed. The torrent cleared out the valley and dumped a deposit of mud, rocks and timber two m deep and 270 m wide on Highway #11. The highway was closed for more than a week as Alberta Transportation crews struggled to clear the road. "There is an eight-foot bank of stuff on the upper side of the highway that keeps coming across as we take it out," one engineer explained. No one was injured during the disaster.

One of the five waterfalls on Mud Creek.

*The spectacular scenery of Allstones Creek gorge is yours to enjoy
if you are prepared to get your feet wet.*

23 Allstones Creek – map p. 87

Duration ~ half day
Distance ~ 5.4 km
Level of Difficulty ~ numerous stream crossings followed by a short, steep scramble
Maximum Elevation ~ 1,400 m
Elevation Gain ~ 80 m
Map ~ 83 C/8 Nordegg

This is a fun splash up Allstones Creek through its impressive gorge as far as a waterfall. Because of the numerous stream crossings, this is definitely an old sneaker hike.

~

You may park anywhere in the informal campsite area. On a hot day, it might be best to consider a spot under the spruce trees. From here you can reach Allstones Creek by backtracking along the gravel access road to the highway, where you turn right and walk as far as the causeway. A shorter, prettier way is to follow the vehicle tracks to the edge of the cliffs overlooking Allstones Cove, a charming, tranquil arm of Abraham Lake. Take a trail to the right of the road and head up to a slope overlooking the highway. Here, there are two options. The recommended option is to scramble down the slope to the highway, turn right and walk north. Cross to the west side of the highway and scramble down the slope to Allstones Creek. Or, for the child in all of us, the upper culvert above the cove begs exploration. Scramble down the fairly steep, but short slope to the upper culvert and walk through it to the other side of the highway. Unless there have been torrential rainfalls and the creek is unnaturally high, the culvert will be dry and not hazardous.

Once in the picturesque gorge of Allstones Creek it is easy to understand how this stream got its name. Allstones' fairly wide streambed is liberally strewn with—you guessed it—stones and boulders. Prior to the flooding of Abraham Lake, cutthroat and Dolly Varden trout were caught in Allstones Creek. Fluctuations in the level of the reservoir mean that fish can only move upstream when the reservoir is full, in the autumn. As the lake level drops over the winter

Access ~ Park your vehicle at one of several informal campsites on the east side of Highway #11. The gravel access road is located just south of the causeway over Allstones Creek. Allstones Creek is located 31 km west of Nordegg, or 52 km east of the Banff National Park boundary.

0.0	trailhead
0.1	Highway #11
0.2	Allstones Creek
2.0	trail and chute
2.6	waterfall
2.7	Allstones Creek above the waterfall
2.8	junction
3.4	Allstones Creek
5.4	trailhead

and following spring, any fish caught above the highway are trapped and most likely die.

The gorge itself is dramatic. Its serrated rock walls tower above you on both sides of the creek. It doesn't matter on what side of the creek you begin your walk upstream, because within a short distance you are forced to cross then recross the creek again and again. Needless to say, this aspect of the hike is best appreciated on a hot day! After zigzagging upstream for several kilometres you come upon a trail on the left-hand side of the creek leading up the side of the gorge. Ignore the trail and continue your splash up Allstones Creek. Within a very short distance you come to a narrowing of the streambed where the water rushes down through a chute. You may be tempted to turn around at this point, but plunge ahead through the chute to the north side of the creek. The water level and footing are neither as high nor as dangerous as they seem.

Continue upstream past a low ledge. You are finally rewarded with a picture-perfect waterfall where Allstones Creek cascades over a six m-high cliff. The action of the water is eroding the cliff, driving it inexorably back upstream. Find a suitable boulder and sit a while to enjoy the scenery.

At the base of the waterfall, cross to the south side of the stream. To the left there is a trail that leads up through the steeply-pitched rocks to the top of the gorge. Here, there is a T-junction. To view the waterfall from the top, turn right and follow the trail 100 m down to Allstones Creek and the lip of the waterfall. Return to the junction. Instead of scrambling back down to the base of the waterfall,

keep to the right and follow the trail as it skirts the edge of the gorge. The trail dips down into the creekbed just downstream of the chute. From here, turn downstream to return to the trailhead.

WHAT'S IN A NAME?

Allstones Creek

This creek was likely named by Stoney Indians due to the rocky creekbed and unique rock formations. The English translation has been in local use since at least 1918. Three other geographic features, Allstones Lake, Allstones Cove and Allstones Rapids, take their name from the creek. The rapids on the North Saskatchewan River no longer exist due to the creation of Abraham Lake in 1972. About 800 m of the creek was also permanently flooded, forming Allstones Cove.

The steeply-pitched walls of the gorge have been eroded into razor-edged ridges.

24 Allstones Lake – map p. 87

Duration ~ full day
Distance ~ 12.9 km
Level of Difficulty ~ steady elevation gain on a good footpath
Maximum Elevation ~ 3,030 m
Elevation Gain ~ 1,710 m
Map ~ 83 C/8 Nordegg

Access ~ Park your vehicle at one of two areas on the east side of Highway #11. The first is directly opposite the Allstones Lake trailhead sign on the north side of Allstones Creek. The better and more scenic site is located off a gravel access road just south of the causeway over the creek. Allstones Creek is located 31 km west of Nordegg, or 52 km east of the Banff National Park boundary.

Although it takes only several hours to climb up to Allstones Lake, do plan to make this a day hike. The views along the way are spectacular and the lake itself offers a restful repose after a steep climb. For the energetic, there is a side trip to the top of the ridge above Allstones Lake for an unsurpassed view of the lake and surrounding valleys.

~

If you have parked south of Allstones Creek follow the gravel road back to the highway. Turn right, or north, and walk up the highway 200 m to the other parking area on the north side of the creek. Cross the highway to the Allstones Lake Recreation Trail sign. The trail is quite visible as it scrambles up the embankment above the highway. You will have to jump across a wet area in the ditch to get onto the trail.

The short spurt up the slope from the highway is a good indication of the steepness of this relatively short hike. The trail rarely levels out as you climb, climb, climb up the valley. At first, it leads to the right of a shallow ravine of a small, unnamed creek. After a short distance, the trail swings away from the ravine to climb steadily through spruce and pine forest. Upon reaching a braid in the trail, there is a choice. If you take the left or lower braid, you descend to a small stream before climbing sharply up the opposite embankment. The stream makes a cool, refreshing rest stop on a warm day. If you choose the right or upper braid, the trail stays level, crosses the stream and reconnects with the main path at 1.6 km.

As you climb you are rewarded with sneak previews of magnificent mountain scenery through the stands of pine. At long last the trail breaks out of the forest onto an open slope where you can take in the surrounding views. Even though you may be tempted to take a short break here, persevere to the top of the open slope. Where the trail enters a stand of pine trees,

0.0	trailhead
1.3	braid
1.5	stream crossing
1.6	braid rejoins
2.3	open slope
3.4	rivulet
4.0	intersection
4.6	Allstones Lake
6.3	circuit around the lake
6.9	intersection
7.9	top of ridge
8.9	intersection
12.9	trailhead

The sparkling waters of Allstones Lake are an invitation to enjoy a rest in the sunshine.

take a well-deserved rest among the wildflowers. Abraham Lake and Mount Michener are spread out at your feet; the Kootenay Plains are in the far distance.

Continue climbing through pine trees and then onto open slopes. Just as the trail begins to level out there is one, last steep spurt to the top of a rocky ridge. Here, the trail takes a 90 degree turn to the left skirting the flank of the hillside. Part way along this exposed slope a rivulet crosses the path. It is a beautiful trot along this part of the trail, with the David Thompson country laying below to your left, and the forested slopes of the surrounding mountains in front. Yarrow, Indian paint brushes in shades of orange and red, vetches, brown-eyed susans, stonecrop and blue harebells are sprinkled liberally along the trail's edges.

A blazed tree stump on the right marks the intersection with the trail that goes to the top of the ridge overlooking Allstones Lake. Ignore this temptation for now and follow the main path to the left as it leads down the slope and through open stands of spruce trees to the edge of Allstones Lake. After a 1700+ m gain, the sparkling waters of this jewel bewitch all who come here. Campsites to the left and to the right of the trail vouch for this statement as those who like to smell the flowers often backpack to the lake for several days of rest and relaxation. Take a stroll along the trail around the lake. There is yet another campsite on the northwest side close to one of the springs that feeds Allstones Lake.

If you want to climb the ridge overlooking Allstones Lake return to the blazed tree stump. At the fork bear left and begin your climb. It is a straightforward pull to the top and one that is well worth the effort. Allstones Lake lies below to the west, while the scar of the slide on Mud Creek dominates the scene to the east. Once you have enjoyed the view return down the slope, then turn left onto the main trail that takes you back to the trailhead and your vehicle.

25 Windy Point Ridge – map p. 87

Duration ~ half day
Distance ~ 3.6 km
Level of Difficulty ~ fairly steep climb with some scrambling
Maximum Elevation ~ 2,060 m
Elevation Gain ~ 656 m
Map ~ 83 C/8 Nordegg

For lovers of rock scrambles and steep, short ascents, Windy Point Ridge makes an excellent half-day hike. The view from The Lookout takes in the North Saskatchewan River valley and surrounding mountains, including Mounts Michener and Abraham. The Lookout is the unofficial name for the first peak along the Windy Point Ridge.

~

From your parked vehicle walk back to Highway #11. Cross the highway and find a path that leads up the grassy slope to the top of the rock cut above the highway. You are now on the spine of Windy Point Ridge. Turn right and begin your climb.

Access ~ Windy Point is located 22 km west of Nordegg, or 61 km east of the Banff National Park boundary, or one km south of the Mount Michener viewpoint on Highway #11. It is unsigned. An access road immediately east of the highway rock cut leads to a parking area overlooking the Point.

0.0   trailhead
0.1   Highway #11
0.7   "sasquatch track"
1.8   The Lookout
3.6   trailhead

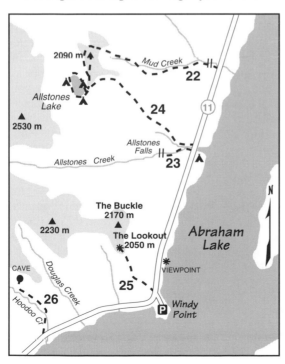

Windy Point Ridge climbs to The Lookout in three steps. The first step begins immediately. Krummholz pines, ground-hugging junipers and kinnikinnick struggle for survival on this rocky, sun-drenched and very windy ridge. Approximately 500 m later you reach the top of the first step. Here, the ground levels for a bit, a welcome relief. Views looking down on Windy Point and across Abraham Lake toward Mount Michener are your reward after a short, but stiff climb.

The longest and steepest pitch is the second step that rises directly in front of you. There is no path over the rock. You have to negotiate your way past the rock faces as best you can. The limestone rocks are marked with rillenkarren, tiny gullies with razor-sharp peaks that tear at your hands and knees as you climb, so pick your way up this pitch with care. En route, if you're lucky, you will find a "sasquatch" footprint—about size eight—embedded in the limestone rock!

After a tough pull you reach the top of the second step. You're much higher up the slope now and you can see north as far as the Bighorn Dam and south to the curve in the lake past the David Thompson Resort. In early fall a dusting of snow can accentuate the tops of the surrounding mountains.

The third step is not as long or as steep as the second pitch. Before you know it, you have arrived at The Lookout, complete with rock cairn. Now you can see as far north as Coliseum and Shunda Mountains and far south into the Siffleur Wilderness. Behind you is the top of Windy Point Ridge, known to local climbers as The Buckle, named after a similar feature, the Buchaille Etive Mor, at Glen Coe in Scotland. The Lookout is as far as most hikers venture. It is possible to scramble along the ridge to the foot of The Buckle, traverse the left side along a game trail, then ascend The Buckle from the back. A shallow cave is visible a little to the right on the scree slope just below The Buckle.

Return the way you came.

WHAT'S IN A NAME?

Mount Michener

Previous Names ~ Eye Opener Mountain ~ Phoebe's Teat

Mount Michener was named in 1979 in honour of the Right Honourable Daniel Roland Michener, Governor General of Canada from 1967-1974. Michener was born in Lacombe, Alberta and raised in Red Deer.

Michener was an active man who enjoyed the outdoors. At the age of 82, he climbed his mountain on Canada Day, 1982, with the assistance of several alpinists and a helicopter. He was dropped off by helicopter several hundred metres below the summit from where he scrambled to the top with the assistance of Lloyd Gallagher, deputy leader of Canada's 1982 Everest expedition.

Mount Michener's earlier name, Eye Opener Mountain, is a sanitized version of another local name, Phoebe's Teat. Phoebe, according to local oral tradition, was a "barmaid" in Rocky Mountain House during the 1930s. She may have, from time to time, visited the miners in Nordegg.

The best view of Phoebe's Teat is from the official viewpoint one km south of Windy Point. With the help of an active imagination you can see Phoebe's profile from her thrown-back head down to her knee. Her teat, incidentally, is not the highest point on Mount Michener. The 2,545 m-high peak is further back, near her head.

Apparently Michener was unaware of his illustrious namesake's...uh..."irregular" background. When told the original name of his mountain, His Excellency was not amused.

Mount Michener.

Opposite: Stand outside your vehicle at the Mount Michener viewpoint or walk onto the point itself, and you need no explanation how this point of land got its name! Stoney Indians gave this location the same name—Ganutha Impa.

The McConnell Thrust Fault

Windy Point ridge.

Driving west along the David Thompson highway, the Front Ranges are the first set of mountains you meet east of the foothills. Dividing the foothills from the Front Ranges is the McConnell Thrust Fault, one of the great thrust faults in the Rockies. Highway #11 cuts across the McConnell Thrust Fault several hundred metres north of Windy Point. Stand by your vehicle, or better yet, walk out to the extreme end of the point and look across Lake Abraham. To your right is Mount Michener. Mount Michener is typical of the mountains of the Front Ranges in that it is highly folded and faulted. East of Mount Michener are the lower, rounded forested foothills. These consist mainly of younger shales and sandstones. This abrupt change of typography demarcates the McConnell Thrust Fault.The massive folds that you see in the rock is evidence of rock's "plasticity." In some places these folds have fractured and have

slid along the fracture, forming what is called a thrust fault. To understand how a thrust fault is formed, take a piece of paper and slowly push the ends of the paper towards each other. Notice how the paper bulges upwards in a fold. The same thing happens with rock. But if you apply more pressure on one end of the paper the shape of the fold changes. The increased pressure forces one side of the fold to bend over the other side. This same phenomenon occurred in the mountain-making process. But unlike paper, rock can only withstand so much pressure before it fractures. As the thrust sheets moved eastwards they overrode younger formations.The McConnell Thrust Fault has placed limestone and dolo rock of the Cambrian period (approximately 530 million years old) over much younger rock of the Lower Cretaceous period (approximately 200 million years old). Along the highway at Windy Point there are some 850 m of exposed Cambrian rock.

26 Hoodoo Creek – map p. 87

Duration ~ half day
Distance ~ 5.2 km
Level of Difficulty ~ rock scramble up streambed
Maximum Elevation ~ 1,740 m
Elevation Gain ~ 400 m
Map ~ 83 C/1 Whiterabbit Creek; 83 C/8 Nordegg

Access ~ Park your vehicle on Highway #11 at Hoodoo Creek three km south of Windy Point. The creek is located 38 km west of Nordegg, or 45 km east of the Banff National Park boundary.

The broad gravel wash that is Hoodoo Creek leads up into an ever-narrowing ravine. Although a 1966 Calgary Power map calls this stream Bear Creek, it is an impressive pair of hoodoos that give this creek its name. Hoodoos are not the only geological phenomenon along this hike. For the spelunker in all of us, there is a shallow cave above the hoodoos that invites a visit.

0.0	trailhead
1.0	chute
1.3	hoodoos
2.4	cave
2.6	fork in Hoodoo Creek
5.2	trailhead

~

There is no discernible trail up the wide, stony and apparently dry creekbed, so pick your way upstream as best you can. On a cloudless summer day the sun's rays bouncing off the rocks can make this a very hot hike and if you haven't filled your water bottle you may be concerned. But don't worry; within a kilometre the stream reemerges to flow through a gorge, giving you plenty of opportunity to replenish your canteen.

The streambed begins to narrow where it takes a lazy bend to the left. It continues to narrow as you climb. Finally, you come to the end of the gravel wash. It is here the stream flows through a small gorge, and it is up this gorge that you must find your way, first on one side of the stream and then on the other. It is not long before you reach two 30 m-high hoodoos, complete with "caps," poised above the gorge on the right-hand side of the creek. Upstream of the hoodoos the rushing waters of Hoodoo Creek sluice over the smooth rocks. An easily discernible trail on the left-hand side of the creek goes past several difficult spots in the streambed, where huge boulders block your path.

It's a scramble along the embankment until you come to a cave above and on your right. Scramble up the short, but steep trail that leads to the mouth of the cave. Caves are always interesting and this two-room cave makes a perfect spot to rest and enjoy the view. Stoney oral tradition speaks of a cave near Windy Point that was home around 1900 to some Metis trappers. This may be the place. In the cave there is a second room and a tunnel. The tunnel extends back about seven m, where it is blocked by debris. It does go beyond this point, possibly breaking the surface, for pine needles can be found on its floor.

Returning to the trail along Hoodoo Creek, turn right and continue to climb steeply to a fork in Hoodoo Creek. Along the left-hand fork there is a picturesque cascade. If you look up the right-hand fork, you can see a window in the ridge.

Return the way you came.

GEOFACTS

Hoodoos

Rising some 10 m above the creekbed the hoodoos that are seen on this hike are evidence that glaciers once spread across the Front Ranges.

Glaciers advanced and retreated a number of times. Each time the glaciers spread their tentacles down the mountain valleys, they dislodged and carried rock, depositing it along the way. This deposit was a mixture of clay- and sand-sized fragments, and occasionally large rocks. This poorly sorted mixture is called till.

In some places dissolved limestone in the till provided calcium carbonate, which cemented the deposits. As water eroded the deposits, pillars of hardened till have remained. These pillars are called hoodoos. Large blocks called cap rocks can often be found perched on top of the hoodoos, further helping to protect the till beneath.

The hoodoos on Hoodoo Creek.

Hoodoo Creek.

Bigfoot!

David Thompson is credited with the first sighting of a sasquatch track on January 7, 1811 near Jasper. Measuring the footprint, Thompson recorded that it was 35.5 cm in length and 20 cm wide. His Indian guides "would have it to be a young mammoth," he wrote. To the Indians, the "mammoth" was an extraordinary and fearsome creature. Present-day cryptozoologists (those who study "hidden animals") would have the "mammoths" to be the elusive sasquatch. Elusive, because although there have many sightings throughout the Pacific northwest, there is little physical evidence to support the existence of a bipedal half-ape, half-human creature. No

This "sasquatch" track discovered in mud flats at Farley Lake is in fact a bear track. The hind paw of the animal has overlapped the front paw, creating an elongated footprint in the mud.

skeletal remains have been found; neither have any faeces, hair, sleeping and/or living quarters been discovered. The sasquatch then, may well belong to a phenomenon that includes UFOs, but for one piece of evidence. Apparently sasquatch leave tracks. Literally thousands of footprints have been recorded since the 1960s. They have been photographed and plaster casts have been made of them. Although the footprints vary in size, they nevertheless can give us some hint about their owners. For example, there is no arch, indicating that sasquatches are flat footed. They have five toes, not claws, which would appear to disprove the argument of those who would have the sasquatch be a bear. However, these disbelievers point out that bear claws do not always show and when a bear's hind foot overlaps with its front foot, the result is a very large, human-like footprint.

The footprints vary in length, the shortest being 28 cm and the longer ones being 46 cm. The stride is generally more than a metre in length. All this would indicate a height of nearly three m. What perhaps is even more interesting is the depth that the impressions have left in the sand and mud; a 38-cm track has been recorded to have sunk 2.5 cm into hard-packed wet sand, indicating a weight of nearly 800 hundred pounds.

All recent Alberta sightings of the mysterious sasquatch have been from the upper North Saskatchewan River valley. Hobbema Cree camped at Windy Point during the summer of 1968 first reported these large, yet eerily human-like footprints after their dogs had been disturbed one night. More footprints were discovered near Whiterabbit Creek and again near Windy Point the following summer. Edith Yellowbird and three other women had seen four creatures near Windy Point, and other Cree camped near Windy Point had noticed huge tracks in the sand. So frequent had the tracks become, that the Cree took them for granted.

Are sporadic sightings and occasional footprints proof of the existence of the sasquatch? So far, no one has been able to prove or disprove its existence. One thing, though, is certain. The "sasquatch" footprints embedded in the Cambrian rock on Windy Point's second pitch are merely a freak of erosion. Or are they?

WHAT'S IN A NAME?

Abraham Lake

Abraham Lake is named after Stoney Indian Silas Abraham and his family. The Abraham family has lived along the upper North Saskatchewan River valley since the 19th century. The creation of the reservoir in 1972 buried a number of features associated with the family. These included the Abraham Flats at the mouth of the Cline River where Silas Abraham and his son, Norman, had built cabins. At Windy Point, there were a number of graves, including one child of Norman Abraham and an unknown number of children of John Abraham, Silas's son.

It was these graves that inspired Jake Jameson, a grade four student at Caroline, to write a winning essay in the government-sponsored Name the Lake Contest. The contest to name the reservoir behind Bighorn Dam was held in the spring of 1972. There were nearly 2,000 entries submitted by Alberta students in grades one through nine. Prizes were awarded for the best entry in each grade. The nine winning names were submitted to the Geographic Board of Alberta, which chose from among them the name for the lake.

Young Jake Jameson's co-winner was grade nine student Karen Schauerte, of Alder Flats, who had also submitted the same name. Both Karen and Jake received a $400 first prize.

Other names submitted to the Geographic Board included Pete Pangman Lake, David Thompson Lake, Lake Walking Eagle, Windy Point Lake, Lake Charlotte, Lake Wesley and Walking Eagle Lake.

Abraham Lake. Courtesy of Robin Chambers.

Cline River Area

The Cline River area includes the confluence of the Cline and North Saskatchewan Rivers and the south side of the Cline River watershed. It contains alpine, subalpine and boreal upland ecoregions and is a significant habitat for elk, mountain sheep, goats and grizzly bear.

The recorded history of the area is one of travel between the Kootenay Plains and its headwaters, especially Pinto Lake. The lake's bull trout population was known to attract Stoney Indians annually. By the time A. P. Coleman visited the lake in 1893, the trail up the Cline River was well established. His visit was part of a quixotic quest.

It began in 1827 when Scottish botanist David Douglas made a mistake. Near Athabasca Pass he described two mountains, which he named Mounts Hooker and Brown, and estimated their heights at about 5,000 m. The report of these two "giants" caught Coleman's attention, and like several other explorers of the Rocky Mountains, he was determined to find them. His 1893 trip past Pinto Lake was his third attempt. He succeeded this time, but felt no triumph: "We had reached our point after six weeks of toil and anxiety, after three summers of effort, to find that Mount Brown and Mount Hooker were frauds."

The "giant" heights of Mounts Hooker and Brown were not frauds. Douglas had made an honest mistake. He had used an earlier computation that put Athabasca Pass at 3,000 m, rather than 1,700 m. So when he climbed Mount Brown his calculations were out by 1,300 m. Exactly who made the original error in calculating the height of Athabasca Pass is unknown.

The other historical figure associated with Cline River and Pinto Lake is Mary Schäffer. Her first visit in 1906 was part of a test. That was the year she and Mollie Adams decided to challenge convention and explore the Rockies. In those days ladies did not travel the back country like men, even if they were Quakers who stressed the equality of the sexes. Their exclamation is famous: "Why not? We can starve as well as they; the muskeg will be no softer for us than them; the ground no harder to sleep upon; the waters no deeper to swim, nor the bath colder if we fall in." Outfitter Billy Warren was aghast. Unable to change their minds he took them on a trial run. From Banff he took them over Bow Pass to the North Saskatchewan River. They forded the river, then continued on to Sunset Pass and Pinto Lake. From Pinto Lake, they went down the Cline to the Kootenay Plains, then up the Siffleur back to Banff.

Schäffer and Adams passed the test and together with Sid Unwin, the four began their annual summer-long expeditions through the Canadian Rockies. Their most famous trip was in 1908 when they reached Maligne Lake. There is a romantic end to this story. Billy Warren, the man who was so determined initially not to take Mary Schäffer into the mountains, married her.

27 Vision Quest – map p. 116

Duration ~ half day
Distance ~ 5 km
Level of Difficulty ~ steady, steep climb
Maximum Elevation ~ 2,165 m
Elevation Gain ~ 765 m
Map ~ 83 C/1 Whiterabbit Creek

This short, but very steep climb up an open spine takes you through an old native vision quest site en route to the top of a ridge overlooking Abraham Lake.

~

Above the waste transfer site is open pine forest. There is no trail, but take the plunge and find a route up through the trees. Once through the pines, you find yourself at the bottom of a long and steep, but open slope. There is no path up the slope, but the route is obvious. This south-facing slope is as dry as it is open, but in spring dainty butter-and-eggs and pussyfoots sprinkle the hillside. If there was any doubt in your mind at the beginning of this hike about the steepness of the climb, the first 100 m should dispel any questions you may have had. The huffing and puffing are worth it, though, as you work your way up. As you rise above the pine trees, the

Access ~ Park your vehicle just off Highway #11 at the Cline Solid Waste Transfer Site located 42 km west of Nordegg, or 41 km east of the Banff National Park boundary. Whitegoat (Cline) Creek is 600 m south of the waste transfer site.

0.0	trailhead
0.6	vision quest site
2.0	ridge
2.5	cliff face
5.0	trailhead

Walking along the top of the Vision Quest ridge you can enjoy a panoramic view of Abraham Lake. Courtesy of Chris Hanstock.

97

view continues to improve. Looking to the north you can see Windy Point and looking south you can see as far as the Kootenay Plains.

Suddenly, when approaching a copse of pines in a notch, the ridge flattens. Here, the trees are festooned with metres of cloth that once were brightly coloured, but are now sadly faded. This may be a vision quest site of at least one native seeking direction in his life. A perfect site to find peace and happiness, the notch invites a stop to enjoy the view before walking on through the knot of pines.

The slope becomes steeper and steeper. Finally, it flattens near the top. Once at the top, continue along the ridge. As you approach the cliff face in front of you, the ridge that you are climbing becomes quite narrow and is not for the faint of heart. From here, there is a glorious view of the North Saskatchewan River valley dominated by the aquamarine waters of Abraham Lake. To the right is the Whitegoat Creek valley, while below on your left is BATUS Canyon.

Return the way you came.

FLORAFACTS

Bearberry

Scientific Name ~ *Arctostaphylos ura-ursi* Other Names ~ Kinnikinnick Stoney Name ~ Siyo Ta Hatha

The Kootenai, Stoney and Cree, who have all at one time lived on or frequented the Kootenay Plains, made ceremonial and medicinal use of many of the plants that grow in these mountains. One plant for which they had many different uses was the common bearberry, or kinnikinnick, as it is also known. A low, creeping shrub, bearberry sports shiny green leaves, a pale pink flower in spring, and small, round red berries in autumn.

Kinnikinnick means "something to smoke," and indeed many native groups gathered and dried the leaves of the bearberry for this purpose. They then mixed the dried kinnikinnick with either dried and shredded inner bark of the red-osier dogwood bush, or tobacco. It was used in most if not all religious ceremonies. The leaves had other uses, too. The liquid from boiled bearberry leaves could be drunk to cure urinary tract infections and women's "disorders." If mixed with the liquid from boiled juniper leaves it was sometimes used to cure dysentery. The berries were eaten, although they are rather dry, or preserved for later use. As a

source of vitamin C, the berries were effective in warding off scurvy. The Cree used the bearberry's stems and roots in treating diarrhea, especially in their children.

HISTORICAL FOOTNOTES

The Vision Quest

"...the Rocky Mountains are precious and sacred to us. We know every trail and mountain pass in this area. We had special ceremonial and religious areas in the mountains.... These mountains are our temples, our sanctuaries, and our resting places. They are a place of hope, a place of vision, a place of refuge, a very special and holy place where the Great Spirit speaks with us."

When Chief John Snow of the Stoney Bighorn Reserve wrote his book *These Mountains Are Our Sacred Places* in 1977, it was at a time when much of what the Stoneys held dear was threatened by the tides of change in the North Saskatchewan River valley. The Bighorn Dam was completed and had flooded much of the historic hunting grounds of the Stoneys, and plans for up-scale resorts in the valley had been presented to the provincial government. Much of the Stoney world at Bighorn had changed forever.

It was, perhaps, against this backdrop of local turmoil and of a growing awareness on the part of native groups across North America that native spirituality underwent a renaissance. In Chief John Snow's sacred mountains that renaissance took the form of sundances, sweats, and vision quests. A vision quest is a solitary experience by one person, almost always a male, who seeks wisdom and guidance by isolating himself from his community. Prior to embarking on his mission, he participates in a sweat lodge ceremony in which he and the others present are purified both physically and spiritually through fasting and praying. The sacred pipe is smoked to Waka Taga, the Great Spirit. It is first offered to the person sitting on the east side of the sweat lodge, then, moving in a circular fashion, to the person on the north side, then the west side, and finally ending by the leader of the ceremony holding the stem of the pipe toward the north.

After this ceremony, the seeker sets off on his vision quest. Finding a secluded spot, he remains there for a number of days, fasting and praying for guidance for his future. His vision often takes the form of communication between himself and a spirit, which can take the form of an animal, bird, or even an inanimate object like a rock. He may even acquire that form as his guardian spirit. Carrying an object of his guardian spirit, such as bones or feathers, then protects him in times of trial.

Once he has received instructions from his spirit he returns to his community, where his experiences will be interpreted for him.

Taking a short break at the vision quest site.

28 Whitegoat Falls – map p. 116

Duration ~ one hour
Distance ~ 2.4 km
Level of Difficulty ~ easy walk with some light bushwhacking
Maximum Elevation ~ 1,445 m
Elevation Gain ~ 45 m
Map ~ 83 C/1 Whiterabbit Creek

For car-weary travellers who want to stretch their legs and see a pretty waterfall without compromising too much of their time, this short, brisk walk might be just the ticket.

~

A chain link fence encloses the waste transfer site to discourage bears from scavenging. If the gates are open, walk through the transfer site compound to the four-wheel drive track visible on the other side. Otherwise, follow the fence

Access ~ Park your vehicle just off Highway #11 at the Cline Solid Waste Transfer site located 42 km west of Nordegg, or 41 km east of the Banff National Park boundary. Whitegoat (Cline) Creek is 600 m south of the waste transfer site.

0.0	trailhead
0.6	junction
0.9	Whitegoat Creek gorge
1.2	viewpoint of Whitegoat Falls
2.4	trailhead

The punchbowl Whitegoat Falls.

around the south side of the compound to reach the track.

The road is not particularly steep, but you cannot mistake the steady climb through open pine forest. Continue along the road to a junction with a trail on the left that goes to Whitegoat Falls. The trail is easy to miss. If you come to a braid in the main road you have gone too far; backtrack 30 m and turn onto the bridle path. The horse trail descends slowly through the woods. Leave the bridle path when you can see the creek's gorge. Here, swing to the right and bushwhack along the top of the embankment. The trail that you left continues to descend another 300 m to a ford that crosses the creek, then connects one km later with the Little Indian Falls loop. On the embankment above the gorge there is no path, but the south-facing bank is lightly forested with only junipers, a few

spruce trees and small bushes to hinder you. Continue as far as an open slope where you can catch the best view of the beautiful punchbowl Whitegoat Falls. The waters cascade down in two steps through a cleft in the rock walls.

If you wish to get closer to these beautiful waterfalls, continue bushwhacking for another 100 m until you are past the elbow in Whitegoat Creek. Watch for a game trail that leads down into the gorge about 30 m below the falls. Prior to the flooding of the Abraham Lake reservoir in the early 1970s, brook trout moved upstream from the North Saskatchewan River as far as the canyon and the waterfalls. Now, there are no fish in the Whitegoat Creek; the highway culvert and fluctuations in the water levels in the reservoir ensure that.

Return the way you came.

WHAT'S IN A NAME?

Whitegoat Creek

Previous Names ~ Cline Creek

If you are looking for a highway sign for Whitegoat Creek, you won't be able to find it. Rather, there is a sign for Cline Creek. The creek's official name is Whitegoat, but the name Cline has been used in the past and is still used today by Alberta Transportation to identify this small creek.

For an undetermined length of time the Cline River was known as the White Goat River, and it appears as though the name of the creek followed suit. When the river's name was changed to Cline, the creek's name changed to Cline as well, despite being officially named the Whitegoat. When Alberta Transportation chose to ignore the official name, some people believed that they wanted to eradicate the name Whitegoat. In

1971, the provincial government had reduced the size of the White Goat Wilderness by about two-thirds, pushing its boundaries well back from the David Thompson Highway.

The present solution, though, does not work well. If you ask for directions to Cline Creek, chances are that you will get directions to Cline River. Or vice versa. This was nearly a serious mistake for one party who were discovered by now-retired Alberta Forest Ranger John Elliott. He reported meeting the party travelling up Cline Creek, heading supposedly for Pinto Lake.

Historically, Whitegoat Creek takes its name from Sir James Hector of the Palliser Expedition, who referred to the nearby Cline River as the "wap-ut-teehk," which is Stoney for Whitegoat.

29 Stelfox Loop – map p. 102

Duration ~ full day
Distance ~ 21.8 km
Level of Difficulty ~ steady climb followed by numerous stream crossings
Maximum Elevation ~ 1,995 m
Elevation Gain ~ 555 m
Map ~ 83 C/1 Whiterabbit Creek; 83 C/2 Cline River

Access ~ Park your vehicle just off Highway #11 at the Cline Solid Waste Transfer site located 42 km west of Nordegg, or 41 km east of the Banff National Park boundary. Whitegoat (Cline) Creek is 600 m south of the waste transfer site.

The many creek crossings on Coral Creek slow you down considerably if you are planning on completing this hike in one day, but it can be done. This hike also requires two vehicles. A second vehicle is left at the Coral Creek Trail staging area located 47 km west of Nordegg or 36 km east of the Banff National Park boundary on Highway #11.

~

0.0	trailhead
0.6	junction
0.7	braid
2.6	Whitegoat Creek
3.0	Whitegoat Creek
3.3	Whitegoat Creek
3.6	Whitegoat Creek
4.4	gravel wash
5.6	junction
5.8	Whitegoat Creek
5.9	informal campsite and braid
6.1	end braid
6.3	gravel wash
8.0	Whitegoat Pass
8.8	gravel wash
10.6	T-junction
10.8	Coral Creek
11.2	Coral Creek
11.9	Coral Creek
12.0	Coral Creek and braid
12.5	end of braid
12.6	gravel wash
13.2	Coral Creek
13.7	Coral Creek
14.2	Coral Creek
14.3	Coral Creek
15.3	gravel wash
16.5	Coral Creek
16.7	Coral Creek and waterfall
16.8	second waterfall and Coral Creek
16.9	Coral Creek

17.4 campsite
17.6 junction
18.1 junction
18.4 junction
18.7 junction
19.7 junction
21.0 junction
21.3 junction
21.7 stream crossing
21.8 Coral Creek Trail
       parking area

The approach to Whitegoat Pass makes a good rest stop.

There is a chain link fence around the waste transfer site to discourage bears scavenging. If the gates are open, walk through the transfer site compound to the four-wheel drive track visible on the other side. Otherwise, follow the fence around the south side of the compound to reach the track.

Although not remarkably steep, the trail climbs steadily through open pine forest. This part of the hike can seem like a bit of a trudge as there are few views until you reach the 2.6-km mark. Continue along the road past a junction with a trail on the left that leads to Whitegoat Falls. As you begin to climb, the road braids three times around boggy areas. Choose the main road since the braids tend to be wetter and more difficult to walk on, especially if carrying a pack. Mount Stelfox peeks from between the trees,

giving you a sense of the time and space. Shortly beyond the point where you first hear Whitegoat Creek, you descend sharply to the creek. This is the first of many stream crossings that you will have on this hike. If you are here before or after the early summer melt and runoff, you should be able to pick your way across the stream without removing your footwear. Otherwise, be prepared to sacrifice a certain amount of time on the crossings. Vistas now come into view with Mount Stelfox keeping company on the left. Three more stream crossings need to be negotiated before you can reestablish the rhythm that carries you for the next two km. A gravel wash marks the approximate half-way point between the last stream crossing and the junction with the Whitegoat Pass trail.

As you approach the 5.6-km mark, keep a sharp eye for the Whitegoat Pass trail that joins your road from the left. The junction is easy to miss. A large, two m-long log to the left of the road may be the best landmark for the junction. Bear left onto the Whitegoat Pass trail. Once on this horse trail it is quite distinct all the way across the pass and down to Coral Creek.

The trail descends to Whitegoat Creek, which, of course, you must cross. The only place where you may have some difficulty in picking up the trail is on the other side of the creek. Once across, it is best to continue straight ahead into what seems at first to be a solid growth of willows. Pick up the trail that goes past an informal campsite. If you have begun this hike late in the day, you may wish to camp overnight at this spot. Otherwise, continue along the trail. What appears to be a fork is actually a braid, so it does not matter which branch is taken. The trail climbs slowly through old-growth forest where calypso orchids and mosses

WHAT'S IN A NAME?

Mount Stelfox

Coral Creek is big, but the Cline is bigger,
They travel parklands of aspen and pine
To join the mighty North Saskatchewan River;
That river, so great, majestic and fine.

Whatever his talents as a poet, Henry Stelfox (1883-1974) was an interesting Albertan. Born in England in 1883, he spent some time as a young man in Africa among the Zulus and Basutos; the latter tribe named him "Ramosoanyi Ramoulili"—the little white man who sees in the dark. He immigrated to Canada and homesteaded near Wetaskiwin in 1907. After being hailed out four years in a row, he moved to Rocky Mountain House, where he tried his hand at a number of occupations. He became a keen outdoorsman and conservationist, serving on the Game Advisory Council from 1945 to 1958. In 1954 he was awarded the Julian Crandall conservation trophy, and in 1956 the Geographic Board of Alberta named Mount Stelfox in his honour.

Poem "Singing River" by Henry Stelfox

The Earl of Southesk called Mount Stelfox a "precipitous wall of mountain…about ten miles [long], its height perhaps two thousand feet [above Coral Creek]; in many places it is nearly perpendicular and the summit forms a continuous serrated line."

form the undergrowth. The trail descends into a gravel wash and follows it uphill before returning to the left side of the gully. Now, as you climb steeply, views open up, especially behind you where the mountains of red and grey rock make a sharp contrast to the verdant meadows and forests on the lower elevations.

Before you know it you are at the lower end of the pass that separates Mount Stelfox from the range of mountains to the northwest. Continuing a little further the trail crosses beneath a scree slope on the extreme north slope of Mount Stelfox. From your vantage point you can see much of this mountain. If you are day hiking, this open, flat spot makes an excellent lunch stop. If backpacking, this location is a good camp site except for the lack of water.

Continue along the trail as it climbs to the pass. It's an easy ascent beneath the scree slopes of Mount Stelfox. The trail cuts through willows and low bushes. No cairn marks the top of the pass, but from here the trail descends quickly toward Coral Creek. The pretty panorama of the Coral Creek valley below keeps you company throughout most of your descent. The trail swings sharply to the northwest, taking you upstream until a final steep pitch takes you over a gravel wash and to Coral Creek. Here, the trail forks. Bear left and follow the horse trail downstream. The other fork crosses the creek and continues to Job Pass. Local outfitters cut the trail over Whitegoat Pass as a way of bypassing the lower reaches of Coral Creek on their way to Job Lake. When you walk down Coral Creek you understand.

The Coral Creek trail is the most difficult part of this hike. Not only is it rocky underfoot, but it crosses and

At the top of Whitegoat Pass.

recrosses Coral Creek as many as a dozen times on the way to the Coral Creek trailhead where you have left your second vehicle. You may be able to avoid some of the fords if you are willing to scramble around rock faces and cliffs, a somewhat difficult feat when carrying a full pack! Beware, too, that some of the fords are deep and the current strong, especially during the early summer runoff.

The trail braids at one point; bear right along the trail for 500 m until the two branches rejoin. Cross a gravel wash. On the opposite bank of Coral Creek there is a view of some hoodoos. Now, you are faced with another series of creek crossings. The trail, though, is less difficult and some time can be made on this stretch. Two delightful waterfalls, one with a triple punchbowl, make an excellent place to rest a little before continuing.

At a junction, bear left and leave the creek bottom by climbing a steep, long hill to the top of the ridge. Here, a secondary trail joins from the right; it leads to a viewpoint overlooking the Coral Creek gorge. Remain on the horse trail. It is wide and very easy to follow. Between here and your vehicle, watch for several junctions. The first junction is with a trail that joins the horse trail from the right. It leads to the gorge viewpoint as well. The next trail joins from the left. Continue along the main horse trail. At the third junction, keep to the left. The trail to the right leads to the junction of the Cline and Coral gorges (see Cline and Coral Canyons Loop). Other secondary trails join the Coral Creek Trail, first one from the right and then one from the left. Ignore them and keep to the main trail. An unnamed creek is easy to cross and is an indication that you are within metres of your second vehicle.

HISTORICAL FOOTNOTES

The Earl of Southesk (1827-1905)

James Carnegie, ninth Earl of Southesk, recently widowed at age 32, was feeling ill and restless. He needed, as he told his friends, to travel to a part of the world where he might find good sport hunting big game and recoup his health. All things considered, his health could not have been that poor, for the part of the world he chose was the rugged Front Ranges of the Canadian Rockies, where neither his Indian guides nor white men had been before.

It was the autumn of 1859 and Southesk, after some refined reading (he took a small library with him), bracing weather and jolly sport, was working his way up Job Creek. His party missed Job Pass and crossed the divide onto Coral Creek via a hair-raising notch, over which they had to drag their horses with ropes. Southesk's September 17 diary entry records: "Breakfasting early, we made our way down a wild and rugged glen, along which we toiled till [sic] evening without rest or food, confined mostly to the bed of a torrent so stony as to hurt the horses' feet; our direction tended always to the southeast. At length we arrived at the valley's end, where the water escaped through a long, narrow, deep gorge

of rock, then crossed the shoulder of a mountain covered with lying-wood, and finally camped near the Saskatchewan, half-day from Kootanie [sic] Plain." The next day Southesk crossed the North Saskatchewan, and worked his way up the Siffleur River and crossed Pipestone Pass. Somewhere along the Siffleur Southesk lost his copy of *Hamlet*.

The identification of Coral Creek as Southesk's route to the Kootenay Plains has been the subject of some debate. However, Coral Creek is the only stream between the Brazeau and Cline Rivers that runs southeast and ends in a narrow, deep gorge. Southesk eventually made his way back to England where, invigorated by his Canadian adventure, he remarried, fathered eight children and lived to age 78. His hunting trophies are still preserved at Kinnaird Castle in Scotland.

As for his lost copy of *Hamlet*, it was found, weather-beaten but readable, almost 40 years later in 1898 by Hugh Stutfield and J. Norman Collie. They were descending the Siffleur River from Pipestone Pass on one of their quests for the mythical "giants" of Mounts Hooker and Brown.

30 Littlehorn Meadows – map p. 107

Duration ~ three days
Distance ~ 26.6 km
Level of Difficulty ~ steady climb to alpine area
Maximum Elevation ~ 2,480 m
Elevation Gain ~ 1,080 m
Map ~ 83 C/1 Whiterabbit Creek;
83 C/2 Cline River; 83 C/7 Job Creek

Leading up Whitegoat Creek to its headwaters just below Littlehorn Pass, this hike proceeds to loop around Littlehorn peak before you return the way you came. If you are very strong and very, very fast this hike can be done in two long days. The scenery is so special, though, that we feel it would be an injustice to recommend this. Do take at least three days to revel in the beauty of the Littlehorn meadows.

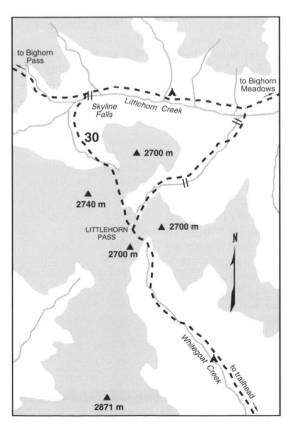

Access ~ Park your vehicle off Highway #11 at the Cline Solid Waste Transfer site located 42 km west of Nordegg, or 41 km east of the Banff National Park boundary. Whitegoat (Cline) Creek is 600 m south of the waste transfer site.

0.0	trailhead
0.6	junction
0.7	braid
2.6	Whitegoat Creek
3.0	Whitegoat Creek
3.3	Whitegoat Creek
3.6	Whitegoat Creek
4.4	gravel wash
5.6	junction
6.0	gravel wash
6.1	stream
6.5	gravel wash
6.7	outfitter's camp
7.6	Whitegoat Creek
7.7	Whitegoat Creek
7.9	Whitegoat Creek
8.3	Whitegoat Creek
9.6	Littlehorn Pass
10.2	notch
11.7	horse trail
12.0	viewpoint of "Skyline Falls"
12.3	stream
12.5	gravel wash
13.0	stream and outfitter's camp
13.3	gravel wash
13.8	gravel wash
14.0	fork
14.1	Littlehorn Creek
14.3	junction
14.9	Littlehorn Creek
15.3	fork

(continued)

Snowfields persist until midsummer, obliterating the path through the talus.

There is a chain link fence around the waste transfer site to discourage bears scavenging. If the gates are open, walk through the transfer site compound to the four-wheel drive track visible on the other side. If the gates are locked follow the fence around the south side of the compound to reach the track.

Although not remarkably steep, the trail climbs steadily through open pine forest and there are few views until the 2.6-km mark. Continue along the road past a junction with a trail on the left that leads to Whitegoat Falls. The road braids three times around boggy areas. Choose the main road since the braids tend to be wetter and more difficult to walk on. Shortly beyond the point where you first hear the rapids on Whitegoat Creek, descend sharply to this pretty, gurgling stream. This is the first of several stream crossings en route to the Littlehorn meadows. Vistas now come into view with Mount Stelfox keeping you company on the left. There are three more stream crossings before you can reestablish your rhythm. Cross a gravel wash. The trail now goes up, then down like waves on an ocean. Views disappear, making this part of the hike a bit of a slog. There are few good rest spots along this part of the trail, but a large log just to the left of the road makes a good seat. It also marks the junction with a smaller horse trail on the left, which leads to Whitegoat Pass.

Press on along the main road, climbing over a gravel wash, across a small stream, and past another gravel wash. The monotony of this stretch is broken by a junction with a trail on your left. It leads to an outfitter's camp complete with several fire pits. This site is the last level ground for six km. Press on to the next outfitter's camp in the Littlehorn meadows, but with a steep climb over two passes there will be little time to smell the flowers and enjoy the alpine meadows. So, with the racing waters of Whitegoat Creek only 20 m away, this first outfitter's camp makes an excellent place to pitch the tent. A sneak preview of the scenery that awaits you can be seen from the creek. In the meadows above the campsite is an array of wildflowers that range from Indian paint brushes and columbines to tiny forget-me-nots. Snow lingers on the opposite ridge.

A harbinger of the scenery to come. Approaching Littlehorn Pass.

From the outfitter's camp, the trail climbs steeply for the next kilometre as you approach the base of the Littlehorn Pass. Better views open up. Behind is Abraham Lake and Mount Stelfox, and ahead is a rock pillar that guards the pass. Whitegoat Creek has to be crossed again at the top of a steep pitch. From here, the magnificent scenery draws you ever upwards. The trail remains quite distinct as it winds through a narrow gorge from first the left bank, then to the right bank and then back to the left bank of Whitegoat Creek. While climbing above the treeline and through the talus slopes on the lower portion of the pass, keep an eye out for mountain sheep and even mountain goats that inhabit the area. A favourite spot for these animals is at a shallow cave and salt lick to the left. Marmots, golden mantled ground squirrels and pikas are also at home among the rocks and scree. It's a tough, but beautiful climb to the top of the pass. Alpine meadows cover the slope just beneath the notch that marks the pass, and in early summer the meadows are a riot of colour as vivid blue forget-me-nots jostle for space and nourishment with yellow alpine poppies and cinquefoils. From the top of the pass you can swing your eyes from Abraham Lake to the southeast, to the mountains and valleys just north of you.

The top of Littlehorn Pass marks both the beginning and end of the loop that leads to the base of Bighorn Pass, down the north branch of Littlehorn Creek, and back up along the south branch of the creek. So, begin your loop by descending into the lush bowl below Littlehorn Pass and climbing up to the notch straight ahead. From the notch the descent into the next meadows is steep. If you

The cairn on Littlehorn peak.

HISTORICAL FOOTNOTES

Skyline Trail Riders of the Canadian Rockies

The growing popularity of trail riding in the Canadian Rockies led to the formation of this Canadian Pacific Railway-sponsored club in 1924. This club was part of the railway's promotion of the tourist industry in the Rockies. Its charter members included Jimmy Simpson and Tom Wilson, who sometimes acted as outfitters and guides on the group's trips.

The organization was a popular one and by 1929 it had about 1,500 members. Its focus was an annual camp where those attending went on a three-day or longer ride on a different route each year. On its inception the club took on the characteristics of an "order." Badges of various grades were awarded to those riding from 80 to 4,022 km of mountain trails.

The Trail Riders have a sister organization called The Skyline Trail Hikers of the Canadian Rockies.

are here in early summer, be prepared for the trail to be at least partially covered with snow. For those who would like to indulge in an easy rock scramble and have an hour or so to kill, climb the grassy slope to the right of the notch. It is a 300-m scramble to a cairn on top of the 2,700 m-high Littlehorn peak. There is a glorious 360 degree panorama that takes in the loop that you will make. If you are lucky you will see mountain goats grazing on the seemingly bare slopes. To get to the meadows from here it is best to return to the notch, since the descent through the talus directly below the peak is rough and slow.

The meadows are an alpine botanist's delight! Watered by the melting snows from the surrounding mountainsides, the meadows support a full range of alpine flowers, including white heather that carpets whole slopes. As you descend through the meadows the footing can be a little wet, especially early in the season. With Bighorn Pass looming in front and above, cross the many braids of the headwaters of the north branch of Littlehorn Creek. Wind through the willows and find the horse trail that leads down from Bighorn Pass. Turn right onto the trail and follow it as it parallels the left-hand side of the creek. The trail drops quickly from the alpine into the trees. En route, a stunningly beautiful waterfall, named by the Skyline Trail Riders after themselves, plunges down a rock slope in a series of steps.

The trail drops through the willows to a small stream and crosses a gravel wash. By now you are well within the treeline. Just beyond the next stream crossing there is an outfitter's camp on the left. This is the only other campsite on this hike. Beyond this point the trail continues to drop quickly past two gravel washes to a fork in the trail. To take the left-hand fork leads you down the Littlehorn to the Bighorn Meadows. However, bear right and descend to Littlehorn Creek. At this point the torrent is at least four m across and there is no easy crossing.

You are now on the return portion of the loop around Littlehorn peak. The trail climbs steeply up a ridge almost from the creek crossing. On top where the trail flattens, you can hear and then see the south branch of the Littlehorn Creek racing to its meeting with the north branch. A junction with a secondary trail on the right leads to a viewpoint overlooking the lower Littlehorn Falls. The descent to the viewpoint is steep and treacherous.

The trail climbs toward Littlehorn Pass in gradual steps through open meadows and spruce trees. The trail leads past several tributaries of Littlehorn Creek and climbs the opposite bank sharply. After a steep

The Littlehorn Falls on the south branch of Littlehorn Creek.

pull the trail flattens a little. Straight ahead is a headwall that appears to block the way. The trail, though, begins a long, long climb that swings to the right. As you climb back above the treeline the scenery is nothing less than spectacular, with the south branch of Littlehorn Creek foaming below on the left. Just above a particularly pretty set of waterfalls along the upper reaches of the creek, the trail flattens again briefly before crossing what is now a small rivulet, then switching up a talus slope. After a tough pull you are once again in the bowl just below Littlehorn Pass. Climb the scree to the top of the pass and retrace your steps down the Whitegoat Creek to your campsite.

From here, continue descending along the Whitegoat to your trailhead.

111

31 Viewpoint Trail – map p. 116

Duration ~ two hours
Distance ~ 4.2 km
Level of Difficulty ~ easy stroll
Maximum Elevation ~ 1,370 m
Elevation Gain ~ 15 m
Map ~ 83 C/1 Whiterabbit Creek

Access ~ Park your vehicle at the David Thompson Resort 46 km west of Nordegg, or 37 km east of the Banff National Park boundary on Highway #11.

This short hike is a pleasant orientation to the area immediately around the David Thompson Resort. Few people can resist the lure of a lake and this walk should satisfy the desire for a close-up view of Abraham Lake.

~

Walk south through the parking lot past the motel, where you pick up a private road that leads down the slope toward Abraham Lake. Through the pine forests you can see Elliot Peak on the left and Sentinel Mountain on the right. There is a junction with a hiking trail near the edge of the slope. Turn left onto the trail and climb a rocky path to a magnificent viewpoint looking south along Abraham Lake. Straight ahead is the Cline fire lookout. To your left is Mount Michener and on your right is Mount William Booth.

0.0	trailhead
0.3	junction
0.6	viewpoint
1.3	gravel road
1.4	Abraham Lake
1.7	trail
2.2	rock cairn
2.9	fork
3.1	helipad
3.3	path
3.6	sewage lagoon
3.9	junction
4.2	trailhead

Mount Michener and Cline fire lookout across the lake.

HISTORICAL FOOTNOTES

Silas Abraham (1871-ca. 1961)

Silas Abraham and his family are almost synonymous with the Kootenay Plains. Some of the most significant features in the area, Mount Abraham, Abraham Lake, the Abraham Slabs and Abraham Flats were named after them by non-natives. The Stoney, like almost all other native peoples in North America, do not name geographic features after people, either living or dead.

Silas Abraham was born in 1871 near the Cline River, probably on the Abraham Flats. It was on the Flats that Silas, and later his son, Norman, built their cabins. Like the other Stoneys, Silas and his family had a preferred hunting area. His region was from Windy Point south to the Kootenay Plains, and the Cline and Siffleur Rivers.

Silas's strategic presence brought him into contact with several famous non-natives who used the Siffleur River to enter the Plains. During the winter of 1902-1903, he and other Stoneys helped construct the cabins and corral at Tom Wilson's ranch. Elliott Barnes, when he was away from his ranch, especially during the winter, hired Silas Abraham to look after his cabin. In 1909, Martin Nor-

degg hired Silas Abraham to accompany him on a coal prospecting expedition. Mary Schäffer met him and his family several times when she visited the Plains.

Silas Abraham died in the early 1960s at the Bighorn Reserve.

From the viewpoint, this well-used trail takes you down along the edge of the hill toward the lake. Hoodoos on the opposite shore of the lake are clearly visible at this point. Numerous footpaths from the campsite join from the left. Ignore them and continue as far as a junction with an old road. Turn right onto the road and descend toward Abraham Lake. If you wish to return to the campground turn left; a 700-m walk brings you to campsite #7. At the lake's edge turn right and saunter along the lakeside. The reservoir is prettiest in the autumn when it is nearly full, hiding the many terraces that mark the different levels of the lake. However, if you are here at any other time, you may enjoy poking about the driftwood that accumulates at the lake's edge. Cut across the meadow toward a low ridge that is in front of you. The hiking trail reappears at the bottom of the slope. Climb the slope and follow the trail as far as a fork. With Abraham Lake and the Abraham Flats below you, this part of the loop is as idyllic as the previous ridge. As you approach Highway #11 the bridge over the Cline River comes into view. Elliot Peak dominates the skyline behind the bridge. A small rock cairn is perched on the height of land before your path dips toward the highway. Below, the braids of the Cline River meander through the Flats, giving you perhaps some idea of what the historic Flats must have looked like before they were destroyed by Abraham Lake.

If you cannot resist descending to the Cline River for a walk along the Flats, bear left at a fork in the trail. Otherwise, turn right swinging away from Abraham Lake and enter a pine forest. Within a short distance you come out onto a helipad complete with wind sock and gasoline drums. Do not cross over to the helipad, but bear right across the flat, open meadow. You should be able to find a roadway that quickly becomes a footpath between the forest on your right and Highway #11 on your left. This path leads back toward the David Thompson Resort. En route, there are two distinct trails that lead up the ridge on the right. In all likelihood, these have been created by motorcycles and ATVs. Pass by the Resort's sewage lagoon. Year after year, mallards and other waterfowl have claimed this as the perfect home to raise their families.

Once past the sewage lagoon, the road climbs a ridge coming steeply upon a junction with a trail on the right. This junction corresponds to 300 m at the beginning of this hike. Keep on the main roadway, or to the left, to return to the trailhead.

WHAT'S IN A NAME?

Abraham Flats

Previous Name ~ Cataract Flats

Abraham Flats was the local and unofficial name for the meadows at the confluence of the Cline River with the North Saskatchewan River. The Flats were inundated by Abraham Lake in 1972 and now come into view only when the reservoir is at low level. The Abraham Flats are named after Stoney Indian, Silas Abraham and his family. Silas and his son, Norman, had their cabins here.

The first mention of the Flats was made by the Earl of Southesk, who camped here the evening of September 17, 1859 after a difficult descent of Coral Creek. He apparently mistook the Flats for the Kootenay Plains when he recorded his disdain: "This so-called plain is merely an inconsiderable enlargement of the valley—a space of some 50 acres, bare of trees, and covered with short grasses."

In the late 1950s, the Alberta Forest Service built the Upper Saskatchewan Ranger station on the Abraham Flats. An all-weather gravel airstrip was also constructed at the Ranger station. Under the charge of Forest Ranger John Elliott, the station remained the regional headquarters for the AFS in the upper North Saskatchewan River valley for about 10 years. The rising waters of Abraham Lake made the site untenable at that time and the station was abandoned.

At the turn of the century the area was called the Cataract Flats. The designation comes from an early name for the Cline River, Cataract River.

HISTORICAL FOOTNOTES

The David Thompson Resort

Courtesy of Doris Magnus.

No doubt, campers at the David Thompson Resort would have found the viewpoint overlooking Abraham Lake and made a trail along the edge of the hill even if the developers of the Resort, Ken and Jim Brown, had not undertaken to develop a formal trail. The Browns first took option on part of a land lease here in September 1971. The Bighorn Dam was nearing completion and Highway #11 had just been rerouted to higher ground, because parts of the old highway were about to disappear under the waters of the reservoir. The entire territory west of Nordegg was opening up to the tourist trade and the Browns wanted to be part of it.

With little capital—only money from the sale of their Calgary homes and a $25,000 bank loan—the brothers first thought that they'd open "maybe a small store, a lunch counter and a campground. We had nothing too ambitious in mind." But when they learned that they had to erect a motel in order to acquire a 24-year lease on the land, the Browns tapped into government incentive loans to finance their resort.

With the help of their father-in-law (the brothers had married two sisters), they levelled the ground for the building sites and roadways that first September. Their wives, with four small children in tow, moved into mobile homes on the site. There was no water or power. For the better part of a year, the Browns hauled water from a spring on the Cline River for personal use and for the construction of the concrete-and-cement-block motel, store and restaurant. When Alberta Hydro informed them that it would cost $200,000 to bring in power, the Browns bought a generator. Even today, the resort's power comes from a generator. To bring in natural gas would have cost $180,000. The Browns opted for propane.

During the summer of 1972, the Browns opened a gas station, a small convenience store and a restaurant. That winter, they marked out campground sites and began construction of the motel. The David Thompson Resort was officially opened on the Labour Day weekend of 1972. As the only services offered on the 87 km-long stretch of road between Nordegg and the Banff-Jasper highway, their enterprise was bound to succeed.

Today, the David Thompson Resort offers a 46-bed motel with swimming pool and whirlpool, a campground, store and gift shop, a restaurant, bar, video arcade, mini golf and children's playground.

32 Little Indian Falls & Whitegoat Lakes – map p. 116

Duration ~ half day
Distance ~ 9.1 km
Level of Difficulty ~ easy stroll with a short, easy scramble
Maximum Elevation ~ 1,385 m
Elevation Gain ~ 30 m
Map ~ 83 C/1 Whiterabbit Creek

Access ~ Park your vehicle at the David Thompson Resort located 46 km west of Nordegg or 37 km east of the Banff National Park boundary on Highway #11.

This pretty loop introduces you to some spots of local interest, namely the Little Indian Falls and the Whitegoat Lakes.

~

From the parking lot, walk up the gravel road leading into the campground. At a fork in the road, turn left and follow the ring road to campsites #7 and #8. On your left is a footpath that leads down an easy slope as far as a gravel road. At the road,

0.0	trailhead
0.3	footpath
0.5	gravel road
0.8	intersection
1.6	windfall area
2.4	windfall area
2.9	Abraham Lake
3.8	promontory
4.8	swamp and stream
5.2	Little Indian Falls
5.3	T-junction
5.8	highway
5.9	trail
6.0	stream
6.4	junction
8.0	junction
8.3	viewpoint over Whitegoat Lakes
8.5	McKenzies' Trails West entrance
8.9	highway
9.1	trailhead

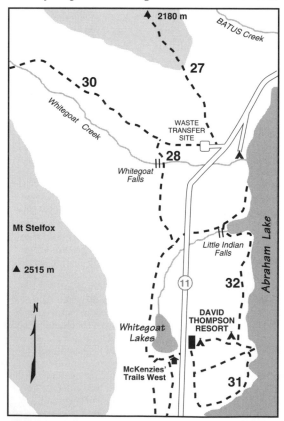

Whitegoat Lakes.

bear to the right and continue down the slope. Look sharply for a footpath on the left where the road cuts through a meadow. Turn left into the meadow. The intersection of the footpath with the road is somewhat indistinct, but the path becomes clearer once you are 30 m or so away from the road. There are no views along this part of the trail as you walk through the open pine forest. Uprooted trees block the path, so follow the orange ticker tape around the windfall area to regain the footpath. After this, the path swings closer to Abraham Lake and you can catch views of the lake from time to time. Finally, break out of the forest to an open slope overlooking Abraham Lake. It is somewhat disconcerting at first to discover that the trail, after it dips down to the lake, disappears, but again, look for orange ticker tape that leads up a slope and back into the woodland. You come upon yet another windfall

WHAT'S IN A NAME?

Whitegoat Lakes

Whitegoat is a colloquial name for the Mountain Goat. This shaggy, white antelope was once common on the slopes above the Kootenay Plains. Over-hunting and habitat disturbance have pushed these animals back into the mountains.

The lake (there is really only one) likely took its name from the nearby Cline River, which at one time, was known locally as the Whitegoat River. Dr. James Hector of the Palliser Expedition, recorded on his 1858 map the present Cline River as the Wap-ut-teehk River. Wap-ut-teehk is Stoney for whitegoat.

area where, again, kindly souls have marked a route with orange tape. Once past the windfall area, the trail brings you to a slope overlooking the entire length of Abraham Lake. Pretty as the view is, the trail soon leads back into the open pines.

Little Indian Falls.

You are now cutting across a point of land that juts out into the lake. The main part of the lake is on the right; a small bay appears on the left as you walk down the point. The open parkland you are walking through allows you to see Mount Michener at your two o'clock and Vision Quest Ridge at your ten o'clock. As you approach the tip of the point, stay high near the trees so you can swing around the promontory toward the bay. Once around, go down the slope to the edge of the water and walk around to the grassy flats on the other side of the bay. Cut across the flats and cross a small stream before turning left and walking toward the hill in front of you. Soon you can hear Little Indian Falls.

This three metre-high waterfall was named by local residents after the Cree children from Smallboy's band who used the waterfall for a shower bath. The waterfalls are a delightful reward for your trot. After a short rest, scramble up the slope immediately to the right of the falls. There is a trail at the top. Turn right onto the trail and within 10 m there is a T-junction. If you are interested in a short detour, turn right. The trail first goes to a bay, then cuts across a point to the next bay. The trail ends here, making this an excellent spot for a snack break as you enjoy the scenery.

Retrace your steps to the T-junction and continue straight along the path to the highway. Cross the highway and find the horse trail that runs along the highway right-of-way. Turn left and walk south. After crossing a small stream there is an intersection. Bear left to stay on the main trail; the trail to the right goes to the Whitegoat Falls. As you walk around the lakes there are some very large poplars and spruce trees. At an intersection bear left along the main, broad trail; if you go to the right you end up at the Coral Creek staging area. Soon, you arrive at a viewpoint over one of the lakes. These lakes are really sloughs, for neither is more than two m deep. Muskrats and beaver have been known to live here, but fish apparently do not.

From here, the trail braids. Take any one for they all lead to McKenzies' Trails West. Turn left onto the rough gravel road and follow it to the highway. Your vehicle and the David Thompson Resort is across the highway and 200 m to the north.

33 Cline and Coral Canyons Loop – map p. 119

Duration ~ half day
Distance ~ 7.7 km
Level of Difficulty ~ easy walk on well-groomed trails
Maximum Elevation ~ 1,510 m
Elevation Gain ~ 155 m
Map ~ 83 C/1 Whiterabbit Creek; 83 C/2 Cline River

Access ~ Park your vehicle just north of the Cline River bridge at the Coral Creek Trail parking area located 47 km west of Nordegg, or 36 km east of the Banff National Park boundary on Highway #11.

This has to be one of the more delightful half-day hikes in the Cline area. From the pretty lower reaches of the Cline, the trail follows an ever-deepening and spectacular gorge that stretches upstream beyond the confluence of the Cline River and Coral Creek. A dramatic view up the broad valley of Coral Creek marks a satisfying conclusion to this hike.

~

Stay on the west side of Highway #11, and walk south toward the Cline River bridge. At the north end of the bridge find the path that leads down

0.0	trailhead
0.2	Cline River
0.3	stream
0.9	lower end of Cline River canyon
1.4	stream
2.9	confluence of Cline River and Coral Creek
3.1	junction
3.5	junction
3.8	junction
4.1	junction and crest of main horse trail
4.2	junction
4.4	top of Coral Creek canyon
4.6	junction
4.7	junction
5.0	junction
6.6	stream
6.9	junction
7.2	junction
7.6	stream
7.7	trailhead

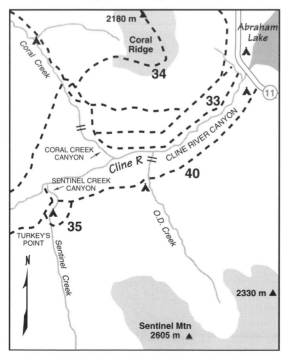

toward the river. As the trail swings away from the bridge, an old beaver dam and lodge are to your immediate right. The trail soon leads to a small bog that is easily crossed. Cross a shallow stream flowing in from your right and continue along what is now a well-defined footpath lined with silver-leaved wolf willow bushes, junipers and buffaloberry bushes.

Passing an Alberta Environment marker, the path soon forks with the lower or left-hand fork leading down to the river. The Cline here is a foaming, racing torrent. Fishermen can often be seen trying their luck for the bull trout that are known to favour the Cline. Continue straight ahead along the path as it skirts the edge of the river's cliff.

The beauty of the lower Cline becomes more spectacular opposite the steep-walled sides of the Cline River canyon. The path soon takes a 90 degree turn to climb a small ridge. At its top, a great view of the gorge awaits you. Shutterbugs will be kept busy trying to capture this magnificent spot on film. Continue along the edge of the canyon, and pass a rivulet, which becomes a small waterfall plunging into the river below. There are numerous braids in the path, so in order not to find yourself heading into the forest, keep the gorge in view on your left. Where the trail makes another sharp 90 degree turn to the right, leave the awe-inspiring Cline River canyon.

Within 50 m you break out upon the scenery of the Coral Creek gorge. Smaller than the Cline River canyon, that of the Coral is nonetheless picturesque. As the trail begins to climb, join the heavily-used horse trail that comes in from the right. Further up the trail a path joins from the right. This path is a shortcut back to the

staging area. Continue along the horse trail. The destination, a viewpoint overlooking the top of the Coral Creek gorge, can be seen on a bench of land nearly one km upstream. As you approach the viewpoint there is a trail to the left leading down to the bench. Resist the temptation to head over to the viewpoint right away and continue straight ahead along the horse trail to the top of the ridge.

GEOFACTS

Cline and Coral Canyons

Each of these two rivers plunges through steep-walled canyons for at least part of their journey to the North Saskatchewan River. The formation of these gorges or canyons began approximately 12,000 years ago with the retreat of the glaciers. Twelve thousand years is, in geological terms, a mere blink of the eye. Nevertheless, the Cline and Coral have had plenty of time to cut through the layers of limestone to form deep canyons.

Looking up Coral Creek.

Numerous trail riders, some out for a day's ride or others on the trail for several weeks, share this trail with hikers.

Here, bear sharply to the left along a path. Within metres you break out onto a dramatic view of the Coral Creek valley.

Upstream of the canyon, Coral Creek wends its way from the snow-caps beyond through gravel beds to the top of the gorge. Then, all views of the creek disappear as it is squeezed between the rock walls of the canyon. Bear left and follow the trail down the slope past a fork to the furthest point on the bench for a view of the chute that marks the beginning of the gorge. This makes an excellent spot to enjoy a light snack and a short rest.

From here, to return to your vehicle, climb back up the path to the fork. Take the right-hand fork that leads across the slope and up to rejoin the horse trail. A 300-m return on the trail brings you to the intersection with a secondary path. Here, leave the horse trail and bear to the left along the path through open pine and spruce forest. At a junction with the old forestry road, turn left. Some 300 m beyond a trail joins from the left. Continue straight ahead. About 100 m before the Coral Creek Trail staging area you must cross one last stream.

WHAT'S IN A NAME?

Cline River

Previous Names ~ Rivière du Meurleton ~ Wap-ut-teehk River ~ Cataract River ~ Whitegoat River

Stoney Name ~ Hahaseegee Wapta (Bad Rapid River)

The Cline River is named after Michael Cline, who joined the North West Company as a fur trader in the late 1790s. After the North West Company and the Hudson's Bay Company joined forces in 1821, he found himself in charge of the Bay's trading post at Jasper House from 1824-1835. During the summer the postmaster and a few men kept the post open, tended a garden and cared for the horses. Meanwhile another group took an extended hunting trip through the mountains to secure provisions for the winter to reduce the amount of subsistence hunting and their dependency on the pemmican trade.

The Kootenay Plains, known for its abundance and variety of wildlife, and as a gathering place among Indians from both sides of the Divide, was a preferred destination. Sir James Hector called the route from Jasper House to the Kootenay Plains "Old Cline's trail." Michael Cline probably crossed over from the Brazeau River to Coral Creek via Job Pass. From Coral Creek he probably entered the valley of the present-day Cline River before debouching onto the Plains.

Sir James Hector of the Palliser Expedition called the Cline the Wap-ut-teehk River, which is Stoney for whitegoat. On his map he gives both Wap-ut-teehk and White Goat as names for the river. The name Whitegoat River remained in colloquial use until at least the mid-1970s.

Another name for the Cline was Cataract River, named by geologist A.P. Coleman in 1892. Cataract River, he said, was a translation of the river's Stoney name, Hahaseegee Wapta. Coleman found this to be accurate when he had difficulty fording the river below the canyon: "...our ponies lurched and slipped, while the foam dashed against the seat of the saddle on the upstream side. One had all the

sensations of pitching and rolling at sea in a very small canoe, so that it was a decided relief when the pony stumbled into shallow water on the other side." Over the next 10 years other travellers, such as J. Norman Collie and Mary Schäffer, called the river the Cataract.

At the beginning of the 19th century, fur traders David Thompson and Alexander Henry referred to the Cline as the Rivière du Meurleton. Meurleton may be a French corruption of a native (perhaps Kootenay) name. Or it may be a corruption of merle d'eau, which means dipper (Cinclus mexicanus). This chunky little bird prefers cascading mountain streams that stay open all year, such as the Cline.

A final possibility is that Meurleton comes from the 18th century French word for battlement: merle or merlet. This theory is based on Henry's analogy of nearby Minster Mountain as a fortress.

Viewpoints along the Cline River thrill hikers of all ages.

34 Coral Ridge – map p. 119

Duration ~ full day
Distance ~ 13.4 km
Level of Difficulty ~ steady walk on hard-packed trail; steep bushwhack; easy scramble
Maximum Elevation ~ 2,380 m
Elevation Gain ~ 1,025 m
Map ~ 83 C/1 Whiterabbit Creek; 83 C/2 Cline River

Proof that ancient seas had inundated what are now the mountainous regions of Alberta can be found on a ridge overlooking the confluence of Cline River and Coral Creek. A tough little climb rewards the intrepid hiker with a magnificent view of these valleys, as well as Abraham Lake and the North Saskatchewan River valley.

~

GEOFACTS

Our Tropical Past

Long before the formation of the Rockies, tropical seas covered much of what is now Alberta. The seas advanced and retreated a number of times. By the late Devonian and early Mississippian periods (375-350 million years ago) seas covered most of what is now Alberta. With each invasion of the sea, another shoreline was created.

During these periods, the warm, shallow water was rich in marine life. Primitive fish, sponges, crinoids (sea lilies) and brachiopods flourished. The warm waters and climate also made a perfect combination for the formation of coral reefs. Then, during the late Devonian period a major disaster struck the reefs and the reef building corals died.

These reefs are very important today. It was in reefs of similar age that Imperial Oil brought in Leduc Number One in 1947 to kick start the Canadian petroleum industry.

Access ~ Park your vehicle at the Coral Creek Trail parking area on the north side of the Cline River 47 km west of Nordegg, or 36 km east of the Banff National Park boundary on Highway #11. A hard-packed horse trail leading up the Cline River valley begins at the west end of the staging area.

0.0	trailhead
0.1	stream
0.5	junction
0.8	junction
2.1	junction
3.1	junction
3.4	junction
3.7	junction and base of Coral Ridge
4.2	deadfall
4.7	avalanche slope
5.2	top of shoulder and cairns
5.7	saddle
5.9	metal reflector
6.3	cairn
6.7	cairn and end of ridge walk
13.4	trailhead

The stems of crinoids are composed of stacks of disks, each disk being grooved.

What appears to be a normal scree slope is, in fact, a rock hound's delight. With the Cline River valley in the background, the author examines a coral fossil.

From the trailhead, the hard-packed horse trail makes the first several kilometres a bit of a trudge as it climbs slowly, paralleling the Cline River valley. Along the way you cross a small stream and meet a number of forks or junctions in the trail. At the first junction with a trail joining from the right, keep on the main horse trail by continuing straight ahead. Three hundred m later there is another junction with a trail joining from the right. This is actually a braid—it rejoins the main horse trail at 3.1 km. Ignore it and continue straight ahead on the main trail to the next junction, which marks the confluence of Coral Creek with the Cline River. Here, take a sharp right-hand turn, staying on the horse trail. At this point, the trail begins to ascend more quickly through lodgepole pine forest. The next junction, a full kilometre later, is the top end of the braid that began at the 800-m mark. It is here that you break out of the open forest onto the vista of the Coral Creek gorge. Continue following the horse trail as it winds its way up along the open ridge. The steep rock sides of the gorge on the left keep you company. Near the trail's highest point is a footpath leading to the left and down to the viewpoint overlooking the top of the Coral Creek gorge. Ignore this secondary path and continue along the horse trail as it climbs straight ahead through spruce and pine forest. At the top of the hill just before the trail begins its sharp dip to Coral Creek is a footpath to the left. Do not take this path; instead, turn right toward the base of Coral Ridge.

It's an easy bushwhack at the base of this, the extreme end of the lowest shoulder of Mount Stelfox. For 100 m climb up a series of easy rock ledges, allowing yourself to drift a little to the left. Then, dip down and enter the pine forest that covers the entire south-facing slope of the ridge. The next 100 m or so are a miserable bushwhack through heavy deadfall, some of which is the remnants of an old forest fire. As you struggle through this area bear a little to the left. The thought of a nearly 360 degree panorama, not to mention the corals and remains of marine life embedded forever in the rocks at the top of the ridge, helps you persevere through this part of the climb. Once through the deadfall area, begin a steep, tough climb through open forest. As you continue to drift to the left you come upon an avalanche slope. Climb straight up through the scree. The slope eases somewhat as you make the final push through open lodgepole pine forest to the top.

The view at the top is nothing less than spectacular. Swinging your eyes from north to south, you take in Mount Stelfox above you and the aquamarine waters of Abraham Lake below set against its backdrop of Mounts Michener and William Booth. Directly south, Sentinel Peak and the anticline of Elliot Peak overlook the Cline River valley. The Cline's dramatic canyon walls are visible even from this height. Protecting the Cline valley are first Purple Mountain, then the glaciers on the Whitegoat Peaks, the majestic Mount Cline itself and finally the Whitegoat Peaks. Continuing the swing to the northwest is the long, glaciated, U-shaped Coral Creek valley with its tributary canyons and finally, the forested lower slopes of Mount Stelfox.

Three rock cairns placed in a triangle on this pleasant knoll indicate that you are not the first to have made the climb. Add a rock or two to show you were here. The best, though, is yet to come, so after a short rest, walk eastward along the ridge, being careful not to get too close to the edge of the cliffs. At the end of the ridge is a saddle that joins this knoll to Coral Ridge itself. It's an easy jaunt down and across the saddle and up the scree slope to a metal survey reflector. Continue to climb the ridge. It eventually flattens out and becomes a grassy ridge interspaced with krummholz. A cairn marks the end of the ridge walk.

In addition to adding Baldy and Coliseum mountains far to the northeast to your vista are the treasures at your feet, for this entire ridge was once a coral reef. It is now uplifted sharply from its ancient sea floor. It is the corals on this ridge that give the creek below its name. Time spent poking among the scree will be richly rewarded.

Return the way you came. Be sure to swing to the left as you descend in order to avoid the small valley on the right.

HISTORICAL FOOTNOTES

Triangle Peak

Triangle Peak is a mountain described and climbed by University of Toronto geologist A. P. Coleman. It may be Coral Ridge. On July 18, 1892, he forded the Cline River near its confluence with the North Saskatchewan River. A. P. Coleman then climbed a mountain and described the following scene:

"A small beautiful lake [Whitegoat Lakes] and white salt licks broke the surface of prairie below us, and looking down on our specks of ponies, we could imagine the brown herds of buffalo drinking at the pond or streaming toward the salt lick, where the hunters lay in wait for them. One could still see their hollow paths and wallows and an occasional whitened skull in 1892."

Triangle Peak remains a mystery mountain. Whether it is Coral Ridge or not, it really doesn't matter. The view is just as great as the one Coleman described 100 years ago.

35 Sentinel Creek – map p. 119

Duration ~ half day
Distance ~ 9.8 km
Level of Difficulty ~ steady walk with steep scramble
Maximum Elevation ~ 1,555 m
Elevation Gain ~ 185 m
Map ~ 83 C/1 Whiterabbit Creek; 83 C/2 Cline River

Access ~ Park your vehicle at the Pinto Lake Recreation Trail staging area 48 km west of Nordegg, or 35 km east of the Banff National Park boundary just south of the Cline River bridge on Highway #11.

This half-day walk introduces you to the Cline River country with its racing mountain streams and steep-walled canyons. A popular hike, you may well meet others en route to or returning from Pinto Lake.

~

The main path to Sentinel Creek begins to the left of the Pinto Lake Recreation Trail sign. It leads down past several informal campsites and through open pine forest. As the trail begins to climb slowly

0.0	trailhead
0.5	junction
1.6	gravel wash
2.0	O.D. Creek
2.6	spring
4.0	junction
4.3	Sentinel Creek
4.5	Turkey's Point
4.7	junction
5.0	junctions
5.1	end of footpath
5.4	confluence of Sentinel Creek and Cline River
5.7	Sentinel Creek
5.8	junction
9.8	trailhead

Sentinel Mountain.

126

WHAT'S IN A NAME?

Sentinel Creek and Sentinel Mountain

Sentinel Creek is the informal name for the creek beside Sentinel Mountain. Although Sentinel Mountain was named by A. P. Coleman, the mountain he saw and named is not the same one shown on the topographic map. On July 16, 1892 when Coleman and his party were descending Whiterabbit Creek they saw: "...straight ahead, jutting boldly into the belt of prairie, stood a beautiful mountain nine thousand feet high, bent into a fold like an 'S', two miles long and a mile broad on its side." Since the mountain could be seen from all the nearby valleys, he called it Sentinel Mountain.

Whether you are standing on the Plains near the mouth of the Whiterabbit, or using your map, one thing is absolutely clear—you cannot see Sentinel Mountain from that angle. What you do see is Elliot Peak and its trademark "A"-shaped anticline. Elliot Peak (2,872 m) is not only taller than Sentinel Mountain (2,600 m), but also blocks any view of Sentinel Mountain.

Today's Elliot Peak, then, is A. P. Coleman's Sentinel Mountain.

up the Cline River valley the vegetation changes to poplar bush, which in autumn, creates a splash of gold against the blue sky. One-half km later, a secondary path joins from the right. This path leads back to the gravel pit and parking area at the trailhead. Continue straight ahead.

Climbing slowly through spruce forest, the trail is a popular one with hikers, mountain bikers and equestrians alike. After one km you come to a dry gravel wash. At this point you can hear to your right, but not see, the Cline River as it foams its way down its canyon. The first real stream you cross is O.D. Creek some 400 m past the wash. Kindly souls have thrown a couple of logs across this pretty creek to aid you. This is a good place to fill your water bottle if you have not already done so. Once across, there is an informal campsite with a fine view up O.D. Creek valley, which boasts of steep sides and a rapid drop. Sentinel Mountain is to the right and Elliot Peak is the promontory at the top of the valley. From the campsite, keep on the main trail by bearing to the right. Secondary trails leading to the left end within a few hundred metres.

For those of you who forgot or prefer not to drink from a creek, a freshwater spring bubbles out of the ground just to the right of the trail 600 m past O.D. Creek. While welcome, the spring also heralds an area, which in a wet year, renders much of the lower part of the Pinto Lake trail muddy and slick. In this stretch, springs have made the trail impassable to the point that it has had to be corduroyed. Shortly beyond here the vegetation changes to that of Engelmann spruce, a sign that you are slowly but surely climbing. The trail has dried out, but now you enter an area where a violent windstorm blew down a number of trees across the pathway. Outfitters, who make heavy use of this trail, were probably responsible for reopening the trail.

At a fork in the trail, bear left. The Pinto Lake trail continues straight ahead, but you want to take the left-hand fork to swing upstream of where the main trail crosses Sentinel Creek. Within metres there is another windfall area and it is quite apparent that outfitters wielding chain saws have not come this way, for you must climb over numerous fallen trees before you are clear of this tedious part of the trail. Once past here, the trail drops sharply to Sentinel Creek.

This pretty mountain stream tumbles over rocks as it twists and turns down the valley before joining the Cline River. After crossing Sentinel Creek you are tempted to stop and enjoy the scenery, but press on to "Turkey's Point" campsite. To find this informal camping spot, go downstream and find the continuation of the trail through the willows. It continues downstream for 50 m, at which point you arrive at "Turkey's Point" campsite set amongst open pines on a

FLORAFACTS

Canada Buffaloberry

Scientific Name ~ *Shepherdia canadensis*
Other Names ~ Soapberry, Soopolallie
Stoney Name ~ Sawin Ta Hatha

Growing more than two m high, the buffaloberry has, in autumn, yellow, orange or red berries. While not poisonous, the berries may be unappealing to our taste buds.

The natives whipped the berries together with water to produce a frothy pink delicacy known as "Indian ice cream." The same substance that allows the berry juice to froth also gives the berries a soapy feel when rubbed between your fingers, hence the shrub's other common name, soapberry.

The Stoneys made an infusion using the plant's berries and leaves as a treatment for a sore face and acne. With the roots, they made a tea for "women's disorders."

The Stoneys also called the fruit of this plant "slave berries," after Peigan women who were badly treated by their husbands.

spit above the creekbed. This is an enticing place to rest while taking in the local scenery of cliffs and countless cataracts. Looking upstream, Elliot and Sentinel Peaks guard the valley on the left.

Return to the footpath and climb up the steep embankment above the creek. At the top there is a T-junction. Left is the Pinto Lake Trail. Turn right and walk down the slope. You are high enough to have a good view of the turquoise waters of Abraham Lake framed by Mount Michener. There are a series of junctions with secondary trails leading down to Sentinel Creek. Ignore these and continue straight ahead along a footpath that winds its way through the spruce trees along the top of the narrow Sentinel Creek canyon. The footpath begins to drop and finally ends at a steep scramble down the slope to Sentinel Creek. The narrowest part of the canyon is just upstream, but high walls on either side of the creek continue downstream. The scenery is nothing less than dramatic. Your jaunt ends at the confluence of Sentinel Creek with the Cline River. This is a good place to stop and enjoy the magnificent scenery.

Retrace your footsteps back up Sentinel Creek to the point where you descended into the canyon. Scramble up the slope and along the footpath to the main trail. A number of braids drop down to Sentinel Creek. The top of the canyon is just downstream. Logs thrown across the creek help keep your feet dry. Find the main trail and follow it as it leads out of the creek valley en route to the trailhead. One hundred m beyond the creek there is a fork in the trail to the right. This is the footpath you took initially to swing upstream of the Sentinel Creek canyon. From here it is a straight jaunt back to the trailhead and your vehicle.

HISTORICAL FOOTNOTES

Robert Smallboy (1898-1984)

In 1968 about 150 Cree from Hobbema followed Chief Robert Smallboy to the Kootenay Plains. They established a camp and attempted to live free from "civilization's evils and death." As a part of this new life, band members attempted to follow a lifestyle modelled as closely as possible on their ancestral ways. Their move to Kootenay Plains attracted national and international attention.

This "back to the land" movement had strong religious connotations. According to Chief Smallboy "Those of us who are camped on the Kootenay Plains, who have established our ties with the Mother Earth and the Supreme Being by living our lives as the Great Spirit had intended man to live, we have once more been made aware of the scheme of things and the purpose of life."

Smallboy's decision was controversial among his fellow Cree. Some who stayed behind in Hobbema resented the innuendo that their life and community were "evil." Others were convinced that Smallboy believed in a coming apocalypse: "This is the real reason for their movement to Kootenay Plains. By going back to the old ways of Indian living they believe they will become the chosen people saved from this disaster."

Over the years, Smallboy's group camped in a number of locations, including along the Siffleur River, at Whitegoat Lakes and beside Two O'Clock Creek. Since the Smallboy camps were near the Kootenay Plains Natural Area, there was concern that the delicate natural grasslands would be damaged due to overgrazing, off-road vehicle use and improper waste disposal practices. By 1972, with wild game becoming scarce, the main Smallboy group moved north, eventually settling in the Coal Branch south of Edson.

In 1980, Smallboy was awarded the Order of Canada in recognition of his efforts to make his band independent, self-supporting and in touch with its own traditions.

36 Landslide Lake – map p. 130

Duration ~ two days
Distance ~ 33.6 km
Level of Difficulty ~ easy climb with some steep, rocky pitches
Maximum Elevation ~ 1,995 m
Elevation Gain ~ 640 m
Map ~ 83 C/1 Whiterabbit Creek; 83 C/2 Cline River

Access ~ Park your vehicle at the Pinto Lake Recreation Trail staging area 48 km west of Nordegg, or 35 km east of the Banff National Park boundary just south of the Cline River bridge on Highway #11.

A long walk through the forest and alongside Entry Creek is rewarded by the scenery at Landslide Lake. Landslide has long been a favourite fishing hole for fishermen casting or fly fishing for cutthroat trout since it was first stocked in 1964. Particularly good fishing can be enjoyed at the south end of the lake where creeks flow into the lake.

~

The main path to Landslide Lake begins to the left of the Pinto Lake Recreation Trail sign. It leads down past several informal campsites and

0.0	trailhead
0.5	junction
2.0	O.D. Creek
2.6	spring
4.0	junction
4.3	Sentinel Creek
4.7	T-junction
6.6	junction of Pinto Lake and Landslide-Lake of the Falls Trails
8.0	outfitter's camp
9.5	outfitter's camp
10.3	outfitter's camp and confluence of Shoe Leather and Entry Creeks
11.5	confluence of Entry and Landslide Creeks
12.8	discharge of Landslide Creek
13.4	Landslide Lake Natural Area boundary
13.5	outfitter's camp
14.1	outfitter's camp
14.6	Landslide Lake
14.7	campsite
14.8	Alberta Forestry Service reclamation site
16.8	campsites
33.6	trailhead

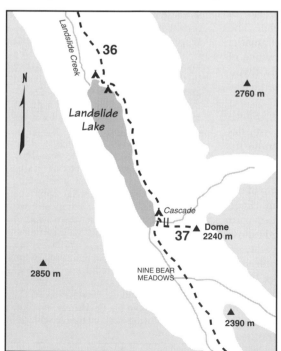

Cline River Area

Landslide Lake from near the
pass above Wildhorse Creek.
Courtesy of Chris Hanstock.

through open forest. One-half km later, a secondary path joins from the right. This path leads back to the gravel pit and parking area at the trailhead. Continue straight ahead. The first stream you cross is O.D. Creek some 400 m past a dry gravel wash. From the campsite, keep on the main trail by bearing to the right. Secondary trails leading to the left end within a few hundred metres. A freshwater spring 600 m past O.D. Creek heralds the beginning of a boggy section that can make the trail both muddy and slick.

At a fork in the trail, bear straight ahead; the trail to the left is the Sentinel Creek Trail. Within 100 m drop sharply to Sentinel Creek, which you cross. Bear a little to the right before choosing one of the braids that scram-

bles up the west embankment. On top, turn left at the T-junction and walk up along the open slope. The trail then swings into the forest before dropping quickly, in a series of steps, to the Cline River. This part of the trail is flat and in no time at all you are at the junction of the Pinto Lake Recreation Trail and the Landslide Lake-Lake of the Falls Trails. Numerous informal campsites to the right of the trail approaching the junction indicate that many hikers choose to rest here before continuing.

The junction of the two trails is signed, so you will have no trouble finding the trail leading to the left and to Landslide Lake. Climb a low ridge before beginning a long swing to the south through open forest. Along the gradual ascent you pass two outfitter's campsites. Near where the trail breaks out of the forest and drops to Entry Creek is another outfitter's campsite. On the other side of Entry Creek, Shoe Leather Creek races in from the west, making this a pretty place to rest. From here, the trail follows Entry Creek up to its confluence with Landslide Creek. The trail is good, if a bit rocky in places, and the scenery promises high peaks and valleys.

The junction of the Landslide Lake and Lake of the Falls Trails is also signed. The trail to Landslide Lake bears sharply to the left and begins a long, fairly steep ascent. The trail is good, rising in a series of steep pitches, until you come to a very wet stretch made worse by heavy horse traffic. Here, the Alberta Forestry Service has thrown down corduroy walkways over the worst sections. In places the trail has widened as hikers and horses alike seek drier ground on either side of the trail. Just past the end of this tedious section, you come

WHAT'S IN A NAME?

Landslide Lake

What this valley looked like before a rock avalanche tumbled from the peak at the northeast end of the lake will never be known. It may be that the avalanche, or slide, happened about 10,000 years when the last glacier that covered these mountains retreated. If so, the glacier undercut the base of the mountain so that when it melted there was nothing to support the rock. Given how slowly vegetation grows at this altitude, the number and size of the trees that grow in the "splash" area indicate that the slide occurred far back in time.

When the rocks were hurled into the valley they blocked a stream, creating a lake. You can search for the outlet of the lake, but you will not find it. The slide forced the outlet stream beneath the rock and debris. The stream emerges from the rock 1.8 km from the T-junction at the north end of the lake.

Removed from the original White Goat Wilderness Area in 1972, the Landslide Lake Natural Area was established the following year by order-in-council and the boundaries extended to the height of land around the lake in 1993.

Early morning at Landslide Lake. Courtesy of Karl Keller.

to a pretty view of Landslide Creek where it discharges from the boulders piled high in the ravine. On a sunny day when the sunlight dances off the tumbling waters the thick moss on the rocks looks particularly verdant. It is a good place to fill your water bottle. The trail continues sharply uphill and becomes rocky and rough underfoot when approaching the slide area. The rocks strewn across the hillside make for an interesting climb. The boundary of the Landslide Lake Natural Area is signed and just beyond here the trail passes through a meadow. Look up to the mountain on the left. It was part of the face of this mountain that sliced off eons ago, crashing rocks the size of small cars down its face and into the valley below. A small rock field, part of the "splash" area of the slide, is just to the left. If you look above the trees behind the rocks you can see a large hill of rock where the main slide settled. Pass several outfitter's campsites in the meadows before coming to a T-junction overlooking Landslide Lake.

This two km-long lake is nestled between high, barren mountains. The scree slopes of the mountain on the right sweep all the way down to the lakeshore. Forested slopes and alpine meadows soften the mountainside on the east side of the lake. At the far end of the lake, you can see the steep scree slope that leads up to the pass above Wildhorse Creek.

Good campsites are found both to the left and to the right of the T-junction. If you turn right at the T-junction you can find two good campsites, the first within 50 m, the second within 100 m. If you turn left and walk about 100 m you come to another campsite perched on a spit of

WHAT'S IN A NAME?

Entry Creek

Previous Names ~ Easy Creek

Entry Creek is a descriptive name for a route into Shoe Leather Creek valley. With the popularity of Landslide Lake and Lake of the Falls among hikers it has taken on a wider connotation.

The stream was originally called Easy Creek, as a contrast to its tributary, Shoe Leather Creek. In 1958, en route to making a first ascent of the Whitegoat Peaks, Alpine Club of Canada members Al Hober, Eric Hopkins and Don Linke, found the walking along Easy Creek much easier than along Shoe Leather Creek. Easy Creek was later changed to Entry Creek since the name Easy Creek was already in use elsewhere.

land jutting into the lake. Beyond here is an Alberta Forest Service reclamation site. This was once a large outfitter's campsite. Now, outfitters are not allowed by the Alberta Forest Service to overnight at Landslide Lake in an attempt to help Mother Nature reclaim the area. So please obey the signs and do not camp here. Three other campsites are located at the southeast end of the lake. To get there, continue along the trail past the reclamation area and cross a boggy area before dropping to the shoreline. The trail along the shore is, in spots, indistinct, but the route along the east shore of the lake is obvious. About halfway down the lake, the trail leaves the shoreline and climbs back into the trees. The first of the three campsites is found 16.8 km from the trailhead or 2.2 km from the T-junction by the lake.

Return the way you came, or leave via Wildhorse Creek.

37 Nine Bear Meadows – map p. 130

Duration ~ half day or full day
Distance ~ 0.6 km
Level of Difficulty ~ no trail, easy stroll with short climbs and scree slopes
Maximum Elevation ~ 2,300 m
Elevation Gain ~ 300 m
Map ~ 83 C/2 Cline River

Access ~ Your trailhead is at the middle of the three campsites at the southeast end of Landslide Lake.

0.0	trailhead
0.1	bottom of waterfall
0.2	top of waterfall
0.3	top of the dome
0.6	trailhead

There are few hikes that can beat this glorious walk alongside an unnamed creek and into the expanse of alpine meadow beyond.

~

From the campsite bushwhack east along the stream. There is no trail, but you should find it easy to reach the bottom of a long cascade where this unnamed creek tumbles over rocks down the face of the slope. Rills and little waterfalls accompany you when climbing the slope along the right-hand side of the stream. Once on top, the dome to the right invites investigation, so bear right and work your way up its slope to the top. From here, there are great views of Landslide Lake and the surrounding area. Bear left and continue climbing slowly.

The name, Nine Bear Meadows, is based upon an incident that occurred to a hiker coming to Landslide Lake from the south along Wildhorse Creek. He arrived at the pass, looked down and counted one, two, three...NINE furry brown shapes in the meadow below. He returned to the trailhead the way he came.

There are a number of options at this point. You may continue climbing along the ridge you are on. Or if your curiosity drives you to verify the name of Nine Bear Meadows, swing to your right toward a large ravine and work your way down to the lush alpine meadows at the south end of the lake. Alpine flowers such as blue beardtongue, purple fleabane, pearly everlastings and the ubiquitous paintbrush are sprinkled throughout the meadows. Other wildflowers are the wild heliotrope and the yellow hedysarum. Grizzlies are quite fond of them so keep a sharp eye for the telltale shoulder hump and silvery hairs rising above the lush vegetation.

Another area worth investigating is the meadows to the north across the stream. From here you can do a ridge walk or traverse northward before dropping down to the campsites at the north end of the lake. For those who have no interest in ridge walking, you can follow the stream into the box canyon to the east.

You can return the way you came, the cascades being an ideal entry and exit point for this easy access to an alpine area.

HISTORICAL FOOTNOTES

The Valley of the Ticked-Off Bears

This is a story that grows with each telling around the campfire.

As is well known, bears that pose a potential risk to hikers and campers are usually live-trapped and transported to remote areas. Each trapped bear is supposed to be moved to a separate area, but this does not always happen. Instead, the same valley may be used again and again to dump delinquent animals. In short time, the place is full of angry, hungry, snarly bears with a craving for garbage, picnic baskets and any other food associated with people. And woe to any hikers who stumble into the Valley of the Ticked-Off Bears.

There is no place to run. There is no place to hide. Everywhere there are bears wanting your food. They may even want you. As you lie awake at night in your tent, your ears straining to every sound outside, you hear a very quiet rip. The thin nylon wall of your tent is being slowly cut open. You can see the claw move down past your face. Then you see the dark hairy paw reach in toward you.

You scream! And realize it was only a dream. Or was it?

This incident did happen. There was a solitary hiker camped in a beautiful alpine meadow. Looking up he saw a helicopter. Slung beneath the chopper was something big. The helicopter came to within 100 m of his camp, hovered and then slowly descended. It released a bear. The hiker ran! Two days later, he reached safety at the warden's office in Banff.

So beware. You may be in the Valley of the Ticked-Off Bears.

38 Lake of the Falls – map p. 136

Duration ~ three days
Distance ~ 33.2 km
Level of Difficulty ~ some steep pitches
Maximum Elevation ~ 2,120 m
Elevation Gain ~ 765 m
Map ~ 83 C/1 Whiterabbit Creek;
83 C/2 Cline River

Access ~ Park your vehicle at the Pinto Lake Recreation Trail staging area 48 km west of Nordegg, or 35 km east of the Banff National Park boundary just south of the Cline River bridge on Highway #11.

A classic mountain beauty, Lake of the Falls bewitches all who go there. While this hike can be done in two days, one day in and return, the beauty of Lake of the Falls is so seductive you may want to linger an extra day or two to truly enjoy this valley.

~

The main path to Lake of the Falls begins left of the Pinto Lake Recreation Trail sign. It leads down past several informal campsites and through open forest. One-half km later, a secondary path joins from the right. This path leads back to the gravel pit and parking area at the trailhead. Continue

0.0	trailhead
0.5	junction
2.0	O.D. Creek
2.6	spring
4.0	junction
4.3	Sentinel Creek
4.7	T-junction
6.6	junction of Pinto Lake and Landslide-Lake of the Falls Trails
8.0	outfitter's camp
9.5	outfitter's camp
10.3	outfitter's camp and confluence of Shoe Leather and Entry Creeks
11.5	confluence of Entry and Landslide Creeks
11.7	Entry Creek
13.0	outfitter's camp
13.6	viewpoint of first waterfall
14.0	Entry Creek
14.4	gravel wash
14.8	junction
15.3	junction
15.6	campsite
16.0	campsite
16.1	Lake of the Falls
16.4	junction
16.6	campsite
33.2	trailhead

At a small bay in Lake of the Falls. Courtesy of Chris Hanstock.

straight ahead. The first stream you cross is O.D. Creek some 400 m past a dry gravel wash. On the other side is an informal campsite with a fine view up O.D. Creek valley. From the campsite, keep on the main trail by bearing to the right. Secondary trails leading to the left end within a few hundred metres. A freshwater spring 600 m past O.D. Creek heralds the beginning of a boggy section that can make the trail both muddy and slick. Past the bog and back on a hard-packed horse trail you continue the slow climb.

At a fork in the trail, bear straight ahead; the trail to the left is the Sentinel Creek Trail. Within 100 m drop sharply to Sentinel Creek, which is crossed via one of the log "bridges" that has been thrown across this picturesque cataract. Bear a little to the right before choosing one of the braids that scrambles up the west embankment. On top, turn left at the T-junction and walk up along the open slope. The trail then swings into the

forest before dropping quickly, in a series of steps, to the Cline River. This part of the trail is flat and in no time at all you are at the junction of the Pinto Lake Recreation Trail and the Landslide Lake-Lake of the Falls Trails. Numerous informal campsites to the right of the trail approaching the junction indicate that many hikers choose to rest here before continuing.

The junction of the two trails is signed, so you will have no trouble finding the trail leading to the left and to Lake of the Falls. Climb a low ridge before beginning a long swing to the south through open forest. Along the gradual ascent you pass two outfitter's campsites. Near where the trail breaks out of the forest and drops to Entry Creek is another outfitter's campsite. On the other side of Entry Creek, Shoe Leather Creek races in from the west, making this a pretty place to rest. From here, the trail follows Entry Creek up to its confluence with Landslide Creek. The trail is good, if a bit rocky in places, and the scenery promises high peaks and valleys.

The junction of the Landslide Lake and Lake of the Falls Trails is also signed. The trail to Landslide Lake bears sharply to the left. Bear to the right and immediately cross Landslide Creek via a log "bridge." On the other side is an informal campsite. A short distance beyond here cross Entry Creek via a wet, slimy log "bridge." Never mind; views open up even more and draw you toward the valleys in front of you. At first it appears as though you will be going up into the valley straight ahead, but when you reach an outfitter's campsite at the base of a mountain you realize that the Lake of the Falls Trail swings sharply to the right, just as does Entry Creek. This may be a good place to rest since two steep pitches separate you from the destination. The first of these pitches begins at the campsite. The trail switches steeply up the shoulder of the mountain, carrying you high above the creek. There is a good view of the first waterfall on Entry Creek, which is now below on the left. In early summer during the runoff, the tremendous amount of water that is hurled over the cliff makes for a photographer's delight. The trail swings out to the edge of the hillside, giving you views up Entry Creek. The valley has narrowed considerably and you can guess how much higher you must climb before reaching the valley of the Lake of the Falls.

Just before descending the slope to Entry Creek, a second waterfall can be seen upstream at a bend in the creek. Another log "bridge" aids your crossing. Now, you begin a very steep pitch that carries you above this second waterfall and beyond. Once on top of the rise cross a gravel wash, swinging a little to the right to pick up the trail again. At a junction, continue straight ahead; if you cross the creek you end at a campsite. Continue straight ahead at a second junction with a trail that also crosses Entry Creek. This trail meanders through the willows until it disappears in the marsh at the outlet of the Lake of the Falls. By now you are enjoying the

WHAT'S IN A NAME?

Shoe Leather Creek

Previous Names ~ Sole Creek

In August 1957, Al Hober and Don Linke made a reconnaissance trip up this stream searching for an easy access to the Whitegoat Peaks. Bad weather and boot failure prevented the two Alpine Club of Canada members from making any climbs that trip. They returned next year by the same route and recorded the first ascent of the highest peak (3,210 m) in the group. They remembered their trip from the year before when their boots fell apart, and named the stream Sole Creek. This was later changed to the more picturesque Shoe Leather Creek.

You gotta have "sole" to hike Shoe Leather Creek. Courtesy of Alfred Falk.

HISTORICAL FOOTNOTES

Alpine Club of Canada

As you look over the mountains and valleys around Lake of the Falls, you see many features that have been named by members of the Alpine Club of Canada. This organization is normally associated with the mountain parks to the west. However, it was also active in the Front Ranges, witness their 1958 expedition that recorded two first ascents, one of Whitegoat Peaks and the other of Resolute Mountain.

The Alpine Club of Canada was formed in 1906 by A. O. Wheeler, a topographic surveyor. At his suggestion Jimmy Simpson and other outfitters, including Tom Wilson, donated some of their horses and services to the club's inaugural camp. Jimmy Simpson was later appointed club Equerry. His job as Equerry was to assist the Master of Horse in arranging the transport of club members to their mountain destinations.

A. P. Coleman was an original member, and in 1907 at the age of 55, made an unsuccessful attempt to climb Mount Robson. Mary Schäffer joined the Alpine Club that same year and later wrote about her explorations in the club's journal.

---

glorious scenery offered by this ever-widening valley. To the right, Purple Mountain guards the entrance to the valley, while straight ahead ice-domed Resolute Mountain entices you onward. A couple of campsites on the left announce your imminent arrival at the north end of the lake.

The Lake of the Falls. With such a name you knew that this had to be a pretty destination, but who could have guessed at such splendour? The chiselled face of Resolute Mountain protects the aquamarine jewel at its base, while on your side of the lake alpine meadows with small copses of spruce trees blanket the slope below the Lake of the Falls ridge. As you bear left along the main trail a spit of land jutting into the lake beckons. Getting there can be soggy, as the trail goes through a bog at the far end of a small bay. Once at the point of land you can look up the lake to where meltwaters cascade down into the lake. If you are lucky you can catch sight of ospreys that prefer to nest on the other side of the lake. Once seriously threatened by pesticides such as DDT, osprey populations appear to be on the rebound. They arrive in late April or early May to raise their young, and leave in September. These birds hover over the lake, then suddenly dive for some unlucky trout that has caught its sharp eye.

Lake of the Falls is a descriptive name. It comes either from the many waterfalls seen cascading off the surrounding cliffs during the spring melt, or from the waterfalls downstream along Entry Creek. This creek gave the lake its earlier name.

Continuing along the main trail that leads up and along the lake, you come to a junction. The right-hand fork leads down to the lakeside. The main trail bears left to climb partway up the meadow. It's a beautiful walk that carries you to the south end of the lake where you can find another campsite. This is also a favourite spot for fly fishermen trying their luck for cutthroat trout that have been stocked in the lake.

Return to the trailhead the way you came.

39 Lake of the Falls Lookout – map p. 136

Duration ~ half day
Distance ~ 10.4 km
Level of Difficulty ~ one steep pitch; high ascent
Maximum Elevation ~ 2,760 m
Elevation Gain ~ 640 m
Map ~ 83 C/2 Cline River

This is an easy ascent of a 2,760 m-high peak. From the top are spectacular views of the surrounding mountains and valleys. For those who don't wish to climb, an exploration to the head of the valley can still make a delightful half-day hike.

~

From the campsite follow the trail to the south end of the lake where a gushing stream enters Lake of the Falls. Do not cross the stream, but climb up beside it and its pretty waterfall. Above the waterfall, the stream slices through pink rock as it churns out a shallow gorge. Beyond this point there is no trail, but an incredibly beautiful alpine meadow that stretches almost all the way back to the head of the valley.

You have to climb a rocky ridge to lift yourself into the meadow beyond. Snowfields linger until late July most years, feeding the stream that hurls itself through a second shallow gorge and over small waterfalls. Rills cascade from the cliffs on Resolute Mountain above you which, when combined with the waterfalls above and below the lake, give the lake its name. As you saunter toward the head of the valley the meadow is broken by rock and scree. Nevertheless your lazy climb remains easy. The head of the valley is hemmed in by precipitous headwalls, but a notch straight ahead indicates the pass. The bowl beneath the pass is strewn with boulders, making your hike somewhat more difficult.

At this point, you can turn around and return to the lakeside. For those who like a rock scramble and ridge walk, bear left and push yourself up the ridge above and to the left of the pass. If you ascend the pass at the end of the valley, bear left along a game trail that traverses the peak. Past the

Access ~ Your trailhead is the campsite on the south end of Lake of the Falls near the stream.

0.0 trailhead at south end of Lake of the Falls
0.3 shallow gorge
0.7 shallow gorge
2.9 head of the valley and pass
5.2 unnamed summit above Lake of the Falls
10.4 trailhead

Lake of the Falls. Courtesy of Karl Keller.

WHAT'S IN A NAME?

Resolute Mountain

Resolute Mountain has two summits rising from its glacier: The Lion and Lioness. The Lioness on the east is the higher (3,150 m) of the two peaks. Since lions, as every stiff-upper-lipped Brit knows, are the most resolute of creatures, the mountain as a whole was named Resolute Mountain.

The names were officially approved in 1959, a year after their first recorded ascent by Alpine Club of Canada members Eric Hopkins, Al Hober and Don Linke. The names were proposed by Eric Hopkins, who viewed them from the north: "Overlooking our camp was a peak with two summits rising out of glaciers...Because of its appearance from camp Eric [Hopkins] suggested the name Lion and Lioness."

peak, the ridge flattens, making for a very comfortable ridge walk. Sheep and hikers have eroded the trail, exposing pink rock and making an interesting variation of a "yellow brick road." There is a 360 degree panorama at the top. To the east are the boggy meadows of a tributary of Entry Creek. In the far distance is Abraham Lake. To the west are the glaciers of Resolute Mountain. Through the gap between Resolute and Purple Mountains are the Whitegoat Peaks.

Return to the lakeside by backtracking along the ridge. Dropping to the lake directly below is slow and hazardous. The mountainside is a giant rock pile strewn with large, unstable talus.

40 Pinto Lake Trail – map p. 143

Duration ~ 4 days
Distance ~ 65.4 km
Level of Difficulty ~ steady hike with some stream crossings
Maximum Elevation ~ 1,750 m
Elevation Gain ~ 380 m
Map ~ 83 C/2 Cline River; 83 C/1 Whiterabbit Creek

Access ~ Park your vehicle at the Pinto Lake Recreation Trail staging area 48 km west of Nordegg, or 35 km east of the Banff National Park boundary just south of the Cline River bridge on Highway #11.

Ever since geologist A. P. Coleman named this lake in 1893 after a cantankerous pack horse, hikers and trail riders have been drawn to this exquisite spot. A two-day straightforward hike leads west along the Cline River valley to the river's very headwaters.

~

The main path to Pinto Lake begins to the left of the Pinto Lake Recreation Trail sign. It leads down past several informal campsites and through open forest. One-half km later, a secondary path joins from the right. This path leads back to the gravel pit and parking area at the trailhead. Continue straight ahead. The first stream you cross is O.D. Creek some 400 m past a dry gravel wash. From the campsite, keep on the main trail by bearing to the right. Secondary trails leading to the left end within a few hundred metres. A freshwater spring 600 m past O.D. Creek heralds the beginning of a boggy section that can make the trail both muddy and slick.

At a fork in the trail, bear straight ahead; the trail to the left is the Sentinel Creek Trail. Within 100 m drop sharply to Sentinel Creek, which you cross. Bear a little to the right before choosing one of the braids that scrambles up the west embankment. On top, turn left at the T-junction and walk up along the open slope. The trail then swings into the forest before dropping quickly, in a series of steps, to the Cline River. This part of the trail is flat and in no time at all you are at the junction of the Pinto Lake Recreation Trail and the Landslide Lake-Lake of the Falls Trails. Numerous informal campsites to the right of the trail, along a braid seen approaching the junction, indicate that many hikers choose to rest here before continuing.

0.0	trailhead
0.5	junction
2.0	O.D. Creek
4.0	junction
4.3	Sentinel Creek
4.7	T-junction
6.5	braid
6.6	junction of Pinto Lake and Landslide-Lake of the Falls Trails
6.8	braid
8.2	Entry Creek
12.7	campsite
13.7	stream and campsite
16.0	Waterfalls Creek
16.2	Waterfalls Creek, junction and campsite
16.6	campsite
18.4	campsite
26.8	meadow and campsite
28.2	meadow, pond and campsite
28.7	Cataract Creek
29.7	junction
29.8	Huntington Creek and ford
30.1	junction
30.6	junctions and ford
31.7	junction
32.2	junction
32.3	Cline River
32.4	Cline River
32.7	Pinto Lake campsite
65.4	trailhead

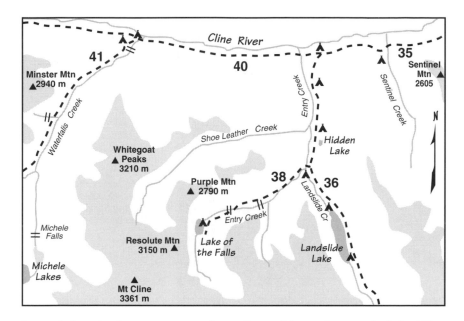

Several hundred metres past the Pinto Lake Recreation Trail sign there is a fork. Keep to the left. The right fork is the end of the braid that passes the campsites. It's a straightforward walk through open forest as far as a log bridge over Entry Creek. Most creek crossings from this point on have been bridged in one fashion or another, eliminating most of the risk of getting your feet wet. For example, the next two stream crossings sport corduroy bridges. The trail next crosses a gravel wash then, gently undulating, rises and falls through dog-hair forest.

Views have been scanty since Sentinel Creek, but where the trail finally leaves the forest and breaks out onto the flats along the Cline River you are treated to a sweeping vista up the valley. You may want to take advantage of a nearby campsite and take a rest to enjoy the great scenery. Ahead is the great tower of Minster Mountain. Walking beside the fast-flowing Cline River you cross a small stream.

Beyond here, the mood of the Cline River changes from one of a river set on cutting its way through bedrock to a more placid stream meandering through gravel beds. The trail, too, marches over flat, gravel meadows. Cross a braid of the Cline by means of a corduroy bridge. The trail leaves the meadows briefly to swing into the bush away from the river. Peek-a-boo views of the valley are enticing. Cross another stream and pass a campsite. The trail once again breaks out of the forest onto the river flats for a few hundred metres before entering an open pine forest. A three-log bridge carries you across the next stream. Another 1.4 km of steady hiking through open forest brings you to the end of the low ridge you have been walking along.

Once again on the gravel flats of the Cline River valley, trot quickly to a braid of Waterfalls Creek. This and the next crossing of Waterfalls Creek have very sturdy bridges, which are blessings, for there would be no way

Trails such as the Pinto Lake Trail were blazed and built by Forestry Rangers. Standard trails, such as this one up the north bank of the Cline River (the White Goat Trail), had to be at least two m wide with no more than a 10% grade, a sometimes challenging feat in the mountains. The rangers also had to bridge the worst streams and corduroy swamps. Courtesy of the Department of Environmental Protection, #10860.

of keeping your feet dry otherwise. Upon crossing the second bridge over Waterfalls Creek there is a junction with a trail that leads to the left up Waterfalls Creek. Keep to the right and almost immediately you come upon a good campsite. It's been a long, if relatively easy, day and you may wish to overnight here. The main campsite, though, is another 400 m along the trail. Its advantages are the toilets and picnic tables that Alberta Forestry Service has provided. You must weigh these comparative luxuries to the disadvantage of backtracking 200 m to the Cline River for water.

From Waterfalls Creek the trail remains straightforward with no steep pitches or treacherous stream crossings. You do, though, get your feet wet once or twice before reaching Pinto Lake. The trail winds slowly up through lodgepole pine forest and crosses a small stream and gravel wash. Not far beyond here there is a horse camp for those who wish to push beyond Waterfalls Creek on the first day. The next several kilometres are not noteworthy as you continue to climb slowly toward Pinto Lake. Looking across the Cline River you can see up McDonald Creek valley. Your next three stream crossings boast corduroy bridges. The fourth crossing, though, does not, but the stream is a narrow braid and you should not have any trouble. You reach the main stream and a two-log bridge a short distance after negotiating the last crossing. The Cline is narrower here as it races through a small gorge. As you trot along above the Cline there are numerous opportunities to walk to the embankment to drink in the views upstream.

The trail drops down from the open forest onto a flat and rocky meadow; an informal campsite is located just off the trail. The Cline River sports a wide and long U-shaped valley that is fringed by high mountain peaks. As you continue in a westerly direction toward the White Goat Wilderness Area, the scenery becomes more and more dramatic. The slopes of Minster Mountain are on the left. From one of its mountain valleys, a large waterfall cascades down the cliff. Another more dramatic waterfall can be seen in the distance along Huntington Creek. Also on your right beside the Cataract Creek valley is a lone narrow wedge-shaped peak called the "Beacon" by Mary Schäffer in 1907.

WHAT'S IN A NAME?

O.D. Creek

This local and unofficial name is an example of military gallows humour. O.D. is short for "Oh Damn!" This memorable phrase is alleged to have been used June 7, 1979 by one or more of the occupants of a Beaver aircraft that crashed that day along the creek. The four occupants of the plane were members of the British Army Training Unit, Suffield. They were reconnoitring the upper slopes of Elliot Peak and Sentinel Mountain when a down draft caused their plane to crash. All four men received minor injuries from the crash. Nothing remains of the plane wreckage. Members of the Training Unit cut the plane into pieces and carried them out.

An informal campsite on the west side of O.D. Creek with a fine view up O.D. Creek.

The next two stream crossings are a breeze as you continue along the flat and easy trail. Pass by a small pond and campsite on the left. Where you have an excellent view across the Cline River of the confluence of Cataract Creek there is a ford. Do not cross the Cline, but continue along its south bank. At a junction in the trail there is a directional sign pointing to the right toward Pinto Lake. You are now within a couple of kilometres of your destination. Upon reaching the confluence of Huntington Creek and the Cline River you are forced to ford the former, as there is no bridge. At a junction bear to the left across a bridge over the Cline River; the trail to the right leads to a campsite.

You are now traversing a swampy section where there are several trails, some more distinct than others. Five hundred m past the bridge over the Cline you come to a series of junctions. At the first junction keep to the left. Almost immediately you come to a campsite and another junction. Here, bear right along the trail; the left-hand fork goes to a rain-collection station. Within metres you find yourself facing a ford across the Cline River, a placid, shallow stream at this point. Once across the Cline you find yourself at a T-junction. Turn left; bearing right takes you to a waterfall, a pretty half-day hike from Pinto Lake. The trail is a little rough, but distinct enough as it leads to another junction where you want to keep to the left; going to the right takes you back down the Cline River along its north bank. At yet another junction continue straight ahead or to the left. Going right will lead to

Sunset Pass. Cross two small log bridges and soon you are at the main campsite at Pinto Lake.

As in the case of the Waterfalls Creek campsite, the toilets, fire pits and picnic tables at Pinto Lake are surprising touches of luxury in the back country. Two days of steady hiking have brought you to this gem of a lake. You can return the way you came the following day, or spend another day or two enjoying the day hikes in the vicinity.

WHAT'S IN A NAME?

Minster Mountain

Minster Mountain was named in 1893 by A. P. Coleman as he passed along the Cline to Pinto Lake. Coleman, a geologist, noted that the Cline River valley and its adjacent slopes had been glaciated: "...two or three thousand feet above the river the polished surfaces are lost and the imposing walls of cathedral like mountains rise to snowy summits. From a striking one which can be seen from the Kootenay Plains, and which we named Minster Mountain, avalanches thundered down as we passed."

Coleman was not the first to notice this striking cathedral-like peak. It was 1811 and Alexander Henry paused in his midwinter dash to Howse Pass to gaze up the Cline River, which he called Rivière du Meurleton. He described a remarkable mountain: "Along this river I observed a high, steep mountain of singular shape, like a wall surrounded by a moat and ramparts, with an elevated central summit resembling a citadel, the whole having the appearance of a commanding fortress."

What is interesting about these two depictions is the contrasting interpretation: where one man saw a fortress, another saw a cathedral.

41 Waterfalls Creek – map p. 143

Duration ~ full day
Distance ~ 15.3 km
Level of Difficulty ~ rough trail with some deadfall and bushwhacking
Maximum Elevation ~ 1,980 m
Elevation Gain ~ 410 m
Map ~ 83 C/2 Cline River

A rather long day combined with some bushwhacking is time well spent for those who enjoy hiking in less popular areas. Waterfalls and cascades along the valley make this a very scenic walk.

~

From the main Waterfalls Creek campsite walk east, downstream, along the Pinto Lake Recreation Trail for 400 m to Waterfalls Creek. Just before the bridge find a secondary path that leads up the right-hand side of Waterfalls Creek. The path soon peters out in the swampy ground around the creek, so keep close to the bank and continue upstream. As you work your way past the bog you emerge on terra firma. There is still no sign of a definite trail, but continue walking along the gravel and stony bank of the stream all the way to a very pretty double-chute waterfall.

Clamber up the slope beside the waterfall and continue upstream. The trail is reasonably good as far as a junction. The left-hand fork fords Waterfalls Creek and swings back downstream. The right-hand fork, marked by several blazes, is a horse trail that heads into the lodgepole pine forest. While horse people prefer this lengthy forest trail to the open banks of Waterfalls Creek, the trail is marred with heavy deadfall and no views. So, do not take either fork, but continue straight ahead along the creek. It's quite open making walking fairly easy.

Approximately 1.6 km from the trailhead and opposite two small cliffs, pick up a trail 30 m or so from the water's edge. The trail leads down an old watercourse past a campsite. The trail is somewhat overgrown here and you must bushwhack your way around trees and shrubs. Fortunately, this tedium is short lived as the trail begins a steep

Access ~ Your trailhead is the main Waterfalls Creek campsite located 400 m west of Waterfalls Creek on the Pinto Lake Recreation Trail.

0.0	trailhead
0.4	campsite and Waterfalls Creek
0.8	waterfall
1.0	junction
2.5	viewpoint
3.3	junction
3.4	stream
3.5	upper trail
4.5	gravel wash
5.0	avalanche slope
5.5	gravel wash
5.6	gravel wash
6.3	avalanche slope
6.8	cave
7.3	trail
11.1	stream
11.4	deadfall area
13.1	meadow and pond
14.3	Waterfalls Creek
15.3	trailhead

This six metre-high waterfall makes the slog through the bog at the beginning of the trail well worth it.

ascent through open forest, eventually carrying you high above Waterfalls Creek. At the top of the ridge the trail breaks out of the forest and you are treated to great views up the valley. Never far out of your sight on this hike is a pointed triangular peak marking the main fork of Waterfalls Creek. The trail dips down a little only to climb again. At a junction keep to the right rather than dropping down to the creek. You come to a stream.

At the stream bushwhack up the slope on the right and find the horse trail that you eschewed above the first waterfall. Turn left onto the trail. From this point, despite the deadfall, the horse trail is much easier to follow than it would be to bushwhack along the edge of the creek. The trail first crosses a gravel wash and then cuts across an avalanche slope. The trail is a little less indistinct as it winds its way through the grass and

shrubs. On your right high up on the cliffs you can see one of the many waterfalls for which the creek is named. In early summer with the melting snow the waterfall is a magnificent sight; by autumn it is reduced to a trickle. A shallow cave can be seen adjacent to the waterfall. At the end of the avalanche slope the horse trail drops over a small ledge onto a very wide gravel wash. What a glorious view! Impressive cliffs loom above and on the right. Across Waterfalls Creek are the Whitegoat Peaks with their perpetual snowfields. Straight ahead is the unnamed triangular peak. Further to the southwest, you can see glaciers that lie astride the boundary of Banff National Park. And falling over the headwall beside the glaciers is a waterfall fed by the Michele Lakes; even at this distance you can see the 300 m-high waterfall quite clearly.

The trail descends from the gravel wash and crosses another, where you lose the trail completely. But once across, you pick it up again near Waterfalls Creek. Looking to the right you cannot help but notice a large waterfall and cave. Continue along the trail until you come to another avalanche slope at the base of the waterfall and cave. Turn right off the trail and scramble partway up the slope for an even better view of Waterfalls Creek valley.

A fun side trip is to continue scrambling up the steep slope to the lowest of the three tiers of the waterfall. The water plummets 30 m from the cave above. To explore the cave and the second tier of the waterfall scramble up the grassy slope to the left. Make no mistake; it's a steep, if short, pull up to the cave. The cavernous mouth yawns above you. The second tier of the waterfall has a drop of approximately 60 m. The cave does not go back very far and is only a large frost pocket, but it's fun to poke around anyway.

Run down the slope back to Waterfalls Creek where you find the horse trail. Turn left for the return trip to your campsite. If you continued along the trail to the right you would swing up the valley to a fork in the creek where the trail climbs a pass before dropping to Pinto Lake. The

GEOFACTS

Gravel Washes

As you hike along Waterfalls Creek you cross several gravel washes. Most washes are, or appear to be, dry. If there is any water it is a mere trickle. It seems strange that such a small amount of water could create such a broad streambed. Interestingly, many streams in the Front Ranges exhibit this same configuration. Why?

Much of the answer lies in the seasonal flow of water. During the late-spring and early-summer melt, the number of waterfalls off the headwalls increases, swelling the streams below. The rushing waters carry with them rocks and boulders, which are tossed up along the banks of the streams. As the season progresses and the meltwaters recede, the volume of water in the streams, of course, drops. But left along its banks is the evidence of many seasons of spring runoffs.

This wide, rocky streambed in Waterfalls Creek valley is typical of streams found in the Front Ranges.

WHAT'S IN A NAME?

Whitegoat Peaks

The three Whitegoat Peaks take their name from an incident that occurred during the first recorded ascent of this mountain in 1958. Five mountain goats, otherwise known as whitegoats, were seen near the base camp at the head of Shoe Leather Creek. Alpine Club of Canada members Don Linke, who proposed the name, Al Hober and Eric Hopkins climbed the highest (3,210 m) peak in the middle, but found the rock on the western summit too rotten to tackle: "We were amazed to find that this imposing rock tower consisted of such poor rock and decided to leave it for others to climb," wrote Linke. Twelve years later this peak was climbed by Tony Daffern, Pete Ford and Chris Smith. The Linke party originally called the mountain Thunder Peaks.

Whitegoat Peaks as seen from Waterfalls Creek.

Waterfalls Creek Trail is an alternative route into Pinto Lake, but is quite rough as it is rarely used by hikers.

When you return to the stream 3.5 km from the trailhead, you have an option. You can drop down to Waterfalls Creek and return the way you came by bushwhacking along the creek. Or, if you wish, you can continue along the horse trail. The remaining description of the hike takes you back to your campsite via the horse trail.

The trail crosses an avalanche slope, then climbs through the forested slope above Waterfalls Creek. The relatively good trail ends 300 m later at a large deadfall area. It's both tiring and somewhat confusing as you clamber around the deadfall; you might have to spend some time finding the trail again. Once back on the trail, you make good time trotting through the forest. Your trail comes out onto a meadow with a small pond, and predictably, the trail disappears as it enters the meadow. The best course of action, since the meadow is quite spongy and wet, is to cross over a low ridge to the right. Here, take a hard right and walk along the ridge away from the meadow. Look sharply for blazes on the trees as you draw near the end of the narrow arm of the meadow. From here the trail climbs along a low ridge and takes you back to the junction at one km. Bear left to return to the waterfall and your trailhead.

HISTORICAL FOOTNOTES

Along the Cataract River

For about 10 years, the Cline River was known as Cataract River. A. P. Coleman followed the Cataract to its headwaters at Pinto Lake in 1893. Forest fires had gone through the valley several years before leaving behind an eerie scene: "We travelled all day through burnt woods where most of the trees were still standing, either covered with blackened bark or yellow-white, like tusks of ivory, where the singed wood had peeled off. The wood had dried out and cracked, and a rousing wind played strange music upon them, hisses and sighs and groans and whistlings, so that the valley was most dolefully bewitched." In 1907 Mary Schäffer followed the Cataract downstream from Pinto Lake to the Kootenay Plains. She also noted the sign of past forest fires, making the route "not altogether an attractive trail."

Lodgepole pine have since covered most of the fire scars. The name Cataract River has been replaced by the name Cline River. But the name Cataract has been preserved in Cataract Creek, a tributary of the Cline and, for a time, regarded as the Cline's headwaters.

In 1924, a lady with the magnificent handle of Ethelwyn Octavia Doble Alford decided to experience the life of a forest ranger. She spent several weeks on patrol in the Cline River and Kootenay Plains country with a group of Forest Rangers from Nordegg led by William Shankland. It took them two days to ride from Nordegg to the mouth of the Cline, then called the Whitegoat River. There they rested the horses on the nearby Abraham Flats. They went across the North Saskatchewan to Tom Wilson's cabin, which appalled her: "It looked very weird and ratty and mousey and dirty and dark."

The rangers checked the trail along the Siffleur River and constructed a switchback on it. Two to three times each season, wrote Ethelwyn Alford, the rangers patrolled and kept clear between 300-500 km of trail. They rode up the Cline River to Pinto Lake. There she was shown and was pleasantly surprised by a pretty waterfall that cascaded "just like steps" over the rock outcrop. Alford called that portion of the Cline River between Pinto Lake and Cataract Creek, Pinto Creek.

Ethelwyn Alford's pretty waterfall.

42 Falls on Cline River – map p. 153

Duration ~ two hours
Distance ~ 3.6 km
Level of Difficulty ~ easy walk with some light bushwhacking
Maximum Elevation ~ 1,750 m
Elevation Gain ~ nil
Map ~ 83 C/2 Cline River

This short hike is just the ticket for those who enjoy an after-dinner walk.

~

With the Cline River on the right walk downstream away from your campsite. Cross two log bridges and continue as far as a junction in the trail. The Sunset Pass Trail goes to the left. Bear right. Cross a shallow stream and continue along the trail. At a second junction, keep to the right again. The trail to the left connects with a trail along the north bank of the Cline, exiting at the Coral Creek Trail staging area on Highway #11. Continuing, the trail is a little rough with some low, boggy spots, but it is generally quite distinct and well used. It's not long before you come to yet another junction of trails. This time bear left to continue with the Cline River on your right. The trail to the right fords the Cline and continues on the river's south bank on its long trek downstream to the Pinto Lake Recreation Trail staging area, also on Highway #11.

The upper reaches of the Cline River are shallow and placid, so the waterfall that you come upon a mere 300 m beyond the last junction is a bit of a surprise. The low ridge marks the western boundary of the White Goat Wilderness Area. The Wilderness Area's southern boundary begins at the waterfall and follows the Cline River downstream.

Return the way you came.

Access ~ Your trailhead is the main campsite at Pinto Lake at the outlet of Cline River.

0.0	trailhead
0.3	bridge
0.4	bridge
0.6	junction
1.1	junction
1.5	junction
1.8	Cline River Falls
3.6	trailhead

43 Pinto Lake Loop – map p. 153

Duration ~ full day
Distance ~ 6.8 km
Level of Difficulty ~ easy walk with some bushwhacking
Maximum Elevation ~ 1,820 m
Elevation Gain ~ 70 m
Map ~ 83 C/2 Cline River

A scramble up and over boulders takes you to a large cave partway around Pinto Lake on what is otherwise an easy walk. A visit to the Trees of Renown, witnesses to a dramatic rescue in 1924, nearly completes your circuit of lovely Pinto Lake.

~

From the trailhead find the footpath that leads counter-clockwise around the lake. For the most part the trail stays very close to the lakeshore where you are in constant view of the precipitous peaks surrounding the lake. The path winds in and out of spruce trees that blanket the entire west slope of the lake. It is not long before you come upon a small secondary campsite. Continue along the sometimes rough trail and soon

Access ~ Your trailhead begins at the main campsite at Pinto Lake.

0.0	trailhead
0.4	campsite
1.0	campsite and spring
2.2	stream crossing, campsite and junction
2.7	cave
3.2	junction
3.3	bog
3.4	stream crossing
3.6	stream crossing
4.3	stream and pond
5.4	campsite, junction and Trees of Renown
5.7	junction
6.8	Cline River and trailhead

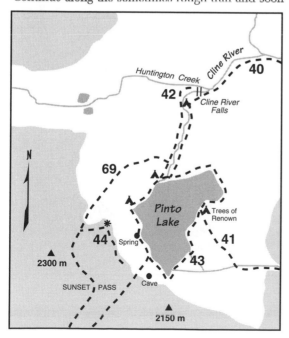

The Pinto Lake Rescue

What began as a well-planned season of trapping at Pinto Lake in the winter of 1923-1924 nearly ended in disaster for a trapper, Frank Pierce, and his wife and teenage daughter.

Winter is the best season for trapping, when the furs are lustrous and thick. Pierce realized that an expedition into Pinto Lake in the late autumn meant a minimum six-month stay, so he hired local Indians to pack in a large quantity of food for him and his family. It wasn't long, though, before his plans were placed in jeopardy. A loaded rifle carried on a pack pony discharged, shattering his left arm. A doctor was summoned, and he found it necessary to amputate the arm near the shoulder. Dr. Shillebeer urged Pierce to leave while there was time, but Pierce argued that if he had another man to help him, he should be able to recuperate and continue his trapping. A helper, Joseph Tansey of Nordegg, went in just before freeze-up.

Not unexpectedly, nothing was heard from the group over the winter months. Then, in the third week of June, Tansey shocked Nordegg when he staggered into town with an urgent plea for help. The Pierce family was near starvation. During the winter, a series of misfortunes befell the group. First, Pierce's horse had died. Then, Pierce had the stump of his amputated arm frozen and, according to newspaper reports at the time, "was having considerable trouble as a result." And finally, all the provisions had been eaten. Pierce himself was in such poor shape that he could not make it out on his own.

The Alberta Provincial Police were galvanized into action. Detective Holmes and Constable English of the Red Deer detachment, and Constable Watson, who was based in Nordegg, departed on June 21st. Surprisingly, they met Pierce who, after Tansey's departure, felt that he could make it out on his own. But he was alone, having left his family at Pinto Lake. Fearing for the family's welfare, the rescue party continued. Before leaving Pinto Lake the rescuers carved their names and that of the Pierce's into two nearby lodgepole pines.

These trees still stand. They are easy to find because the Alberta Forest Service has fenced off what remains of them. The Trees of Renown are among an inventory of Alberta trees that have either historical or botanical distinction. A depression marking Pierce's log house is directly east of the Trees of Renown.

The Trees of Renown tell a tale of a close call for one family.

Pinto Lake from the Lookout. Courtesy of Julie Hrapko.

you come to another much larger camping area. The trail beyond this campsite can be rough in places as it dips down to the lakeshore and winds its way through the trees. Adjacent to yet another camp spot is an interesting pool and spring that must be high in nutrients judging by the algae that grow at this location. The trail becomes quite rough with deadfall often blocking the path. Where the trail hugs the lakeshore a little too closely it threatens to disappear into the lake altogether. Yet despite these annoyances, this is a pretty hike.

At the next campsite by a gravel wash you come to a junction in the trail. You can continue straight ahead. But why not turn right and scramble up to the mouth of a large cave that you can see on the cliffs above? Find the trail that leads up on the left-hand side of the wash or, if you think that it might be easier, walk up the dry streambed. There is water in the creek, as you discover when you climb, but on its lower reaches it flows under the rocks. A good, but quite rough trail leads up over the steep pitches to the left of the stream. As you climb, small cascades tumble over boulders in the streambed. Looking up, the black entrance to the cave dominates the view.

The last pull into the entrance to the cave is over scree, large boulders and a stream that gurgles out of the mouth of the cave. The entrance is very large. Inside, water plops from the roof into a pool that extends back about 15 m from the cave mouth. The water, by the way, is very clear, cold and delicious. Fill your water bottle here! There is a great view of Pinto Lake, so enjoy a rest and the view before carefully picking your way back down the slope to the campsite and junction.

At the junction turn right onto the path and continue walking along the trail, which is not as distinct now. At the far end of the lake, the trail crosses a large boggy area. If in doubt, hug the lakeshore since the trail always returns there. You can then pick up a good trail as far as a stream, which you must cross. As it is shallow it presents no real challenge. The next section is a bushwhack since the trail disappears while crossing another bog and stream. The trail reappears at a gravel wash. Cross another shallow stream. The shoreline beyond this point is blanketed with labrador tea, with its pretty white flower in spring and its yellow-red leaves in autumn. The trail now passes a small pond on the right and continues to where it widens into a large campsite. At the south end of the

camping area there is a junction. Continue straight ahead to complete your circuit around the lake. The trail on the right leads up to a pass and down to Waterfalls Creek.

You are now about three-quarters of the way around the lake so continue swinging to the left at a junction. The trail from the Trees of Renown is quite good and will take you quickly back to the Cline River. Your campsite is located directly across the river, which you have to ford. The Cline is about 30 m across, but is very shallow so you will have no trouble.

GEOFACTS

Caves

The Front Ranges are composed primarily of limestone. Where there is limestone, there are often caves. Caves are formed from the dissolving of the limestone by slightly acidic groundwater. Surprisingly, despite the limestone topography, there are few known caves in the Canadian Rockies. This is probably due to the work of glaciers, which either eroded away the caves, or left thick layers of gravel and rock over cave entrances. Only the southern Rockies have been systematically combed by spelunkers for their caves and much is yet to be learned about the possibility and location of caves in the Rockies. The best-known cave close to the David Thompson corridor is the Wapiabi Cave located in the Bighorn Range.

Stoney Indians associate caves with a race of immortal little people called makutibi. These little people are males only. Hunters, on occasion, may see traces of these creatures, their tiny footprints or that of their tiny dogs. At night, they may hear these dogs barking. Little people normally shun human contact, but from time to time they will speak to people. They are credited with being instructors to the Indians, and they live in villages beneath the mountains. These villages may be reached through the caves. According to the Stoney, not all

caves lead to underground villages, but because they did not know which caves did and which did not, they treated all caves with respect. Before approaching a cave, Stoneys traditionally conducted a brief ritual to assure the dwellers within that no harm was intended. This was wise since there was the risk of captivity among the little people.

Shamans or medicine men could contact the little people by telepathy or dreams. The little people would instruct the shaman and give him power to see into the future or perform miracles. Like all gifts from the supernatural, this power had a twin edge: if used for good, the shaman would prosper, if used for evil, he would suffer.

Scrambling up to the cave above Pinto Lake.

44 Pinto Lake Lookout – map p. 153

Duration ~ half day
Distance ~ 13.2 km
Level of Difficulty ~ steep ascent followed
by an easy walk
Maximum Elevation ~ 2,010 m
Elevation Gain ~ 260 m
Map ~ 83 C/2 Cline River

Access ~ Your trailhead is the
main campsite at Pinto Lake.

0.0	trailhead
0.3	bridge
0.4	bridge
0.6	junction
0.8	bog
5.7	Lookout Ridge
5.8	cairn
5.9	cairn
6.6	end of ridge
13.2	trailhead

For those choosing to hike into Pinto Lake via Sunset Pass, this half-day hike repeats the last few kilometres of the trail. For those coming up the Cline River, there is a tough little climb ahead of you. However, the steep pull up the Sunset Pass Trail offers wonderful panoramic views of the lake, the Cline River valley and the mountains of White Goat Wilderness Area.

~

With the Cline River on the right walk downstream. Cross two log bridges and continue as far as a junction in the trail. The Sunset Pass Trail, which you want, is on the left; the trail on the right leads down the Cline River. Turn left and follow the trail as it enters a boggy, wet section. The trail becomes indistinct, but persevere and pick up the trail on the other side. Almost immediately, you enter the spruce forest and within 50 m begin the long pull up to the Lookout.

The trail switches numerous times before you haul yourself above the switchbacks. The trail continues its steep climb through forest and across avalanche slopes as it traverses the shoulder of the unnamed mountain on the right. As you break out of the trees great views open up of the surrounding mountains and Pinto Lake below. A particularly steep ascent across scree brings you to a rocky outcropping. The trail switches up through the outcrop and continues its climb. Cross the scree as the trail snakes around cliffs and up to the ridge overlooking Pinto Lake.

At the ridge, the Sunset Pass Trail climbs more gently. Before entering the Engelmann spruce that dot the north end of the pass, turn left off the trail and head across the open alpine meadow. There is no trail, but it doesn't matter. Looking below, you see the lake snuggled amongst a carpet of ever-

A rock cairn overlooking Pinto Lake.

greens. Add a rock to either of the two cairns located on separate points overlooking Pinto Lake. When walking in a southerly direction across the meadow you see different views of the lake; at first you can only see the north end of the lake, the south end directly below is hidden by cliffs. Walk to the end of the meadow and gaze down on the extreme south end of Pinto Lake.

It's been an effort to gain this ridge, so you may want to relax in the meadows before returning to the campsite the way you came.

HISTORICAL FOOTNOTES

Bull Trout

Since its first recorded visitors, Pinto Lake has been famous for its fishing. Both A. P. Coleman in 1893 and Mary Schäffer in 1906 reported that Stoney Indians came here to fish. Schäffer wrote: "hundreds of speckled trout could be seen lazily swimming about or lying in the bottoms of pools, all averaging fourteen inches in length. So heavy was our catch, that even our bacon-palled appetites refused to devour all we got, and we smoked them as did the Indians, in a dense smudge of spagnum moss."

The "speckled trout" were Bull Trout, a species of char. Pinto Lake has a localized population of Bull Trout as the rapids and falls along the Cline bar any movement of fish from the North Saskatchewan to the lake. Bull Trout are slow maturing and easy to catch. This combination plus habitat degradation have reduced their numbers across Alberta. The fish usually mature and are ready for spawning in their fifth year. At Pinto Lake, however, they grow and mature at a slower rate. Therefore, it takes longer than usual to recoup any population losses. The Bull Trout at Pinto Lake are unique in that they are unusually brilliantly coloured during spawning.

45 BATUS Canyon – map p. 102

Duration ~ two hours
Distance ~ 2.6 km
Level of Difficulty ~ steady climb followed by a steep scramble
Maximum Elevation ~ 1,555 m
Elevation Gain ~ 125 m
Map ~ 83 C/1 Whiterabbit Creek

The British Army Training Unit, Suffield, BATUS for short, practised rock climbing in this gorge. One soldier lost his life here. Walk on the ridge above the creek to access the viewpoint of the gorge.

~

Scramble up the gravel slope to gain an open ridge overlooking the north bank of the creek. It's a relatively easy walk uphill for the first 500 m.

Access ~ Park your vehicle on Highway #11 at an un-named creek seven km south of the Cline River. The creek is 55 km west of Nordegg, or 28 km east of the Banff National Park boundary. Your trailhead is the base of the gravel slope on the west side of the highway.

0.0   trailhead
0.6   log ruins
1.1   base of ridge
1.3   canyon viewpoint
2.6   trailhead

Knowing that one British soldier lost his life in the canyon should discourage you from attempting a scramble down to the creek and the waterfall.

Below on the left is the creek with its rapids and small cascades racing toward the North Saskatchewan River. This is a south-facing slope with sparse, heat-loving plants such as kinnikinnick, junipers and yellow butter-and-egg flowers. Even though this is quite a short hike, take your water canteen, especially on a hot day.

As you climb, you pass the remains of a log shelter tucked among the pine and spruce trees on the right. Straight ahead you can see BATUS canyon, a narrow cleft in the rock wall. The ridge becomes steeper as you approach the base of the rock face. Looking behind you, a wonderful view opens up of the Kootenay Plains.

The ridge you have been climbing ends at the base of a broken rock face. Bear right, away from the creek, and begin working your way up the steep slope. Once on top of the slope, turn left and work your way back toward the creek. It's a bit of a bushwhack through bushes and trees, but an open lip at the extreme west end of the ridge offers a terrific view of BATUS canyon. There is a small waterfall that plunges from the cleft into the creekbed below.

Return the way you came.

HISTORICAL FOOTNOTES

The British Army Training Unit, Suffield

Each year from May to October, units of the British Army come to Alberta to train and practise. Between 1979 and 1992, the Brits were headquartered for the six-month period at Suffield, which is the only live firing range in the northern hemisphere. Part of their Suffield posting included a rigorous training course in the Bighorn-Cline River area. For three weeks, the soldiers ran up mountain passes carrying full packs, scaled headwalls, practised water craft skills, and cycled up horse trails. There was no one more physically fit than a British soldier who came off this course!

Although most of the soldiers stayed in the David Thompson corridor only for the duration of the three week course, there was a "permanent" staff that provided leadership and support for soldiers on the course. Initially, BATUS set up its base camp just east of the David Thompson Resort, but in 1986 the base camp was moved east to Dry Haven. There, the soldiers put up a temporary cookhouse, pub, canteen, sleeping quarters for 100 men, and storehouses for equipment and hardware. Over the years, BATUS soldiers involved themselves in the local community by cutting deadfall wood and clearing trails. The Shunda Creek Hostel near Nordegg is built in part by volunteer labour from BATUS.

In 1992 logistical problems of organizing and setting up the Dry Haven auxiliary training camp forced BATUS to reevaluate the Suffield-Dry Haven plan. The decision was made to move from Suffield to Seebe, and from Dry Haven to Morley, west of Calgary. Concrete pads located north of Highway #11 near the Dry Haven campground (located 28 km west of Nordegg or 67 km east of the Banff National Park boundary) are the only reminder that BATUS soldiers were once an annual presence here.

Kootenay Plains

The Kootenay Plains stretches between two ridges, Windy Point to the east and Whirlpool Point to the west. Between them is one of the largest, unspoilt montane regions left in Alberta. This landscape is characterized by a pattern of open forests and grasslands caused by low rainfall and many chinooks. The Kootenay Plains is the warmest and driest region within the Rocky Mountains.

The mild temperatures and shallow snow cover make this a critical wildlife winter range for elk, mule deer, mountain sheep and moose. In the past, mountain caribou wintered here, as well as the now locally extinct wood bison. In all over 60 species of birds, 14 mammals and over 240 species of vascular plants live here. Among the plants are many that are uncommon in Alberta.

The pleasant temperatures and abundant wildlife made this an attractive hunting area for Indians. The first were the Kootenay. They are the region's ghosts. When fur traders David Thompson and Alexander Henry were recording their presence on the Plains they were already nearly gone. They were being pushed west across the Divide by the better-armed Peigan. They left behind their name, empty campsites and a vacuum soon to be filled by another group, the Stoney.

The Stoney, also called Assiniboine, were originally part of the Sioux nation. Sometime in the late 17th century they split from the Sioux, then began to migrate westward from the Lake of the Woods-Lake Nipigon region. It was during this westward migration that they split into different groups. One group, today called the Wesley Band, moved northwestward along the parkland before entering the foothills west of Edmonton. From this region along the Athabasca River they filtered down to the Upper North Saskatchewan and Kootenay Plains.

There is a biblical flavour to the Wesley Band history: their migration to the Kootenay Plains, exile and "Egyptian captivity" at Morley, followed by "Exodus" back to the Plains. The migration period began with a man named Abraham, who, according to son John Abraham, sometime around 1820 "went up in the mountains to what is now known by the name of Kootenay Plains and there settled, growing vegetables with success." Abraham was present at Blackfoot Crossing in 1877 for the signing of Treaty Number Seven. Under this treaty, the Stoney bands were gathered together on a number of reserves near Morley. No reserve land was set aside along the upper North Saskatchewan, though the Wesleys present at the Treaty signing later insisted that they received verbal assurances that this would be done.

The Wesley Band continued to make annual summer forays to the Kootenay Plains area to hunt. With food supplies and living conditions at Morley deteriorating, about 100 Stoney followed Peter Wesley in 1894 back to their "promised land" on the Kootenay Plains. Several years later they petitioned the federal Department of the Interior for a reserve.

In 1910, the Stoney land claim to the Kootenay Plains was accepted. It was cancelled next year due to the discovery of coal along the Bighorn River and Whiterabbit Creek. The federal government for a time considered forcing them back to Morley. By 1947, however, they received a reserve with conditions attached. The land they received at the confluence of the Bighorn and North Saskatchewan Rivers was not part of their original land claim. The provincial government stated that they had given up their claim to the Plains while the Stoney assumed, due to the smallness of the reserve, that more land would be forthcoming. They continued to use the Kootenay Plains to support themselves, their horses and cattle.

The construction of the Bighorn Dam and creation of Abraham Lake flooded most of the land claim area, including cabins, graves, campgrounds and pastures. The Stoney asked for compensation, which included reserve land on what remained of the Kootenay Plains. In 1974, the federal government agreed that they should be given another 7,300 hectares. The provincial government, however, rejected the federal government's request to provide land to meet the outstanding treaty obligation. The matter is before the courts.

In the meantime, two blocks of land have been transferred by the provincial government to the Stoney as compensation for the lost grave sites caused by the flooding behind the Bighorn Dam. One block of about 480 hectares lies directly across the highway from the Two O'Clock Creek Recreation Area campground. The other block of about 700 hectares lies across the highway from the Siffleur Falls Staging Area parking lot.

HISTORICAL FOOTNOTES

The Stoney Cemetery

Windy Point, with its spectacular view of the valley, was a popular location for the Stoney Indians to bury their dead. At least five children were buried there. The creation of Abraham Lake threatened to cover these and other grave sites. The Stoneys at the Bighorn Reserve were thus faced with an emotional and religious quandary. Stoney Chief John Snow summed up their dilemma:

"While we do not want to move the graves, as the spirits of our dead relatives do not like to have their place of rest disturbed, we also feel that it would be a greater sin to leave the graves where they are to be covered and flooded by water. Many of our people believe that at the time of the resurrection, the spirits will not be able to rise up through the water when the body was originally buried on dry land."

In total, there were 24 known grave sites to be covered by Abraham Lake. In 1972, 20 of them were disinterred by the Provincial Government and reburied at the Stoney Indian graveyard and memorial beside Two O'Clock Creek. Two Stoney families asked that four graves not be moved.

Indian burials and water have a close association. Natives nearing old age often asked their families to take them to a mound near the confluence of two streams, or a stream and a lake. There, after the family sang songs and offered prayers to their Great Spirit, the elder was left alone to commune with the Great Spirit and to die. One stream represented life and the other death. When the elder died, both streams carried away the spirit to heaven. It is because of this belief that some Indians have a dread of dying a long distance from a flowing stream.

46 Bridge Creek – map p. 163

Duration ~ half day
Distance ~ 6.4 km
Level of Difficulty ~ scramble along rocky streambed; some stream crossings
Maximum Elevation ~ 1,475 m
Elevation Gain ~ 90 m
Map ~ 83 C/1 Whiterabbit Creek

Access ~ Park your vehicle on the levee on the north bank of Bridge Creek located two km north of Two O'Clock Creek, or 59 km west of Nordegg, or 24 km east of the Banff National Park boundary on Highway #11.

Possibly once the scene of a violent fight between warring Indians, Bridge Creek today is an idyllic mountain stream. Some light bushwhacking and numerous stream crossings lead you to a pretty waterfall that will keep shutterbugs content.

~

A distinct path takes you from your vehicle along the stony levee on the north bank of Bridge Creek. This

0.0	trailhead
0.3	fork
0.5	creekbed
2.6	hoodoos
3.2	gorge and waterfall
6.4	trailhead

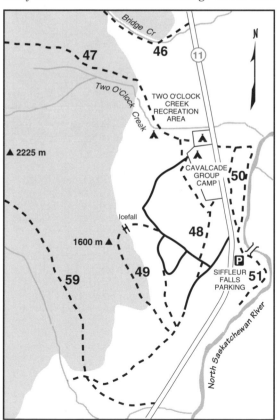

WHAT'S IN A NAME?

Bridge Creek

Courtesy of Doris Magnus.

Previous Name ~ Indian Creek
Stoney Name ~ Kootenahyoo Waptan
(Kootenay Creek)

This stream is named after the Upper Saskatchewan River bridge. This bridge, also called Edwards Bridge, was dismantled in 1972 with the creation of Abraham Lake. There is a now a ford at the former bridge site.

Another local name still in use is Indian Creek. This name comes from the fact that the creek mouth was a favourite fishing spot for members of Chief Robert Smallboy's band of Cree who used to live on the plains.

The Stoney name, Kootenahyoo Waptan, or Kootenay Creek, recalls a purported massacre of Kootenay Indians by the Stoney. There was one survivor, a pregnant Kootenay Indian woman. In another version of the story, there was no massacre. A hunting party of Stoney came across a group of Kootenay Indians who, upon seeing the Stoney approach, took fright and ran away over the mountains to the west. There was one Kootenay who couldn't run since she was pregnant. She was therefore taken prisoner by the Stoney.

Alberta Forest Ranger John Elliott reported attending a sundance ceremony on the plains where Chief Robert Smallboy pointed out one of the dancers to him. The dancer's grandfather, according to Smallboy, was the "baby in the belly" of the captured Kootenay woman who had been acquired from the Stoney by the Cree Indians.

164

sun-drenched slope supports low-lying junipers, wolf willow with its heady scent in early summer, small spruce trees and the pretty yellow aven flowers. At a fork in the trail, bear left to stay as close to the creek as possible. The trail dies at a large boulder field on the right. A light bushwhack between the boulder wash and the stream takes you across a point of land and back out to Bridge Creek. Here, the trail dips into the creekbed. Cross Bridge Creek and continue walking upstream, this time on the left-hand bank. Depending upon the water level, you may have to recross the creek within metres of the first crossing. This is the first of many stream crossings. Unless there have been heavy rains all the crossings should be relatively easy and you should not have to get your feet wet.

The high cliffs on either side of the creek make the scramble upstream interesting. Your interest is further piqued when the stream cuts through a shallow gorge. At times you have to bushwhack along either embankment and there are numerous crossings and recrossings of the stream. Finally, you are past the gorge and into a valley that has opened up with great views of Mount Ernest Ross upstream. A short walk brings you to a high gravel slope, where you can see hoodoos being formed as the less resistant gravel is eroded into the streambed. Past the hoodoos is a small gorge where Bridge Creek cuts through heavy shale. It is punctuated at the end with a delightful waterfall.

Although it is possible to work your way along the left side of the gorge past the waterfall, we recommend that you turn around at this point and retrace your steps to your vehicle.

WHAT'S IN A NAME?

Mount Ernest Ross

Previous Names ~ Twin Peaks ~ Elliot Peak ~ Kootenay Plain Peak

This 2,450 m-high peak was named after Ernest Ross (1883-1963) in 1969. He was also known as The Overlander or Trailblazer, as for almost 40 years he followed his vision of pushing a highway west from Rocky Mountain House to Golden, British Columbia.

Ross's method was straightforward—punch a vehicle through the bush and a road will soon follow. In 1928 he was the first to travel by car to Saunders. In 1931 he was the first to reach Nordegg by car. And in 1940, with four companions, he was the first to reach the Jasper-Banff Highway by car from the east.

Twin Peaks is a local unofficial name based upon the mountain's most significant feature, its two-coloured double peak.

Originally called Elliot Peak, it was given this name after eight year old Elliott Barnes climbed the mountain with his father, Elliott Barnes Sr., in 1906. Elliott Sr. was a photographer who operated a ranch from 1905-1908 on the Kootenay Plains. The peak's name was later transferred to the higher mountain to the north, present-day Elliot Peak, originally called Sentinel Mountain.

This may also be the mystery "Kootanis [sic] Plain Peak," climbed September 17, 1858 by Sir James Hector. He describes following a long ridge composed of different types of stone: dark shale, light grey sandstone, white limestone and shale weathered to a dark vermilion. Hector followed this ridge to its summit where it was formed of "black calcareous shale, with flattened nodulated masses of sandstone that resist the action of the weather."

Ross did not live to see all his achievements recognized. The David Thompson Highway was officially opened in 1968, five years after his death.

47 Two O'Clock Ridge – map p. 163

Duration ~ full day
Distance ~ 18 km
Level of Difficulty ~ long, steady climb to alpine area
Maximum Elevation ~ 2,515 m
Elevation Gain ~ 1,150 m
Map ~ 83 C/1 Whiterabbit Creek

Access ~ Park your vehicle close to campsite #12 at the Two O'Clock Creek Recreation Area campground, located 61 km west of Nordegg or 22 km east of the Banff National Park boundary on Highway #11.

This is a great day hike for those who like to give their legs and their lungs a good stretch. The reward for a long and relentlessly steep climb is a gloriously panoramic view on top.

~

Your well-defined, gravel trail begins across the road from #12 campsite. The trail leads up a set of stone steps to a gate and cattle guard that takes you into the Kootenay Plains Cavalcade Group Camp. At the gate the trail forks. Bear to the right and walk along the road toward the toilets. Behind the toilets is a fence and another cattle guard. Here, you intersect with a broad footpath. Turn left and begin a slow, easy climb up through open bush of poplar, spruce and some pine trees. Taking the right-hand fork takes you back to the campground. In late spring and early summer the grasslands abound in Indian paint brushes, purple and white asters, wild roses, the lovely blue harebell and yarrow.

Within 100 m a secondary trail joins the main footpath. Turn right onto this narrower path; the trail to the left leads into the Sundance Lodge Loop hike. Continue your slow climb upwards through open poplar stands. At a fork in the trail keep to the left; going right returns you to the campground. Continue to climb. At yet another fork keep to the right along the main path. To the left is an informal campsite. Shortly beyond this point you come to Two O'Clock Creek. Cross the log "bridge" and find the trail as it leads upstream along a low ridge. You have gained a little elevation by now and Mount William Booth and Excoelis Mountain are visible behind you. At a fork in the trail there is a choice. You can keep on the main footpath by taking the right-hand fork, or if you wish to keep Two O'Clock Creek in sight, take the left-hand or lower fork. The latter connects with the main footpath at 1.5 km. There are several braids in

0.0	trailhead
0.1	junction
0.3	junction
0.4	junction
0.7	junction
0.9	junction
1.0	Two O'Clock Creek
1.2	junction
1.4	braid
1.5	junction
2.0	junction
2.5	junction
2.9	junction
3.4	cliffs
9.0	rock cairn
18.0	trailhead

In early spring you will probably have to hike through some snow to reach the top of the ridge and its glorious view. Courtesy of Chris Hanstock.

the main trail as it climbs along the ridge. Keep to the left until a junction in the trail; it is here that Two O'Clock Creek takes a 90 degree turn to the right and this is where the lower trail along the creek joins the main footpath. At the junction turn right and continue to climb steeply. A faint footpath joins from the right at the two-km mark; ignore it and bear to the left to remain on the main trail. As you climb, an open ridge above you to the right comes into view. That is your destination.

The trail becomes even steeper after a major intersection with a trail from the left. If you are low on water nip down the left fork 100 m to the creek, for this will be the last chance to fill your water bottle. Otherwise, keep to the right and climb, climb, climb. Spruce trees and junipers make this a pretty hike, giving the slope a park-like setting above the creek valley. Two O'Clock Ridge is straight ahead. The trail climbs sharply to the top of the ridge, offering great views ahead. It then descends into a boggy area where the beautiful round-leaved orchid and purple violet can be found. Climbing

out of the bog, the trail swings onto another ridge to continue its relentless march upward. When you arrive at the edge of the ridge there is a fork in the trail. Bear to the right and continue the ascent; the trail to the left is a game trail that descends to the creek. When returning, this junction is easy to miss. Watch for the surveyor's tape in the trees that marks the way.

Stop occasionally to catch your breath and to enjoy the glorious view. The top of Tuff Puff is on your left. Below are cliffs of red shale that herald

---

WHAT'S IN A NAME?

Two O'Clock Creek

This is a descriptive name for a phenomenon common in mountain streams. It also is a consideration for cautious travellers.

On warm, sunny days in late spring and early summer, meltwater from ice and snow upstream increases in volume as the day progresses. By midafternoon creek crossings can be downright dangerous. Early travellers and wise hikers plan to cross creeks before or after two o'clock when the creek has crested.

the Two O'Clock Creek gorge. As the trail approaches a set of low cliffs, it peters out. Climb on top of the grassy slope to avoid the cliffs. From here, the trail becomes faint as it winds through the trees and open areas. From time to time there is surveyor's tape in the trees to mark the way. Stay within 30 m of the edge of the gorge. As you reach the base of the first knob below Two O'Clock Ridge the trail veers to the right away from the gorge. After the trail swings back to the left the hike becomes a bit of a scramble up through the scree. At the top of the knob you can see the destination so continue up the open ridge. In late spring, the lichen-covered scree slope is sprinkled with wild strawberries, purple sweet vetch and pretty miniature snapdragons called butter-and-eggs.

Two rock cairns confirm your arrival at the peak of Two O'Clock Ridge. Below, to your left, is a large lush meadow with a small stream running through it. The top of Tuff Puff is beyond the meadow, and far, far below is Highway #11, the confluence of the Siffleur and North Saskatchewan Rivers, and the Kootenay Plains. If you had an early start, or if you intend to camp in the meadows below, continue along the ridge. From atop the peak ahead you can see Landslide Lake.

Remember to add a rock or two to the cairns before returning the way you came.

FLORAFACTS

Prickly Wild Rose

Scientific Name ~ *Rosa acicularis*
Stoney Names ~ Hupe Warphen (the leaves) ~ Ozirta (rose hips) ~ Hupe Pe (the bloom)

Alberta's floral emblem, the prickly wild rose, can be found along roadsides as in the case of Two O'Clock Creek Recreation Area campground, dry south-facing slopes and in open woods. The pink blooms of late spring give way in late summer to red fruit called rose hips.

Today, we use the hips to make jam, jelly and tea. The Stoneys and other Indian nations made wide use of the leaves, hips and roots of this plant. When boiled, the leaves produced an infusion used to cure stomach aches. Also, a paste made by chewing the leaves was applied to bee stings. High in vitamins A and C, rose hips were used in soups and mixed with grease to be eaten with dried meat.

The hips also have medicinal qualities. When made into a poultice, the hips were found helpful in relieving the pain of boils. Also, the Stoneys drank an infusion of the hips as a treatment for tuberculosis. A rather bitter drink made from the roots was made to cure diarrhea. If peeled and scraped, the inner bark when boiled was found to be an excellent treatment for sore eyes.

It is difficult to distinguish the Prickly Rose from another common Alberta species, the Wood Rose. Usually the Prickly Rose has a smaller and thicker covering of prickles than those of the Wood Rose. Hybridization between these two species also makes identification difficult. But then, a rose by another name is still a rose.

48 Sundance Lodge Loop – map p. 163

Duration ~ two hours
Distance ~ 4.9 km
Level of Difficulty ~ easy stroll
Maximum Elevation ~ 1,415 m
Elevation Gain ~ 80 m
Map ~ 83 C/1 Whiterabbit Creek

Access ~ Park your vehicle at the Siffleur Falls Trail staging area 62 km west of Nordegg, or 21 km east of Banff National Park boundary on Highway #11.

This is a perfect walk for anyone interested in aspects of First Nations' culture, for you pass through an area favoured by both Stoneys and Cree for their ceremonies of thanksgiving. A low but pretty ridge walk overlooking the Kootenay Plains completes your experience.

~

From your parked vehicle retrace your route back to Highway #11 and then north along the highway for approximately 200 m to where, on the west side of the highway, there is a gravel track. Walk up the gravel road through a gate. The track, cut deeply into the fragile soil, snakes through open stands of spruce trees, low bush cranberry and junipers. There are two quick junctions with secondary four-wheel drive tracks; keep to the right

0.0	trailhead at Siffleur Falls Trail parking lot
0.2	cart track
0.7	junction
0.8	junction
1.1	junction
1.3	sundance lodges
1.5	junction
1.6	sundance lodges
1.7	fork
1.9	sweat lodges
2.0	junction
2.5	junction
2.6	T-junction
3.1	junction
3.7	T-junction
4.1	T-junction
4.9	trailhead

A former Stoney chief, Walking Eagle, once explained that the centre pole represents the tree of life, its rafters being the branches.

A Stoney sundance encampment, ca. 1950. Courtesy of Glenbow Archives, #NA 4212-69.

in both cases to stay on the main road. The road braids from time to time around mud holes or other obstacles to vehicular traffic.

Continuing forward at another junction into an open field with copses of pine trees you catch a glimpse of two sundance lodges on the right. Notice that the lodges are in various states of disrepair. Part of the reason is that a new one is built each time there is a ceremony of thanksgiving. After the ceremony, the lodges are simply abandoned. Secondly, other than the centre pole, which is cut fresh each time, elements of the lodge such as the ridge poles and even some of the walls are often borrowed from older lodges. At this first group of lodges, one of them still has most of its walls, ridge poles and even the remnants of coloured cloth tied to the top of the centre pole.

A short distance beyond these lodges is a junction of tracks in the open field. Bear to the right along the main cart track. Another group of

sundance lodges, older than the previous ones, dot the plains on either side of the trail. At a fork in the track, keep to the right to swing in a northerly direction. Just beyond the 90 degree turn in the road, there are remains of sweat lodges where the participants in the sundance ceremony first go to purify themselves. At yet another junction, continue forward through open stands of aspens. More sweat lodges are tucked in amongst the trees; if you're lucky you may find a sweetgrass bundle left in one of them. There are footpaths to the left and the right. If you wish to examine another sundance lodge and several other sweat lodges, follow a cutline on the left for approximately 200 m. Return to the main cart track.

At a junction keep to the right along the main cart track; the track to the left intersects 100 m later with a trail leading to the Kootenay Plains Cavalcade Group Camp. Climb a low ridge that leads to a great view of the camp below, the Kootenay Plains and the highway.

HISTORICAL FOOTNOTES

The Sundance

Traditionally held in midsummer, the sundance was and still is a major religious ceremony among Plains Indian cultures. It was arranged and conducted by an individual who wished to give thanksgiving, or wished to request aid or intervention on the part of the spirits, or in response to a vision. The festivities also used to mark an opportunity to renew family ties, to arrange marriages and to exchange property. Today, however, the sundance is more an expression of joy and gratitude to Waka Taga, the Great Spirit. Very strict rules govern the behaviour of all who are present.

Interestingly, those practising the sundance have never referred to the ceremony as such. The Stoney word for the ceremony, wahiambah-wagee-cheebee, does not use the words "sun" or "dance" at all. The term appears to have been used by non-Indian traders and missionaries who tried to articulate the mysticism of the ceremony.

The form of the sundance differed from tribe to tribe. Among the Stoneys on the Kootenay Plains, a medicine man is responsible for the success and completion of the ceremony, while among other tribes, like the Blackfoot and Sarcee, a woman takes the lead role. Up to three days of preliminary ritual can precede the selection of the site for the erection of the ceremonial lodge where the celebrations are held. Tipis for the medicine man's helpers are set up with others camping in a large circle around the lodge site. Then, the medicine man chooses a suitable poplar tree to be the centre pole. Green boughs are tied with lengths of brightly coloured cloth to one end of the pole. Next, the centre pole has to be placed upright. It is most important to the medicine man that the centre pole be erected properly, for if it fails to stand upright, the virtuosity of the medicine man is called into question. Then, following a private ceremony in the medicine man's lodge, the ceremonial lodge is built. Prior to the mid-19th century, the lodge looked more like a large tipi with the wall poles leaning against the centre pole. But at some point the design changed so that now the roof poles connect to freestanding walls of woven willow. There are two doorways, one in the east wall and another in the west wall. Inside, there is another half-wall of woven willow placed close to the west wall. It is from these two walls that the medicine man, his helpers and the ceremonial dancers come and go during the ceremonies.

After fasting, prayers and songs of thanksgiving, the dancing begins. Many of the men and women's societies perform dances and none of the dancers break the fast until the ceremony is finished. The dancers each in turn emerge from behind the inner wall to perform their ritual dances. Perhaps the best known dances among the tribes of the Blackfoot Confederacy were those of self-torture; the Stoneys, however, do not appear to have indulged widely in the practice. Self-torture by young men seeking admission into the warrior society occurred often enough, though, for the Dominion government to ban the sundance in 1885—no doubt in response to the urgings of missionaries. Around 1900, with a revival among the Indians in traditional religious practices, the sundance was salvaged from possible oblivion and has been performed annually ever since.

Only a few non-Indians have had the opportunity to witness a sundance. Prior to the 1950s, the Stoneys on the Kootenay Plains occasionally allowed non-Indians to watch from a distance once they had presented a gift. Money was accepted, but only as a sign of friendship and never as admission to the ceremonial lodge. There is a story of a local merchant who was given permission to watch a sundance of the Sunchild Cree. He was told to bring a gift in proportion to his sins. He arrived at the lodge and presented a roast of beef as a gift. The medicine man accepted the gift, but having known the merchant for a number of years, suggested that a couple of fat cows would have been more appropriate!

The curiosity of non-Indians led the Stoneys and Cree in the 1930s and 1940s to stage a separate dance to satisfy their uninvited visitors. Building a lodge near the road, they charged an admission of $.15 or the equivalent in bread, butter or jam.

Here, there is a T-junction. If you go to the left you will end up at the group camp, so instead, turn right and walk along the footpath that parallels the edge of the cliff. This is a most pleasant walk, especially in early spring when the croci are in bloom. At one point, the trail dips down through stands of spruce trees where there is a junction with another footpath from the group camp joining on the left. Keep to the right and climb up the ridge to continue in a southerly direction. At a fork, turn left to stay along the ridge; if you take the right-hand fork you will intersect the main gravel track 400 m later at the two km point. Even the left-hand trail now leaves the ridge and swings down through pine trees to a T-junction. Bear to the right along a broad footpath and continue downhill. The trail passes to the right of a rock outcropping before coming to another T-junction. Bear to the right. The trail now becomes a broad path that intersects with the main gravel track at 800 m. Turn left and return to the highway and to your vehicle.

The purification of the dancers and others involved in the sundance is an important adjunct to the ceremony. Some sweat lodges are used by a single person; this one accommodated two or more. Usually, stones are heated in a fire and then placed inside the sweat lodge where the participants pour water on them to produce steam. The framework seen here was covered with plastic or a tarpaulin.
Courtesy of Gillian Daffern.

49 Icefall Trail Loop – map p. 163

Duration ~ half day
Distance ~ 7.2 km
Level of Difficulty ~ easy stroll with a steep scramble
Maximum Elevation ~ 1,540 m
Elevation Gain ~ 205 m
Map ~ 83 C/1 Whiterabbit Creek

Access ~ Park your vehicle at the Siffleur Falls Trail Staging Area parking lot 62 km west of Nordegg, or 21 km east of the Banff National Park boundary on Highway #11.

In springtime, if you want to check out a stunning, yet easily accessible icefall, this is the hike for you. A scramble up beside the icefall leads to a delightful return ridge walk.

~

From your parked vehicle retrace your route back to Highway #11 and then north along the highway for approximately 200 m to where, on the west side of the highway, there is a gravel track. Walk up the gravel road and through a gate. The track, cut deeply into the fragile soil, snakes through open stands of white spruce, low bush cranberry and junipers. Follow the main track as it swings slowly to the right. There are two quick junctions with secondary four-wheel drive tracks. These form two angles of a major triangular-shaped intersection. Keep to the right in both cases to stay on the main road. The first track coming up the slope on the left is the exit point to the Icefall Trail Loop. Continue on the main road past a footpath that joins from the right. The road braids from time to time around mud holes or other obstacles to vehicular traffic.

Continue forward at another junction. In an open field with copses of pine trees there are two sundance lodges on the right. A short distance beyond these lodges the cart track forks. The right fork is the Sundance Loop. Take the left-hand fork and follow it through the open field. There are more sundance lodges to the right. Shortly, the cart track you are following loops into the forest, where it immediately becomes a footpath. The trail climbs through stands of pine. In early spring, the upper part of the trail can be wet from the icefall runoff. In places the trail straddles two braids of the meltwaters. At a junction, bear left, because the trail to the right returns to the meadow. Continue to climb. Suddenly, you find yourself at the base of the icefall.

0.0	trailhead
0.2	cart track and gate
0.7	junction
0.8	junction
1.1	junction
1.3	sundance lodges
1.5	junction
1.6	sundance lodges
2.2	junction
2.4	icefall
2.8	footpath
4.6	junction at base of ridge
4.7	junction
4.8	braid
5.0	junction
5.3	braid
5.5	junction
5.6	junction with cart track
5.7	junction
6.1	junction
6.3	junction
6.4	junction
6.5	junction
7.0	gate and highway
7.2	trailhead

Looking down to the valley from above the icefall.

This frozen seepage, commonly called an icefall, is an interesting geological feature. It is a challenge for many icefall climbers. If you're here in March or April, you may find one or two climbers working their way to the top, even though the best season for ice climbing is the dead of winter. Some use slings; others prefer to free climb. Take a moment or two to enjoy this quirk of nature.

To complete the loop you must scramble up the cliff to the left of the icefall. It is fairly steep, but mercifully short, and you soon find yourself at the top of the icefall where, remarkably, there is no ice at all! Rather, the area near the cliff is marshy and wet from numerous springs, some of which are sulphurous judging by the whiffs you may catch from time to time. The next

GEOFACTS

Icefalls

In early spring this icefall dominates the view to the west when driving south on Highway #11 near the Siffleur Falls Staging Area. You would not be the first to think that the icefall is a frozen waterfall. Yet, if you were to return here in summer you would not be able to see any waterfall at all.

So, how do you explain the "disappearing" waterfall? The answer lies in the springs and seepages at the top of the icefall. These continue to bubble and ooze from the ground even during the winter. As the water trickles down the cliff face it freezes, and over the course of several months a huge

icefall builds up. Come spring and summer, the icefall melts, leaving only a small trickle of seepage water to keep the face of the cliff moist and wet.

When you are on top of the icefall you may catch a whiff of the familiar "rotten egg" smell of hyrogen sulphide. As the water moves upwards through rock fractures it carries with it dissolved sulphates. The hydrogen sulphide usually oxidizes near the discharge point, giving off its distinctive odour. The sulphide lends a milky appearance to the pools of water that form where the spring bubbles out of the ground.

challenge is to locate the trail that loops back toward your vehicle. Because of the springs no trail can be easily discerned. Keep the bog on your right and continue straight ahead up through the thick grass. Soon you pick up two distinct paths that swing to the left through the trees and break out onto the open ridge. There is a survey marker beside the second path about 200 m from the top of the icefall. Follow the footpath down the ridge as it swings through open pines to a lookout point. Here, there are glorious views to the south and east. Continuing your walk down the ridge, Mounts Siffleur, Loudon and Peskett beckon you.

From time to time the path braids. When you reach a junction at the base of the ridge, you are now back on the Kootenay Plains with its myriad tracks and trails. Turn left onto the well-defined footpath. The trail to the right goes to Tuff Puff.

Within metres paths from both the left and right join the footpath. Continue straight along the main path to the beginning of a long braid. Bear to the right to stay on the edge of the low ridge that you are now on. Bearing left takes you into the trees where, of course, there are no views.

At the next intersection, keep to the right and go down the slope. The next junction is the end of the long braid. Bear right at this junction, and at the one afterwards. At the 5.6-km mark, there is a junction with a cart track. Bear to the left onto the cart track. At the next two intersections, keep to the right along the cart track, but left at the third intersection. At the bottom of a slope there is yet another junction of tracks. Go to the right and up the slope to yet another junction. This territory should look familiar as this junction is the same as the one at 700 m at the beginning of the hike. Turn right and return to the trailhead.

HISTORICAL FOOTNOTES

Chief Walking Eagle (ca. 1883-1965)

For over 20 years he was the great forecaster. His long term weather predictions were published in hundreds of newspapers across Canada and the United States. He was called Chief Walking Eagle. His real name was Morley Beaver.

Chief Walking Eagle was born on the Abraham Flats and lived on the Kootenay Plains and Bighorn Reserve. His ability to interpret nature's signs made him world famous. He said that he could learn more about weather trends in one day's walk through the mountains than a white man could learn from his "high-priced machines."

Walking Eagle had other powers besides weather forecasting. Early on in World War II, during a sundance ceremony on the Kootenay Plains, he formally cursed Adolf Hitler. During the same ceremony, he sponsored a decision by the Stoney to charge the whites present as tourists an admission fee. The money was donated to the Red Cross. As for Hitler, he lost the war.

Walking Eagle's fame as the great Indian weatherman made him, at times, a bit of a caricature in the media. But he could turn the joke. He once claimed that he would carefully observe industrious white men laying down woodpiles for omens of upcoming winter weather conditions. Large woodpiles meant a severe winter was forecast. With the advent of natural gas heating, however, he said he had fewer woodpiles to predict from so he kept his prognostic abilities focused upon the more "traditional" animal hides, tree bark, fish habits and bird migratory patterns.

Walking Eagle lies buried at the Stoney cemetery on the Bighorn Reserve.

50 Heritage Trail – map p. 163

Duration ~ half day
Distance ~ 3.9 km
Level of Difficulty ~ easy stroll
Maximum Elevation ~ 1,360 m
Elevation Gain ~ 25 m
Map ~ 83 C/1 Whiterabbit Creek

This delightful walk leads you to a Stoney Indian cemetery with its heart-wrenching story, and past remains of structures that relate to early ranchers on the Kootenay Plains.

~

Find a four-wheel drive track behind the washrooms at the Siffleur Falls Trail Staging Area parking lot. Almost immediately it forks. Bear to the left to keep closer to the fence and the highway. At another fork bear left again. Continue your pleasant walk through the meadows past the bluebird boxes. On the stroll through the meadows you may see three different kinds of bluebirds. The most common bluebird on the Kootenay Plains is the Mountain Bluebird. The male is startling blue, while the female is brownish-grey with blue on the wings, rump and tail. They arrive on the Plains in mid-March to occupy the nest boxes and begin migration in mid-August. If you are very, very lucky, you may see an Alberta rarity—the Western Bluebird. The male sports a brighter, deeper blue than the Mountain Bluebird. He often has a chestnut-coloured patch on its back and reddish-brown sides, flank and breast. The female is somewhat similar, but much duller. Up to 1992, there have been only two

Access ~ Park your vehicle at the Siffleur Falls Trail Staging Area parking lot 62 km west of Nordegg, or 21 km east of the Banff National Park boundary on Highway #11. The trail begins to the left of the public washrooms.

0.0	trailhead and fork
0.2	fork
0.8	fork
1.0	Kootenay Plains Ecological Reserve boundary fence and remains of a chimney
1.1	Barnes's Ranch corral
1.2	intersection
1.8	Tom Wilson's cabin and the Stoney Indian cemetery and memorial
1.9	Kootenay Plains Ecological Reserve boundary fence
2.0	North Saskatchewan River
2.5	braid
2.7	braid
2.8	junction
2.9	junction
3.3	junction
3.4	junction
3.6	junction
3.9	trailhead

Barnes's beloved fireplace today.

WHAT'S IN A NAME?

Excoelis Mountain

Courtesy of Doris Magnus.

Previous Names ~ Kadoona Mountain ~ Siffleur Mountain

Excoelis is Greek for "Out of the Clouds." This is the motto of the 1st Canadian Parachute Battalion after which this mountain with five peaks was named in 1994. The battalion was formed in 1942 and was the first force on the ground during the 1944 Normandy invasion, parachuting shortly after midnight and hours before the dawn beach landings.

The five peaks local, unofficial name is the Kadoona Peaks or Mountain. They were named by Mary Schäffer and appear in 1911 on her Old Indian Trails expedition map. Kadoona is Stoney for windy. This mountain name likely comes from the Stoney name for the nearby Kootenay Plains—Kadoona Tinda or Windy Plains.

These peaks may have also been the original Siffleur Mountain. Early maps show a nonexistent mountain at the same latitude on the west side of the Siffleur River. This misplaced peak disappeared in later editions and Siffleur Mountain moved further to the south.

confirmed reports of their nesting on the Kootenay Plains. It is even possible that you might see Laxuli Buntings. Males are a lighter blue than Mountain Bluebirds and have white wing bars. The female has a brownish-blue back and rump. They arrive on the Plains in late May and migrate south in late August. They nest in low bushes, preferring thick shrubbery along water courses or on hillsides.

At a fork, turn right to swing away from the highway. The trail leads through open spruce forest, which offers some relief from the heat on a summer's day. Where another track joins from the left, continue straight ahead on the main track. Almost immediately you cross the Kootenay Plains Ecological Reserve boundary fence and come upon the remains of a stone chimney on the left.

This is the ranch site of Elliott Barnes, who spent three summers here after the turn of the century attempting to raise Clydesdale horses. A short

HISTORICAL FOOTNOTES

Elliott Barnes

It is a gentle photograph and self-portrait of the man. Barnes was an excellent photographer and as usual, he set it up well. Sitting in front of the fireplace in his cabin, which he built with the help of local Stoney Indians, he wears his trademark leather jacket. Running from his right heel is the string he attached to the camera to activate the shutter.

This quiet, peaceful man is Elliott Barnes. He spent three years (1905-1908) on the Kootenay Plains raising horses, operating a small packing and guiding business, and taking photographs. By and large his photos have been forgotten and he never received the attention given his contemporary and for a short time (1907-1908) partner, Byron Harmon. Barnes's photographs of the Kootenay Plains area and the Stoney Indians indicate his fine technical ability.

Barnes lived at his Kadoona Tinda Ranch beside Two O'Clock Creek only during the summer. He wintered in Banff while Stoney, Silas Abraham, minded the cabin. It was in Barnes's cabin, one autumn evening in 1907 that another Stoney, Samson Beaver, drew his route map to Maligne Lake for Mary Schäffer.

The horses Barnes tried to raise on the Plains were purebred Clydesdales. They apparently did not adapt well to winter conditions so, in 1908, Barnes sold his ranch and a five year old Clyde stallion named "Duke," to Tom Wilson for $450. Barnes took the remaining herd to his new ranch near Calgary.

Barnes's cabin deteriorated over the years and was eventually burned in 1960 by the Alberta Forest Service. The corral was left standing. An examination of the site today reveals the outline of the walls of his cabin, and the fact that Barnes built the chimney outside the end wall, rather than inside his cabin.

Elliott Barnes at his Kootenay Plains cabin, ca. 1907. Courtesy Whyte Museum of the Canadian Rockies, Banff.

The sod roof and notched corners of an outbuilding of Tom Wilson's were typical construction features of early cabins.

walk farther down the track brings you to Elliott Barnes's octagonal corral. The corral is in remarkably good condition, perhaps due to Barnes's attention to detail in its construction. Look for the dowels that hold the rails and the gate posts together.

With Excoelis Mountain on the right, continue along the road to an intersection and make a sharp right-hand turn. The Stoney cemetery and memorial, and the remaining cabin of guide and outfitter, Tom Wilson, are 600 m further down the road. Until 1994, there were two cabins here. Unfortunately, the main cabin burned down with only the chimney remaining.

Both the Stoney graves inside the log corral and the Wilson cabins were moved here by the provincial government in 1972, when it became apparent that individual grave sites and the Wilson cabins would be flooded by Abraham Lake. The Tom Wilson ranch operated for eight years on the other side of the North Saskatchewan River near the confluence with Whiterabbit Creek. Wilson, with the assistance of local Stoneys such as Silas Abraham, constructed the

buildings and horse corral during the winter of 1902-1903, where they remained until the government dismantled the buildings and moved them across the river.

Continue past the cemetery and memorial to the Kootenay Plains Ecological Reserve boundary fence. Turn left and follow the fence down to the North Saskatchewan River. At the cliff's edge, turn right to follow the footpath. This pretty trail dips into a number of ravines and braids more than once, the lower braids leading down to the river. At a junction bear to the left to avoid a bridle path. The hiking trail, which hugs the banks of the river, offers superior views up the river's valley. To remain on this trail as long as possible, keep to the left at the next two junctions. If you want a shortcut back to the trailhead, turn right at the second junction. Otherwise, continue along the river's edge, keeping to the left at yet a third junction. After 200 m or so you come to a junction with the main, broad path from the Siffleur Falls Trail Staging Area. Turn right and return to your vehicle in the parking lot.

51 Figure Eight Walk – map p. 163

Duration ~ one hour
Distance ~ 3.4 km
Level of Difficulty ~ easy stroll
Maximum Elevation ~ 1,345 m
Elevation Gain ~ 10 m
Map ~ 83 C/1 Whiterabbit Creek

Access ~ Park your vehicle at the Siffleur Falls Trail Staging Area 62 km west of Nordegg, or 21 km east of the Banff National Park boundary on Highway #11.

This short but very pretty walk is ideal for young families who wish to experience the parkland beauty of the Kootenay Plains.

~

Follow the broad, well-used trail as it leads down from the Siffleur Falls Staging Area parking lot to the suspension bridge across the North Saskatchewan River. Do not cross the bridge. Continue past the bridge along the footpath that cuts through the sandy soil as it follows the bend in the river. Low-lying junipers, spruce trees and, in early spring, yellow butter-and-eggs flowers sprinkle the landscape. This path is also frequented by trail riders, so watch for "buns" deposited en route! As the path follows the cliff at the river's edge, pretty vistas of the upper reaches of the North Saskatchewan River come into view.

0.0	trailhead
0.6	suspension bridge
0.9	junction
1.0	fork
1.2	junction
1.6	ford
2.4	junction
2.9	suspension bridge and T-junction
3.4	trailhead

The entire river valley must have looked like this prior to the construction of the Bighorn Dam.

The path quickly becomes a four-wheel drive track that slices through the meadows. After nearly one km, another track intersects from the right. Continue straight ahead. Within a few metres there is a fork. To follow the river's edge more closely, bear to the left. It's a lovely walk through the meadows as the track climbs a low, rocky outcropping. You are presented with a panoramic view of the river and the broad meadows for which the Kootenay Plains have long been famous. Follow the four-wheel drive track as it swings down from the outcropping through the meadows. The air is heavy with the aroma of wild sage. Just after the track nips between a copse of spruce trees, you find yourself at an old ford across the river. It's unknown when and for how long this ford was used.

Return to the rocky outcropping. Follow the track along the crest of the outcropping to the left, away from the river. After a few metres the track will swing down to the right and return to the fork at one km. Rather than returning along the river's edge the way you came, complete the figure eight by turning to the left at the next junction. Follow the footpath to the suspension bridge and the main path back to the parking lot and your vehicle.

WHAT'S IN A NAME?

Kootenay Plains

Previous Names ~ Cottonnahow Plain
Stoney Name ~ Kadoona Tinda (Windy Plains)

The word "Kootenay" is an anglicized form of the Kootenay word "ktunaxa," which may be a dialectical version of "tunaxa," the name given to the Kootenays who inhabited the eastern slopes of the Rockies prior to the early 19th century. Around 1802, fur trader Peter Fidler phonetically spelt ktunaxa "cotton na hew." Thus there appears on an 1806 map of the area the "Cottonnahow Plain." By the end of the decade, the name had settled into its present version, albeit under a number of spellings: Kootones, Kootenae, Kutenai, etc. It was the North West Company fur traders who affected this change, naming the plains after the Kootenay Indians who at that time lived there.

By about 1810, the Kootenay were driven out by the better-armed Peigan. Replacing them on the eastern slopes were the Mountain Cree and Stoneys. These nations involved themselves in the fur trade, becoming middlemen between the Kootenay, now west of the Rockies, and the Rocky Mountain House trading post. The Kootenay Plains became the location for an annual trading mart held between the Cree and Stoney, and the Kootenays.

Stoney oral history relates that the plains received their name from a battle between themselves and the Kootenay, in which the Kootenay were defeated and driven across the mountains. Stoney Tom Kaquitts tells the story: "One day the Kootenay were nearly wiped out, so the remaining Kootenays fled to the west. They headed up the valley and over the ice field back to the interior of the mountains. In those days they had no horses, just dogs for packing. They had only spears and snares to hunt with; that was how they made a living. They never came back."

A characteristic of the plains are the prevailing westerly winds. Hence the Stony name "Kadoona Tinda," meaning the Windy Plains.

HISTORICAL FOOTNOTES

The Lost Serengetti

When you look out across the Kootenay Plains there is something missing. The large herds of ungulates are gone. Habitat loss and disturbance caused by the reservoir and highway are one set of reasons for the loss; over and off-season hunting are the other.

During the first half of the 19th century, travellers crossing the Plains reported a Serengetti-like scene. There were herds of bison, wapiti, mule deer and mountain caribou in the valley. There were bighorn sheep and mountain goats on or near the slopes. In the woods there were moose. The Kootenay Plains were a magnet to the wintering animals, as relatively mild temperatures, light snow cover and habitat variety ensured an adequate food supply. Apart from the bison, the large ungulates are still present, albeit in lesser numbers.

David Thompson described the Kootenay Plains as "the land of the Bison" and depended upon successful hunts in this area for provisions. Both Alexander Henry and Sir James Hector identified the bison as wood buffalo. Hector saw ever fewer bison signs along the upper Siffleur and North Saskatchewan. He reported in 1858 that their numbers, as well as that of other large game, were depleted due to over-hunting and a strange disease:

"...the Indians told us that not many years ago there were many of these animals [bison] along the valley of the North Saskatchewan, within the mountains. Eleven years ago, they say, there were great fires all through the mountains, and in the woods along their eastern base; and after that a disease broke out among all the animals, so that they used to find wapiti, moose, and other deer, as well as buffalo, lying dead in numbers. Before that time there was abundance of game in all parts of the country; but since then there has been great scarcity of animals, and only the best hunters can make sure of killing."

Bison were present on the Plains as late as the late 1850s, but by 1892, when A. P. Coleman came through, all that remained were old, unused bison trails, wallows and the occasional bleached skull. Local outfitter, Ed McKenzie, reports seeing bison skulls up to the 1940s, and speculates that they were present in the area into the 20th century.

The large wapiti herds were apparently shot out by 1900. Remnant herds are still present and may be seen either on the Plains or along the Coral Creek valley. You can see small groups of bighorn sheep at Windy and Whirlpool Points as well as near Bridge Creek.

With the ban on shooting mountain goats, their numbers have rebounded and can now be seen along the upper Whitegoat and Littlehorn Creeks, as well as on Sentinel Mountain and other mountains along the Cline River. Mule deer and moose still seem to be abundant. And the mountain caribou? The last small herd was reported decimated by hunting from the highway sometime in the 1970s.

52 Terrace Walk – map p. 187

Duration ~ half day
Distance ~ 5.9 km
Level of Difficulty ~ easy bushwhack
Maximum Elevation ~ 1,445 m
Elevation Gain ~ 110 m
Map ~ 83 C/1 Whiterabbit Creek

Access ~ Park your vehicle at the Siffleur Falls Trail Staging Area parking lot located 62 km west of Nordegg, or 21 km east of Banff National Park boundary on Highway #11.

This short, easy walk that can be enjoyed by the whole family takes you to a terrace above the North Saskatchewan River, giving you a little elevation from which you can enjoy views up and down the river valley.

~

Follow the broad, well-used trail that leads down from the parking lot to the suspension bridge across the North Saskatchewan River. Cross the suspension bridge. The sandy soil and semi-dry conditions support a variety of sun-loving wildflowers, including prairie groundsel and daisy fleabane. Northern bedstraw, with its clusters of small white flowers, is also common. It was once used to stuff mattresses, perhaps because of the sweet fragrance of its flowers. Another wildflower to watch for is white camas which, while not as poisonous as death camas, nevertheless can make you quite ill if you munch its leaves.

Continue along the trail to a junction with a road on the right. Turn right onto the road. Bearing left takes you to the Siffleur River bridge. After a short distance, the road climbs a little above the North Saskatchewan to give satisfying views to the south and west. In summer, this part of the hike can be a trudge, especially if the day is hot, for there is little shade along the road. Continue straight until reaching a cutline that joins from the left. Bear left onto the cutline. Going straight along the road takes you to Loudon Creek. A four-wheel track along the cutline eases the walk as you climb slowly through open pine and spruce forest. At a fork, keep to the left and you soon arrive at an abandoned horse corral, probably used at one time by outfitters. Outfitters still favour this access into the Siffleur Wilderness; otherwise they have to travel up the Siffleur Falls Trail adding several kilometres to their journey.

0.0	trailhead
0.6	North Saskatchewan River suspension bridge
1.3	junction
2.0	cutline
2.7	fork
2.9	abandoned horse corral
4.5	end of terrace
4.6	junction
5.9	trailhead

Descending from the terrace to the Siffleur Falls Trail.

Leave the cutline and scramble up the open slope on the left to gain access to the terrace. Bear left along a game trail that takes you to the edge of the terrace. On the stroll northwards you can enjoy the views of the North Saskatchewan River valley on your left. The top of the terrace sports typical Kootenay Plains' vegetation, with copses of pines, some krummholz and bearberry bushes. After more than one km the trail dips down to a lower terrace, from where you can see the blue suspension bridge across the river. Continue to the end of the terrace. From here you can see the Siffleur River on your right and northwards along the North Saskatchewan River valley to Abraham Lake.

Take one of the braids that leads down the slope to the junction of trails at the bottom. This junction corresponds to that at 1.3 km. To return to the trailhead turn left.

HISTORICAL FOOTNOTES

Mary Schäffer (1861-1939)

"To appreciate them one must breathe their breath deep into the lungs, must let the soft winds caress the face, and allow the eye to absorb the blue of the surrounding hills and the gold of the grasses beneath the feet.... Here the air is sweeter, dryer, and softer than anywhere I know, and here the world could easily be forgotten and life pass by in a dream."

You are reading Mary Schäffer's description of the Kootenay Plains, the one place in the Canadian Rockies she loved above all else. Mary Schäffer was introduced to the Rockies by a decade of annual excursions into the region with her husband, Dr. Charles Schäffer, a medical doctor with an interest in botany. Together they worked on a book of botany for the Canadian Rockies. When Charles died in 1903, Mary continued with the project, seeing its publication in 1907.

It was a specimen-gathering trip in 1905 that first brought Mary Schäffer to the Kootenay Plains. She travelled from Banff to the Plains via the Pipestone Pass and Siffleur River. Accompanying her was Stewardson Brown, botanist and Curator of the Herbarium of the Academy of Natural Sciences of Philadelphia; future husband Billy Warren, then a guide assigned to her by Tom Wilson; Mollie Adams, her constant travel companion; and three other women who, according to Schäffer, began pining for a bath and soap a few days into the trip. The group spent 17 days in the field and relations became somewhat strained. One of the women, Henrietta Wilson, a mountaineer in her own right, found Mary Schäffer to be somewhat domineering and short on patience.

It was during this trip that Schäffer first met Stoneys' Silas Abraham, Samson Beaver and their families. This meeting had an important consequence two years later when Schäffer returned to the Plains. Samson Beaver drew a map showing the

way to Maligne Lake and fame. The 1907 trip to the Kootenay Plains was for a time the pack trip from hell, since Schäffer became snow-blind at Cataract Pass. Four days on the Plains were heaven and she restored her strength and spirits, took some lovely photographs and played with Frances Louise, Samson Beaver's daughter.

Someone, probably Elliott Barnes, took a photograph of Mary Schäffer atop her pony Nibs. It is a good picture of Mary as she leans over and pats Nibs's neck. She is just days away from her birthday, October 4. She looks happy; her snow blindness gone. She has been a widow for four years. She is in the second year of her new life as an explorer of the Rocky Mountains. Her famous expedition to Maligne Lake is one year ahead. She is 46 years old.

Mary Schäffer on the Kootenay Plains, 1907. Courtesy Whyte Museum of the Canadian Rockies, NG-10.

Samson Beaver (ca. 1875-1934)

This is one of the most famous photographs to come out of the Canadian Rockies. It was taken about 1907 by Mary Schäffer and is a family photo. Seated on the left is Shamosin and on the right is his wife, Leah. Standing in between, cute as a button and holding a spray of poplar leaves, is their daughter Frances Louise.

Shamosin is Stoney for Samson, Samson being Samson Beaver, youngest son of the great explorer of the Canadian Rockies, Job Beaver. Reading about Samson, the one characteristic that stands out about the man is his unfailing good humour. A. P. Coleman described one scene: "Samson had to drive [the] pack pony, a mare with a foal that was always getting into mischief. The two were most exasperating, but the boy [Samson] rode smilingly after them into the worst thickets without a hard word or look of annoyance."

The boy was about 16 years old at the time. Both Coleman and Schäffer described him as a slightly built, handsome and graceful man. It was he who drew the map to Maligne Lake after a dinner-party at Elliott Barnes's cabin. Present that late September evening in 1907 were some of the most famous names associated with the Canadian Rockies: Stoneys' Samson Beaver and Silas Abraham, photographer and host Elliott Barnes, and that mixed foursome of tourist-explorers: Mary Schäffer, Mollie Adams, Billy Warren and Sid Unwin.

Mary Schäffer seemed fascinated by Samson Beaver that evening and recorded a riveting image: "As Sampson [sic] crouched forward on his knees to light his pipe at the fire, his swarthy face lighted up by the bright glow, his brass earrings and nail-studded belt catching the glare, and his blanket breeches, I was glad for even this picture which in a few years can be no more."

Samson Beaver and his family were part of the group that followed Peter Wesley from Morley to the Kootenay Plains in 1894. He lived on the Plains until his death in 1934.

Courtesy of Whyte Museum of the Canadian Rockies, Banff, Alberta, V469 2771.

53 Siffleur Falls Trail – map p. 187

Duration ~ full day
Distance ~ 14 km
Level of Difficulty ~ easy walk; dangerous slopes
Maximum Elevation ~ 1,456 m
Elevation Gain ~ 126 m
Map ~ 83 C/1 Whiterabbit Creek

Access ~ Park your vehicle at the Siffleur Falls Trail Staging Area parking lot located 62 km west of Nordegg, or 21 km east of Banff National Park boundary on Highway #11.

This is by far the most popular hike in the Kootenay Plains so be prepared to share the trail with seniors and young families. This hike offers two options. The most common option people take is to follow the trail up the east side of the Siffleur River as far as the first waterfall and then return to the trailhead. There are, though, two other waterfalls on the Siffleur River that are reward enough for your efforts if you continue along the trail.

~

Follow the broad, well-used trail as it leads down from the parking lot to the suspension bridge across the North Saskatchewan River.

0.0	trailhead
0.6	North Saskatchewan River suspension bridge
1.3	fork
2.0	Siffleur River bridge
3.9	Siffleur Falls viewpoint
5.0	gravel wash
6.2	viewpoint of the second falls
6.9	stream and viewpoint of the third waterfalls
7.0	boundary of the Siffleur Wilderness Area
14.0	trailhead

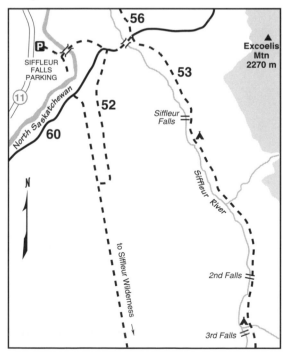

Siffleur Falls. Courtesy of Gillean Daffern.

Cross the suspension bridge and continue along the trail to a fork where you want to keep to the left. This is open, dry parkland with copses of white spruce trees intermixed with junipers, bearberry and willows. The next checkpoint is the green bridge over the Siffleur River. If the day is warm, the sun's rays radiating off the sandy soil can make this a very hot hike, so if you forgot to fill your water bottle, do so at the Siffleur bridge, because you will not have another chance until you are at the first waterfall.

Cross the bridge. Within 20 m there is a junction of trails. Keep to the right at the trail sign and turn south to follow the Siffleur River upstream. The trail climbs steadily through open parkland as the river falls away below you. Your first glimpse of the Siffleur River's gorge is a thrill, for it is truly awesome. As you approach the gorge, the trail braids many times. The trail to the right leads to the edge of the gorge. Beware, since the slope is dangerous. In 1994, a person died after sliding down the cliff into the river below. A safer route is to keep to the left; there are viewpoints of the gorge along the way so you need not feel cheated of the magnificent scenery.

It's a grand walk up the gorge to where the Siffleur River plunges 15 m through a narrow channel in the rocks to its gorge below. The flat rocks just above the falls are a favourite place for hikers to sit and enjoy the view. However, if it has been raining do not attempt this as the rocks are very slippery and therefore dangerous. There have been two deaths at the falls. One, in 1994, occurred when an individual attempted to rescue his dog, who had gone into the water. The current pulled both him and his pet over the falls. Years ear-

---

WHAT'S IN A NAME?

Siffleur River and Falls

It was Sir James Hector of the Palliser Expedition who named the river after the siffleur or whistling marmot, a small mammal that lives in rocky crevices and on scree slopes. Hector followed the Siffleur River down from Pipestone Pass on his way to the Kootenay Plains in 1858 and 1859. The river valley was one of the major access routes to the Plains from what is now Banff National Park. Siffleur Mountain in 1912, and Siffleur Falls in 1979, take their name from the river.

There are three sets of waterfalls along the Siffleur. Early maps show the largest, the second falls, as the Siffleur Falls. The name then moved north to the first falls, which today bears the official name and is the official tourist destination. Despite its scenic qualities, it is interesting to note that none of the early traders or travellers mentioned its waterfalls or gorge.

---

lier, a member of the British Army Training Unit, Suffield stepped past the guard rail to take a closer photograph of the falls. He slipped and fell into the gorge.

It is at these falls that most people turn around and return to their vehicle at the trailhead. If you have several hours to spare, continue upstream along the trail. This is one of the routes that backpackers, hunters and equestrians use to access the Siffleur Wilderness, so the trail is relatively well used and easy to follow. In late spring, the small yellow flowers of the wolf willow scent the air with their heavy, sweet aroma. Rounding a corner in the river where the Siffleur River is cutting its way through the rock, you witness another gorge in the making. Once past a series of rapids and cascades, the trail climbs away from the river and its dangerous embankments. The

The second waterfall on the Siffleur River.

After crossing a gravel wash, a walk through the cool woods soon brings you to a view of the second waterfall. You can actually get a better photograph of this waterfall than you can of the more popular first falls. Continuing past the viewpoint the trail winds over to the ridge immediately above the waterfall. You can't see the Siffleur as it plunges over the five-m ledge below, but there is a wonderful vista of the Siffleur Wilderness to the south.

The trail climbs and drops into two ravines. At a stream crossing, turn right and walk down the streambed as far as its little waterfall, then scramble down to the edge of the Siffleur River. This is the first time since leaving the first waterfall that you have a chance to be at the river's edge. The much smaller, but nonetheless pleasing, third waterfall is just upstream. This makes a fitting conclusion to this day's hike. Obviously, many other people have thought so too, for there is a good campsite on the bench just above the river.

trail undulates along the ridge above the river as it climbs toward the Siffleur Wilderness. At times the trail comes quite close to the edge of the precipice, so exercise prudence and caution in these areas.

HISTORICAL FOOTNOTES

Trail of the Deep Snow

The Stoneys called it the Trail of the Deep Snow. Non-natives called it the Pipestone Trail. It was one of three main access routes into the Kootenay Plains until roads pushed west of Nordegg after World War I. The Trail began near Banff, ascended the Pipestone River, crossed the Pipestone Pass, then descended the Siffleur River to the Plains.

At one time or another, practically every person associated with the region came this way. Sir James Hector, the Earl of Southesk, A. P. Coleman, Mary Schäffer, Job Beaver, Tom Wilson, Elliott Barnes and Martin Nordegg were all here, as were countless and nameless others.

In 1859 that patrician hunter, the Earl of Southesk, came by and dropped his copy of *Hamlet*. In 1898, explorers Hugh Stutfield and J. Norman Collie found it. Sir James Hector, of the Palliser Expedition, used this route twice in 1858 and 1859. On his second trip, he missed meeting Southesk by one month. Tom Wilson and Elliott Barnes had ranches on the Plains and went this way to and from Banff. A midwinter trip in 1908 almost killed Tom Wilson. Martin Nordegg came down the Siffleur in 1908 and 1909 to prospect for coal along the Bighorn River. Hunter and trailmaker, Job Beaver, used it as an access before ranging throughout the Rockies. Mary Schäffer wrote that the Siffleur was her favourite way of entering the Kootenay Plains. For the Wesley Band, this was their preferred route to attend the Indian Days celebrations in Banff.

54 Farley Lake – map p. 195

Duration ~ two days
Distance ~ 32.4 km
Level of Difficulty ~ backpack; steady walk with one steep pitch
Maximum Elevation ~ 1,935 m
Elevation Gain ~ 600 m
Map ~ 83 C/1 Whiterabbit Creek

Access ~ Park your vehicle at the Siffleur Falls Trail Staging Area parking lot located 62 km west of Nordegg, or 21 km east of Banff National Park boundary on Highway #11.

This long but easy hike, with the exception of a three-km pitch, takes you into the back country to a jewel of a lake snuggled in amongst the lodgepole pines and spruce. Farley Lake is also the trailhead for a day hike to Hummingbird Pass.

~

This hike begins like a number of day hikes on the Kootenay Plains. From the trailhead walk down the broad pathway that leads southeast from the parking lot. Cross the suspension bridge over the North Saskatchewan River and continue along the sandy trail to a fork. Keep to the left. A walk of a little more than 500 m brings you to the bridge over the Siffleur River. Cross the bridge. Within metres there are three trails, two of which are signed. The one that you want is the Whiterabbit Recreation Trail that leads straight ahead. The other signed trail is the Siffleur Falls Trail that turns to the right. The trail on the left, much fainter and unsigned, leads to Survey Hill.

Almost immediately the Whiterabbit Recreation Trail begins to climb up the ridge in front of you. Excoelis Mountain is directly ahead. On a sunny day this part of the hike can be very hot, so make sure that you have enough water with you and that you are wearing a good sun hat. Part way up the pitch cross the boundary of the Kootenay Plains Ecological Reserve. Beyond this point you are outside the Reserve. The old road continues to climb. The next couple of kilometres is a bit of a trudge; hard-packed old roads are rarely kind to hiker's feet. The road braids 3.2 km from the trailhead. Keep to the right. Although this braid is steeper than if you continued straight ahead or to the left, the right braid is a shortcut that saves you several kilometres. Within 500 m the other braid

0.0	trailhead at Siffleur Falls Trail parking lot
0.6	North Saskatchewan River suspension bridge
1.3	fork
2.0	Siffleur River bridge and junction
2.6	Kootenay Plains Ecological Reserve boundary
3.2	braid
3.6	end of braid
5.3	junction
6.7	junction
6.8	junction and campsite
7.0	junction
7.7	Whiterabbit Creek
11.4	T-junction
12.1	junction
14.3	talus slope
16.2	Farley Lake
32.4	trailhead

rejoins the trail, which continues to climb. Finally, the old road flattens and starts to swing to the left.

From here there are two routes you can take. If you are confident of your bushwhacking skills, the next intersection will be of interest to you. A narrow footpath on the right less than two km from the end of the braid takes you into the bush, across Wilson Creek and to a hunter's campsite. From the campsite it's a bushwhack slightly to the right through open forest to Whiterabbit Creek. Your crossing is an excellent opportunity to rest a little and replenish your water bottle before continuing your bushwhack through wolf willow and alders. Within 100 m you should come across the Whiterabbit Recreation Trail, now a distinct horse trail. Turn right onto the trail.

If this option unnerves you, opt to continue along the road for another 1.4 km to the first of two junctions. On the right is a horse trail that goes about 100 m to a large campsite. If you miss this junction, 100 m further down the road is a second junction, this one with an old road. Bear to the right, otherwise you continue down to the Kootenay Plains. Within a short distance you come to the large campsite. If it is unoccupied you can enjoy a good rest before continuing across the log bridge over Wilson Creek on the left. There is an excellent view of Mount William Booth from this bridge. In a meadow past the bridge, ignore an intersection with a faint trail on the left unless you are interested in checking out a precipitation station. Your trail leads you across several delightful

---

WHAT'S IN A NAME?

Farley Lake

Previous Names ~ Mud Lake ~ Allium Lake ~ Headwaters Lake

Farley Lake is named after John Farley, who has led many groups to this pretty spot. Farley is a member of the Non-Association of Ramblers and Rhinoceros Trackers, commonly called NARRTs, a hiking club affiliated with the Canadian Hostelling Association in Edmonton. During its heyday during the 1970s and 1980s, this band of gentle anarchists partied, then tracked the noble rhino on foot, by bike, in canoes and kayaks, and on cross-country skis across Alberta, British Columbia and the Northwest Territories. The Shunda Creek Hostel near Nordegg was built in part by NARRT's volunteer labour.

Two other unofficial names, Mud Lake and Headwaters Lake, describe two features: the lake is muddy and lies near the head of the North Ram River. Another unofficial name, Allium Lake, comes from the nodding onion (*allium cernuum*) found growing in a nearby meadow.

John Farley at Farley Lake.

Farley Lake.

meadows for which the Kootenay Plains are famous. At the Whiterabbit Creek thoughtful souls have thrown across several logs to save you from getting your feet wet. From here, the horse trail cuts through several smaller meadows before it enters the open forest.

Whether you choose to bushwhack or to follow the trails outlined in the previous paragraph, now begin to climb slowly between a ridge on your left and the Whiterabbit Creek on your right. At one point, you can see hoodoos forming in the gravel cliffs on the other side of the Whiterabbit. En route, the trail crosses several springs, rendering the trail a little mucky. After nearly four km you reach a T-junction.

Here, you have a choice. The most direct route to Farley Lake is to follow the unsigned Farley Lake/Hummingbird Pass trail to the left. If, however, you miss the junction and continue along the Whiterabbit Recreation Trail, all is not lost. Within 30 m of the junction, the Whiterabbit Trail crosses a gravel wash and begins to switch up a slope. Seventy m or so up the switchback you come to a fork where you keep to the left. This swings around the right-hand side of the ravine with its gravel wash. This trail rejoins the main trail at 12.1 km.

Up to this point it has been a long but easy walk. Now, though, as you head along the left-hand fork from the junction at 11.4 km, you begin to climb. Most of the elevation gain made on this hike occurs over the next 3.5 km, so make no mistake; it's a tough little pitch. Your trail crosses and recrosses the gravel wash numerous times. At 12.1 km the secondary trail leading off the Whiterabbit Trail joins your path from the right. Keep to the left and follow the trail as it climbs a steep pitch. The trail continues to cross and recross the gravel wash until you finally end up on the right-hand side. A last pull and you are finally out of the ravine and at the bottom of a massive talus slope.

For the first time since beginning your climb views begin to open. High limestone cliffs pockmarked with frost pockets and shallow caves rise on both sides of the talus slope. At the top of the first talus slope, the trail levels somewhat and crosses a small meadow before crossing over another, smaller talus field. Before leaving the talus field take a moment to enjoy the scenery behind you. Beyond the defile you just puffed up lie Whiterabbit Creek valley and the many peaks of Excoelis Mountain.

Upon leaving the talus, the trail enters the forest for barely 100 m before it emerges onto a willow thigh-slapping meadow. Now that you are on the flat you can enjoy the scenery, which becomes especially pretty when you finally reach Farley Lake. Depending on the time of year, Farley Lake may or may not be full of water. By high summer the melt waters that help feed the lake are gone and the lake shrinks to half its springtime size. Nevertheless, the lake is nestled below the treeline in a delightful valley. A good campsite above the lake is located in the pine and spruce trees to the right. Return the way you came.

WHAT'S IN A NAME?

Mount William Booth

High on the mountain where few have trod
From solid rock he's been sculptured by God
With hand on the chest as if in eternal repose
But no! he has been vigilant longer than time ever knows,
Has watched o'er the Plains through the aeons span
So the beauties of nature won't be ruined by man.

by Alan Lewis

Previous Names ~ The Sleeping Indian ~ Face Mountain ~ Saw Back Range

This 2,728 m-high mountain was named after William Booth (1829-1912), founder of the Salvation Army, in 1965 on the centenary of the Army's founding. The dedication service was held on the Kootenay Plains during the 1966 David Thompson Cavalcade. Major Fleur Booth, William Booth's great granddaughter, unveiled the highway marker. Other Salvation Army dignitaries present included Colonel Leslie Russell, Chief Secretary for Canada and Bermuda, and Brigadier H. Roberts, Divisional Commander for Alberta.

A local name still in some use is The Sleeping Indian. The profile of the Indian's repose can be seen best from Highway #11 west of the Siffleur Falls Trail Staging Area parking lot. A legend relates that he was the last Kootenay Indian on the Kootenay Plains. He was hunting when the rest of his band was chased across the mountains by the Peigan. Not knowing the band's plight, he decided to winter on the Plains and await their return in spring. The Kootenay did not return to the Plains the next year, or the next. Meanwhile, he sleeps on his mountain until they do.

There is an unconfirmed report that this peak was previously called Face Mountain. This is descriptive of the mountain's unique feature. The 1860 Palliser Expedition map calls this mountain and its adjoining range the Saw Back Range.

55 Hummingbird Pass – map p. 195

Duration ~ full day
Distance ~ 14.4 km
Level of Difficulty ~ steady climb to alpine area
Maximum Elevation ~ 2,300 m
Elevation Gain ~ 365 m
Map ~ 83 C/1 Whiterabbit Creek

The scenic approach and stark alpine terrain at Hummingbird Pass makes this the most popular day hike for hikers spending an extra day at Farley Lake.

~

From the campsite at the south end of Farley Lake, retrace your steps back to the horse trail. Turn right onto the trail and follow it as it skirts the left side of the lake. If the lake is not full and you find that the talus is too rough, drop down to the mud flats. Walk to the end of the lake (or the mud flats), ignoring the cutline to the left. The horse trail disappears at this point. Swing to the right and find a gravel wash. Turn up the wash and continue walking until you see the horse trail reappear between the willows on your left and a talus slope on your right. Immediately begin a steep climb, first beside the talus and then in the forest.

Access ~ Your trailhead is the continuation of the horse trail at the south end of Farley Lake.

0.0	trailhead
1.0	Hummingbird Pass horse trail
2.7	North Ram River
4.2	stream
4.3	stream
4.5	stream
5.6	stream
7.2	Hummingbird Pass
14.4	trailhead

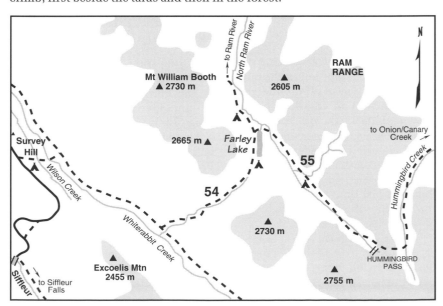

195

The trail levels briefly before snaking up a second pitch. This part of the trail is almost always wet due to the springs that ooze from the rocky slope. The mud is rather slippery so some caution is advised for those who prefer clean knees. After one km or so hints of views can be seen to the left. At the same time, you can hear the North Ram River below. The trail flattens as it crosses the top of the ridge, then drops down to the North Ram. The river is a mere stream at this point and your crossing is an easy hop and a skip. High limestone ridges and peaks of the Ram Range on the left now keep you company all the way to the pass.

Climb through beautiful alpine meadows, interspersed with willows and small spruce. On your right, across the valley, are impressive peaks, precipices and scree slopes. As you cross a gravel wash, bear slightly to the left to regain the trail. Cross a small side stream twice within a few hundred metres. The trail climbs stiffly through a spruce copse before finally breaking out onto an open slope. The trail then dips down to the right side of the

The last pull up Hummingbird Pass.

North Ram before ascending the scree and talus slope below the pass. As you continue to climb, the grey limestone wall on your left and the brown shale cliffs on your right come closer and closer together. A small waterfall cascades from the shale cliffs on the right, even in autumn. The trail crosses the North Ram one last time before switching through the talus and scree to the top of Hummingbird Pass.

What stark beauty presents itself as you climb over the top! You are hemmed in on three sides by impassable headwalls. Below is an enticing meadow, the headwaters of Hummingbird Creek. To drop down to the meadow to discover where Hummingbird Creek goes entails a long climb back up. Instead, if you wish a view of Hummingbird Creek valley climb the ridge to the left. From your vantage point high above the creek you can look down onto Hummingbird Creek and the horse trail that continues down the valley to Onion Creek.

After soaking up a few rays, munching your lunch and enjoying a snooze, return to Farley Lake and your campsite the way you came.

FLORAFACTS

Mountain Slopes and Passes

On the climb from Farley Lake to Hummingbird Pass you walk through two ecoregions—the subalpine and alpine. Both ecoregions share similar factors that determine the type of flora found here. For example, both ecoregions are found at high elevations that are dominated by limestone and shale peaks, and by eroded, more rounded slopes. The type of terrain determines, in part, the amount of soil that can support plant life. Little soil can cling to steep slopes, and where the bedrock is exposed there is no soil at all. On the other hand, at the base of gentler slopes accumulated material eroded from above forms a thin layer of soil.

Another commonality the two ecoregions share is the climate. Cool summers and cold, wet winters are as much factors in the determination of plant species as is the elevation and type of terrain. Snow does not melt at these elevations until early summer, and can return to stay for the winter months as early as September. In addition, snow is possible any month. The growing season, then, is remarkably short. Yet, the overall climate is not as severe as it might seem. The ameliorating factor are the chinooks that funnel through the North Saskatchewan River valley. While the chinooks in the dead of winter do not lay bare the mountain tops as they do the Kootenay Plains below, their warm Pacific air does lessen the severity of the climate.

The type of vegetation that these ecoregions support changes with location. Elevation plays an important role in determining plant species. The pine and spruce forests of the subalpine become thin and stunted the higher you climb. Near the timberline the proud Engelmann spruce is dwarfed to a gnarled, low, shrub-looking tree called krummholz. Unable to withstand the winds that whip near the mountain tops, krummholz spruce and fir grow slowly outward instead of up. In the alpine, with less soil and greater winds, they disappear completely. As you climb into the alpine region, the broad valleys and slopes are home to an array of wildflowers such as mountain cinquefoil, moss campion, and alpine varieties of forget-me-not, harebell and poppy.

Another factor determining the type of plants found here is the direction of the mountain slopes. North-facing slopes receive much less direct sunlight and are more protected from the prevailing winds than south-facing slopes. In the subalpine, these slopes are thickly forested with lodgepole pine and, as you climb to the alpine, Engelmann spruce and fir. Heavily-shaded forest floors support mosses and moisture-loving woodland flowers such as orchids. In contrast, south-facing slopes are often open and exposed to wind and sun. Lodgepole pine is the dominant tree found here. There are more varieties of wildflowers on south-facing slopes, and you can spend considerable time trying to identify the Indian paint brushes, avens and dryads.

The alpine meadow below Hummingbird Pass. Courtesy of Alfred Falk.

56 Survey Hill – map p. 198

Duration ~ full day
Distance ~ 14 km
Level of Difficulty ~ easy walk
Maximum Elevation ~ 1,445 m
Elevation Gain ~ 110 m
Map ~ 83 C/1 Whiterabbit Creek

Access ~ Park your vehicle at the Siffleur Falls Trail Staging Area parking lot 62 km west of Nordegg, or 21 km east of Banff National Park boundary on Highway #11.

Nestled in the rain shadow of the eastern slopes, the Kootenay Plains charm all who venture through its fragile ecosystem. The park-like setting, with meadows interspersed with copses of aspens and pines, though, can confuse the first-time visitor, so it is necessary to follow directions carefully.

~

Follow the broad, well-used trail as it leads down from the parking lot to the suspension bridge across the North Saskatchewan River. Cross the

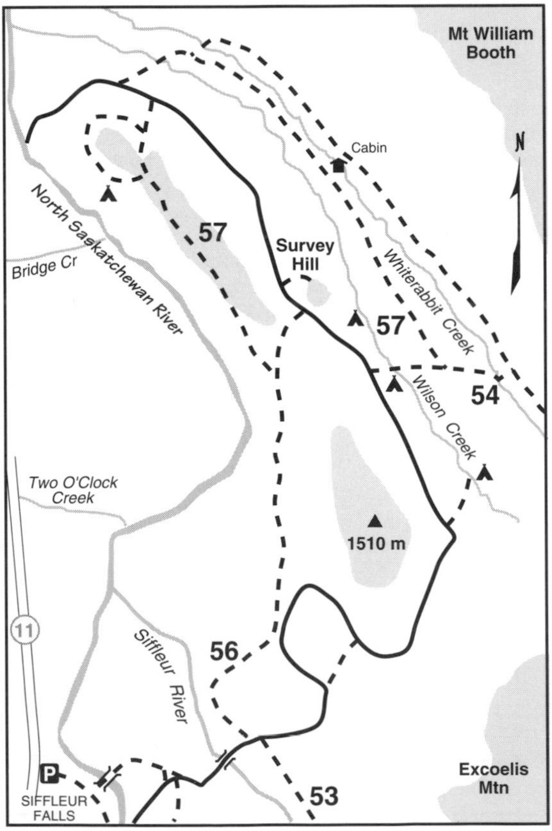

0.0 trailhead
0.6 suspension bridge
1.3 junction
2.0 Siffleur River bridge and junction
4.0 near junction
6.0 junction
6.8 junction with Whiterabbit Recreation Trail road
6.9 Survey Hill
7.0 survey marker
14.0 trailhead

Survey Hill as seen when entering the meadows.

suspension bridge and continue along the trail to a fork where you keep to the left. In spring or during a rainy season, bouquets of blue hare-bells and flax, and yellow hairy golden asters are sprinkled through-out the sandy, desert-like plain. Cross the bridge over the Siffleur River. A scant 10 m past the bridge you come to a junction of three trails. Take the footpath on the left. Walk past a junc-tion about 20 m later and continue through wolf willow and open spruce forest downstream along the Siffleur River. The river's bank, where the footpath used to be, has eroded, so you must bushwhack through the dense wolf willow until the footpath reappears. The path turns sharply away from the river and climbs a ridge. Follow the switchbacks to the top of the ridge, ignoring any foot-paths that bear to the left. From the top of the ridge the trail swings left and follows the edge of a south-facing open slope before entering the lodgepole pine forest.

Buffaloberries and black-eyed susans accompany you on this part of the hike. After one km the footpath comes to within 20 m of the Whiterabbit Recreation Trail road on the right. Continue along the footpath for another two km. Take the right fork at a junction. Continuing to the left takes you up the slope to a ridge overlooking the North Saskatchewan River. After about 800 m the trail disappears as you approach a broad meadow. Do not be alarmed for straight ahead is Survey Hill. Cross through the meadow. In spring, the meadow is a riot of colour and sweet smells that emanate from white and purple asters, clover, harebells and even the wild purple onion.

You soon reach a cart track; this is the Whiterabbit Recreation Trail. Turn left onto the cart track. Skirt Survey Hill to its north end. It is impossible to access Survey Hill earlier due to the beaver dams that have flooded much of the land be-tween the Trail and Survey Hill. At the north end of Survey Hill, turn right off the Whiterabbit Recreation Trail. Within metres you come to Wilson Creek. Find a convenient crossing. Once across, work your way around the base of the hill and find the trail that leads up the slope. It's not a long or steep pull up this 35 m-high hill so you soon find yourself at the top. A survey marker gives this hill its name.

The earliest record of anyone on top of Survey Hill goes to Bessie Wilson, daughter of Tom Wilson, a local horse rancher and guide/outfitter. In 1916, when she rode her horse to the top of the hill for a view, she called this lookout "Horse Hill." As the highest point in this part of the meadows, Survey Hill certainly does command a view overlooking the park-like setting of the Kootenay Plains. There are great views of Abraham Lake to the north. Casting your eyes to the west you can see Vision Quest Ridge and the ridges of Two O'Clock

Creek and Tuff Puff. Below, Wilson Creek, which has been dammed by beavers, splits and goes around both sides of Survey Hill. Looking down on the left you can see a rather large beaver pond. To the south between Whiterabbit Creek and the Siffleur River is Excoelis Mountain.

Survey Hill makes an excellent place to stop and rest and enjoy a snack before returning to the trailhead. If, after you have walked to the south end of Survey Hill along the Whiterabbit Recreation Trail, you feel that you may have difficulty finding the trail out of the meadow, continue along the old road all the way back to the bridge over the Siffleur River. Just as the road enters the forest there is a fork. Bear right. This is a somewhat longer route, but perhaps safer for those who are unfamiliar with the Kootenay Plains. If you bear left you come to a campsite and a log bridge over Wilson Creek. This trail takes you up Whiterabbit Creek.

WHAT'S IN A NAME?

Whiterabbit Creek

Previous Names ~ Rabbit Creek
Stoney Names ~ Musteenaskan Waptan (Whiterabbit Creek)

Whiterabbit Creek takes its name from an incident that occurred beside it in 1894. That year Peter Wesley led the exodus of Stoney families from Morley to the Kootenay Plains. This was a defiant, perhaps risky venture. The people needed reassurance and beside an unnamed stream they found it. They saw an omen. A white rabbit came into view.

Among Indians, the colour white has strong religious overtones when seen in an abnormal situation. As an example, the skin of an albino buffalo is a sacred object. The rabbit, by virtue of its being white out of season, made a powerful impression upon the band. The creek, therefore became known as the Whiterabbit.

Rabbit creek is a variation of the original name.

Remains of Silas Abraham's cabin on the bank above Whiterabbit Creek.

Kootenay Plains

HISTORICAL FOOTNOTES

Kootenay Plains Ecological Reserve

The Kootenay Plains Ecological Reserve was established in 1987 to protect 3,204 hectares of montane habitat. This area originally came under provincial protection in 1968. The Reserve represents one of the most northerly regions of montane habitat in Alberta. Strong chinook winds from the west have modified the climate to create a semi-arid region characterized by grasslands and open forests.

The dry grasslands are dominated by June grass, pasture sage, prairie groundsel and blue flax. In the more moist areas northern wheatgrass grows with the June grass. The aspen forests have a well-developed underlayer containing buffaloberry, prickly rose, creeping juniper, hairy wild rye and northern wheatgrass. On the drier sites, the open white spruce forests have a sparse understory consisting of bearberry, creeping juniper, June grass, pussytoes and grey daisy. On the exposed ridges and riverbanks limber pine grow. The forests surrounding the meadows are dominated by lodgepole pine, much of it formed after a forest fire about 45 years ago. On west-facing slopes of the North Saskatchewan River Douglas fir can be found.

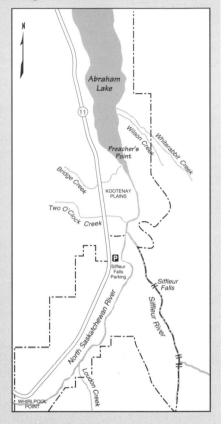

The variety of topography and vegetation supports a large diversity of animals. It is a significant winter range for elk, mule deer, mountain sheep and moose. Occasionally mountain caribou come down the Siffleur River from Banff National Park. Over 60 species of birds and 240 species of plants have been surveyed in the area. These include some that are uncommon in Alberta.

The region is very sensitive to wind erosion once the vegetation cover is disturbed. Due to the dryness of the climate, reestablishment of vegetation is slow and difficult. Active wind erosion occurs both naturally and as a result of off-road vehicle traffic. This traffic, caused by motorcycles, four-wheel drives, ATVs and mountain bikes, plus uncontrolled camping, is damaging the area.

In 1994 the Reserve boundaries were adjusted. It now includes Whirlpool Point and the Siffleur River south to the Siffleur Wilderness boundary. The Reserve's eastern boundary now follows the Whiterabbit Recreation Trail.

201

57 The Meadows – map p. 198

Duration ~ full day
Distance ~ 20.8 km
Level of Difficulty ~ easy walk
Maximum Elevation ~ 1,460 m
Elevation Gain ~ 125 m
Map ~ 83 C/1 Whiterabbit Creek

Access ~ Park your vehicle at the Siffleur Falls Trail Staging Area parking lot 62 km west of Nordegg, or 21 km east of Banff National Park boundary on Highway #11.

Although somewhat long, this hike reveals the charm and diversity of the Kootenay Plains' meadows. The beauty of this parkland once graced all of the upper North Saskatchewan River valley. Now, much of the original Kootenay Plains lie under the waters of Abraham Lake.

~

Follow the broad, well-used trail as it leads down from the parking lot to the North Saskatchewan River suspension bridge. Cross the suspension bridge and continue along the trail to a fork. Keep to the left. In spring or during a rainy season, bouquets of blue harebells and flax, and yellow hairy golden asters are sprinkled throughout the sandy, desert-like plain. Cross the bridge over the Siffleur River. A scant 10 m past the bridge you come to a junction of three trails. The road straight ahead is the Whiterabbit Recreation Trail; the trail to the right is the Siffleur Falls Recreation Trail. Ignore them and take the trail on the left. Walk 20 m and pass a junction with a fainter trail to continue downstream along the Siffleur through wolf willow and open spruce forest. The river has eroded the bank and footpath so you have to bushwhack until the footpath reappears. At a fork, bear right. Here, the path turns sharply away from the river and switches up a ridge.

Climb up the slope and ignore any trails that join from the left. Close to the top of the ridge the path swings to the left to skirt around the shoulder of the hill. Buffaloberries and black-eyed susans accompany you on this part of the hike through open forest. At one point, the path parallels the Whiterabbit Recreation Trail, a four-wheel drive track. Ignore the Trail and stay on the hiking path for two more kilometres. The Trail loops around hills, making it the long way into the meadows. At a junction bear to the right; the

0.0	trailhead
0.6	suspension bridge
1.3	junction
2.0	Siffleur River bridge and junction
4.0	near junction
6.0	junction
6.8	junction with Whiterabbit Recreation Trail road
7.4	junction
7.5	campsite and Wilson Creek bridge
7.7	junction
7.9	precipitation station
9.9	cabin
11.2	junction
11.4	Wilson Creek
11.8	Whiterabbit Recreation Trail
12.5	junction
14.8	junction
20.8	trailhead

The walk along the ridge overlooks the North Saskatchewan River and part of the Kootenay Plains.

left-hand fork leads along an open ridge, which is the return route.

The path becomes fainter and dies completely upon reaching an open meadow. Don't worry; cut straight across the meadow to the Whiterabbit Recreation Trail road. Straight ahead is Wilson Creek and Survey Hill. The meadows are interspersed with copses of poplar, aspen and spruce and it is easy to confuse one meadow for another. There are also many paths that crisscross through the meadows, further challenging your navigational skills. At the Whiterabbit Recreation Trail turn right and walk as far as an intersection with another old road. The junction appears just as you enter the forest. Turn left. Within metres you come to a large campsite. If you stay right you return to the Siffleur River bridge. Cross Wilson Creek bridge and pick up the trail. On a warm day the meadows can be very hot, so if you are low on water fill your canteen before continuing your exploration.

Yet again, you soon come to another intersection. Bear a hard left onto the joining path to avoid going to Whiterabbit Creek. You pass a precipitation station on the left. Your path wanders through groves of aspen and poplar. In spring the area is an amateur botanist's delight. Nodding purple harebells, kittentails, yellow locoweed, and the pretty white daisy fleabane are among the wild flowers that are scattered throughout the meadows. Another point of interest on this part of the hike is the remains of a log cabin that is perched on the banks of Whiterabbit Creek. Over the years, the creek has changed its course, cutting back into its west bank and threatening to topple the cabin. The cabin probably belonged to either Silas Abraham, who lived in the area, or to Tom Wilson. Wilson spent his first winter on the Kootenay Plains in a cabin built beside Whiterabbit Creek. The next year he moved to a location beside Wilson Creek and now under Abraham Lake.

With Mount William Booth on the right, continue along the well-defined trail as it now swings away from Whiterabbit Creek to cross grassy woodlands and open fields. Before entering a broad meadow overlooking the reservoir there are wild rose bushes and sweet-smelling clover, which add their colour and scents to the fragrance of the meadows. Here, the path becomes indistinct. Watch for an intersection with another footpath. To begin the loop back to the trailhead, turn left onto the path; the trail to the right goes to Whiterabbit Creek and the trail straight ahead soon peters out. Cross Wilson Creek. The trail becomes faint after passing a small thicket of trees and a low terrace, but continue straight through the broad meadow past a lone spruce tree.

The views up and down the North Saskatchewan River and Abraham Lake make you want to linger in these sun-drenched meadows. Better views, though, are found on the ridge ahead and slightly to your left. So, continue to a cart track that is the Whiterabbit Recreation Trail. Turning left onto the Trail takes you back to Survey Hill and turning right takes you to a ford across the North Saskatchewan River. You want to do neither; instead, cross the Trail and head toward the ridge in front of you. The best way to gain its crest is to bear to the left and walk between the ridge and the Trail until you see a trail leading up the slope. If you miss the trail or cannot find it, bushwhack up the slope before the forest cover thickens. Once on top, find the well-used path on the other side of the ridge. You are now walking in a southerly direction through open meadows with the beautiful river valley spread below you to the right. At a junction with a path on the right that leads down the ridge, continue straight along the edge of the ridge. The panoramic view remains with you all the way back to a junction that corresponds to the one at the six-km mark. Bear right and return to the trailhead.

Excoelis Mountain. Courtesy of Robin Chambers.

HISTORICAL FOOTNOTES

Tom Wilson (1859-1933)

Christmas dinner at the Wilson's in 1903 had some added bite. First, there was the main course: a bighorn sheep with rum standing in for the trimmings. Then there was the after dinner conversation: "When the hell are you going back?" "Right now!" retorted his guest, Jimmy Simpson, who then left immediately.

Tom Wilson was a character. He later patched things up with Jimmy Simpson and they became partners at his ranch on the Kootenay Plains. Before arriving on the Plains, Tom Wilson already had a varied career, including being a North-West Mounted Police constable and packer. He helped A. B. Rogers find Rogers Pass, and had his photo taken while standing in the crowd behind Donald Smith, who was driving the Last Spike. He also, with the help of his Stoney guide, discovered Lake Louise.

It was the growing tourist trade at Banff and Lake Louise that inspired Wilson to establish a ranch on the Kootenay Plains. The Tom Wilson Ranch, otherwise known as the Kootenay Plains Ranch or Powderhorn Ranch, operated for eight years. Wilson, with the assistance of local Stoney Indians such as Silas Abraham, constructed his buildings and horse corral at the junction of the Whiterabbit Creek and North Saskatchewan River during the winter of 1902-1903. From this base Wilson traded flour, bacon, yard goods, guns and ammunition to the Stoney in return for fresh meat, sheep heads, buckskin articles and horses. During the summer, Wilson was a guide and outfitter in Banff-Lake Louise, wintering his horse herd as well as that of other outfitters on the Plains. Wilson's animals carried the powderhorn brand.

His relationship with the Stoneys was mixed. The Stoneys helped Wilson establish himself on the Plains and traded with him. At the same time they bickered over grazing rights, and Wilson accused his neighbours of killing all the game in the region. Wilson's presence on the Plains, according to the Stoneys, forestalled their land claims to the area.

It appears that some of the conflict was also due to a cultural clash. A case in point was Wilson's vegetable garden. Wilson had planted a garden near his cabin one spring, then left for the summer. He returned in the autumn to find about 50 Stoneys camped nearby and very few vegetables left. Wilson, furious, stormed at the Stoneys about his garden and his vegetables. To Wilson, at issue was respect for private property. The Stoneys, though, like other hunter-gatherer societies, regarded food as a commodity to be shared wherever and whenever it was found.

In 1910, Wilson sold out to his son, John, and Jimmy Simpson. They continued to operate the ranch until 1919 when the Forestry Department took over the land. Wilson had never obtained title to the property and was technically a squatter. The location of the Tom Wilson Ranch and the contentious little vegetable garden is under water now. The original buildings were dismantled in 1972, then moved across the river to the site of the Elliott Barnes's Ranch.

Tom Wilson at his cabin on the Kootenay Plains ranch, ca.1906. Courtesy of Glenbow Archives, #NA 66-764.

58 Cline Fire Lookout – no map

Duration ~ three days
Distance ~ 38 km
Degree of Difficulty ~ long flats and uphill bushwhack
Maximum Elevation ~ 2,055 m
Elevation Gain ~ 720 m
Map ~ 83 C/1 Whiterabbit Creek

Access ~ Park your vehicle at the Siffleur Falls Trail Staging Area parking lot 62 km west of Nordegg, or 21 km east of the Banff National Park boundary on Highway #11.

The first and last days of this hike cover most of the distance that you travel on this three-day outing. The second day you bushwhack up from Canyon Creek to the Cline Fire Lookout, where incredible views north and south along Abraham Lake greet you. A pleasant visit to this remote lookout will leave you with an understanding of the work and life of its personnel and the importance of their job of fire detection.

~

Follow the broad, well-used trail as it leads down from the parking lot to the suspension bridge across the North Saskatchewan River. Cross the suspension bridge and continue along the trail to a fork, where you keep to the left. Cross the bridge over the Siffleur River. A scant 10 m past the bridge, you come to a junction of three trails. Take the footpath on the left. Walk past a junction about 20 m later and continue through wolf willow and open spruce forest downstream along the Siffleur River. The river's bank, where the footpath used to be, has eroded, so you must bushwhack through the dense wolf willow until the footpath reappears. The path turns sharply away from the river and climbs a ridge. Follow the switchbacks to the top of the ridge, ignoring any footpaths that bear to the left. From the top of the ridge the trail follows the edge of a south-facing open slope, then enters the lodgepole pine forest.

After one km the footpath comes to within 20 m of the Whiterabbit Recreation Trail road on the right. Continue along the footpath for another two km. Take the right fork at a junction. Continuing to the left takes you up the slope to a ridge overlooking the North Saskatchewan River. After about 800 m you break out from the trees onto a meadow, with the Whiterabbit Recreation Trail road and

0.0	trailhead
0.6	suspension bridge
1.3	junction
2.0	Siffleur River bridge and junction
4.0	near junction
6.0	junction
6.8	junction with Whiterabbit Recreation Trail road
8.4	lone spruce tree
8.8	Wilson Creek
9.0	junction
9.2	Whiterabbit Creek
10.5	Abraham Lake
15.5	Canyon Creek
15.6	campsite
16.6	horseshoe bend in the creek
16.8	ridge
18.8	sawtooth ridge
19.0	Cline Fire Lookout
38.0	trailhead

Approaching the Cline Fire Lookout

Survey Hill directly ahead. Turn left onto the Trail as it begins its gradual slope down to Abraham Lake. The trail becomes a mere cart track through the long grass, but is still fairly obvious. Where the track narrows as it cuts through low wolf willow bushes, cross a metal culvert. Continue along the swath and you will soon come out onto one of the broad meadows for which the Kootenay Plains is famous. Near the end of the ridge to the left, the track leads past a lone spruce tree and beyond to the ford across the North Saskatchewan. Near the spruce tree, bear right onto a very faint footpath that leads northeast through the grass. The footpath becomes clearer at a line of trees and a small ledge. Within several hundred metres, cross Wilson Creek and continue along the path. At a junction, continue straight ahead to the Whiterabbit Creek.

Once across the creek, turn left off the trail and walk down to Abraham Lake. The approach is through meadow, poplar bush and wolf willow copses. The David Thompson Highway is just across the river and you can easily see the traffic passing by. If you are hiking this trail in the spring or summer, the lake levels will be low. You approach Abraham Lake through unimpressive mud flats. If you are looking for the confluence of Whiterabbit Creek and Abraham Lake, don't bother, since the creek has disappeared into the gravel wash and reaches the lake underground.

Abraham Lake dominates this part of the valley of the North Saskatchewan River. It is hard to imagine now, but beneath its azure-coloured waters once lay most of the open grasslands of the Kootenay Plains. Instead of scenic parkland abounding with wild game, the valley has become a reservoir that stretches 32 km north to the Bighorn Dam. The impression that the lake leaves on you depends upon the season you are hiking. In spring and summer when the reservoir is low, the lake's beauty is compromised by the gravel terraces left behind when the reservoir is drained during the previous winter. Not only are the terraces an eyesore, but they make walking along the lakeshore a chore. Also, on a warm day the sun radiates from the terraces, making this part of the hike very hot. Unfortunately, flotsam along the shoreline and the silt-laden waters discourage any ideas of a refreshing swim. For those who are tempted to go for a dip anyway, don't. Abraham Lake is very dangerous to swimmers and boaters alike. The prevailing westerlies can whip the waters of this shallow lake into good-sized whitecaps in a short period of time. Warning signs are posted along the west side of the lake by the highway, but none are posted along this side of the lake. On the other hand, those who choose to climb to the Cline Fire Lookout in autumn when the reservoir begins to fill will be more favourably impressed with the lake and its shoreline.

After a five km trudge along the lakeshore, the gravel confluence of Canyon Creek and the reservoir herald the beginning of the end of the first day's hike. The shade offered by the trees is welcome after a hot hike. Walk up the creek to a hunter's campsite. This is an excellent place to pitch the tent, fill your canteen and relax before tomorrow's climb. If the hunter's campsite is occupied, cross Canyon Creek to its left bank and continue upstream for one km to the flats at a horseshoe bend in the creek, to another good camping spot.

To reach the fire lookout you must bushwhack most of the way up through open forest. Sometimes you are on game trails and other times you simply follow the ridge. To begin, keeping within 50 m of the creek, bushwhack upstream from the bend onto an open ridge. From this vantage point you can look behind and down to Abraham Lake, and upstream to the magnificent steep rock walls of Canyon Creek. Find a game trail that

The lookout as seen from across Abraham Lake.

follows the ridge upstream for about 200 m to another ridge. Bear a sharp left onto this ridge, moving away from the creek and into the open forest. As you climb, bearing north-northwest, you find game trails. From time to time as the ridges peter out, or the opportunity presents itself, bear right to climb onto a parallel ridge and continue uphill. There are few views to be seen as you climb, but at the base of a long sawtooth ridge you can look down on Canyon Creek and Abraham Lake. Scramble up the sawtooth ridge. Turn left and continue to climb. At the top of this ridge, bear right and climb over a saddle in order to reach the fire lookout. It's a bushwhack all the way, but near the top where the forest falls away, a path finally becomes discernable. A surveyor's stake announces that you have nearly arrived, and from here

you can see the mountain lookout straight ahead and up slope.

The view is well worth the bushwhack. With Mount Michener to your back, Abraham Lake and the Cline River country lie at your feet far below. To the extreme left you can just make out the lower edges of the Kootenay Plains. It's a magnificent sight. The lookout, a one-room affair, is occupied by a lone person from May until September or October, depending on the fire hazard. Unlike Baldy Lookout, few visitors ever climb to the Cline Lookout, so a hearty welcome is almost guaranteed. Don't forget to ask to sign the guest book before leaving.

Return the way you came, remembering to swing to the right to cross two ridges in order to return to the bend in Canyon Creek. Return to your trailhead the following day after a good rest.

HISTORICAL FOOTNOTES

Jimmy Simpson (1877-1972)

Jimmy Simpson is most famous as the founder, builder and operator of Num-Ti-Jah Lodge beside Bow Lake in Banff National Park. Simpson visited the Kootenay Plains many times, and between 1910 and 1918 was a partner on the Tom Wilson Ranch. Simpson was a guide and outfitter in Banff-Lake Louise. The ranch on the Plains was an ideal spot for Simpson to winter his horses, and it was the scene of several stories that built this "Legend of the Rockies."

Simpson was invited by Wilson to spend Christmas at the cabin on the Kootenay Plains in 1903. Simpson snowshoed over 120 km in five days to accept Wilson's invitation. They made terrible companions, and the day after he arrived Simpson was heading back to his trap-

per's cabin. He almost did not make it. En route he fell into an open stream; later he almost poisoned himself with strychnine.

Jimmy Simpson's relationship with Tom Wilson was a difficult one. The two men were stubborn individualists who had a hard time seeing eye to eye on many matters. The break-up of their partnership was a mess, with both Wilson and Simpson together suing a third party, and Wilson suing Simpson for the balance owing on the original $4,000 Simpson was to pay Wilson for half-interest in the ranch.

Simpson left the Kootenay Plains region for his new home beside Bow Lake, but he still returned from time to time. In 1927, at the age of 50, he climbed his last mountain. It was a first ascent of Mount Cline.

Building the Lookout

In response to a 1953 brief entitled "Forest Fire Protection in Alberta," or simply "The Fire Brief," the Alberta Fire Service (AFS) was reorganized and expanded to better detect and control fires in the Green Zone, which covers 65% of Alberta and encompasses the Rocky-Clearwater Forest Reserve, which takes in a large territory west of Rocky Mountain House. One of the 22 recommendations in "The Fire Brief" was to build more mountain fire lookouts.

So it was that on April 25, 1960, Ranger John Elliott found himself taken by helicopter from the Upper Saskatchewan Ranger Station on the Abraham Flats to a site on the east side of the North Saskatchewan River. The fire season was about to commence and the AFS wanted a new lookout built as soon as possible. Elliott, an experienced Ranger with the Service, must have wondered about the wisdom of this decision. The crown of the Cline lookout hill was covered with 18 m-tall spruce trees and a metre of snow. The helicopter could not land and Elliott had to be lowered by sling. Armed with a portable radio, provisions, a sleeping bag and a power saw, Elliott set up camp and then began the work of clearing a space large enough for a helicopter to land. That night as he snuggled into his sleeping bag next to a campfire, his wife watched the fire through binoculars from the Abraham Flats below. The next day, his job finished, Elliott was taken out.

Nothing more could be done for another month until the snow had melted and the frost was out of the ground. Then, a crew was lifted in to begin the work of clearing the rest of the hilltop and building the lookout. The helicopter pilot, Jack Lunan, worked as hard as the crew, bringing in materials and supplies. In a four-day blitz, the little two-man helicopter made 58 round trips and hauled in 64 tonnes of building material. Lunan proved extremely adept at using winds and rising air currents to his advantage. Prevailing easterly winds striking the west face of the lookout mountain created a powerful updraft. Lunan piloted his 'copter to the base of the face, caught the air current and then rose like an elevator to the summit unloading platform. On return trips he used the updraft to cushion his descent. The total project cost was $1,139. Once completed, the Cline Lookout became the 17th mountain lookout in the province, joining 72 firetowers in the fight against fire.

Life In The Clouds

Mountain lookouts and fire towers across the province form the first line of defense against forest fires. The work carried out at the lookouts and towers is known as "fixed" detection; this remains the backbone of the detection system of the Alberta Forest Service (AFS). For areas not covered by lookouts and towers, fire detection relies on regular aircraft patrols. Of the 135 towers and lookouts in the province, 25 are mountain lookouts such as the Cline Lookout. Each has a working radius of approximately 40 km with some "slopover" into another lookout's area. The area covered by the Cline Lookout, for example, overlaps with that of Baldy Lookout near Nordegg. This "slop-over" is useful in pinpointing a fire more accurately.

Most lookouts are remote. As you can imagine, it takes a special kind of person to be on a lookout. Needless to say, a critical criterion for the job is sharp eyesight! But equally important is the ability to live alone for long periods of time. A brief chat with the helicopter pilot who drops in with the mail once a week, is all the human contact these people often have in the four to six months that they are at these isolated vigils. To occupy the time, some paint or make crafts, which they sell during the winter months. Usually at the end of a season, they are quite happy to leave, uncertain whether they want to return. But just as commonly, when the AFS sends out letters of application in midwinter for the next season, they are ready to return for another season among the clouds.

59 Tuff Puff – map p. 163

Duration ~ full day
Distance ~ 14.6 km
Level of Difficulty ~ unrelenting climb
Maximum Elevation ~ 2,330 m
Elevation Gain ~ 975 m
Map ~ 83 C/1 Whiterabbit Creek

This hike is perfect for those who enjoy stretching their legs on a steep climb. The best time of year to do this hike is late spring or early summer when there is still snow on the surrounding peaks. The magnificent scenery is nothing less than inspiring!

~

From the trailhead at the unnamed creek on the west side of the highway, walk along the levee on the north (right-hand) side of the creek. In late spring, the levee supports yellow butter-and-eggs, lupins and fragrant wild sage. At the end of the levee continue along game trails that parallel the creek. At a rock cairn on a low, open slope, take a 90 degree turn to the right and climb uphill to intersect with a footpath. Turn left onto the footpath. If you turn to the right you reach the lower end of the Icefall Loop hike.

Access ~ Park your vehicle at an unnamed creek 65 km west of Nordegg, or 18 km east of the Banff National Park boundary on Highway #11. This unnamed creek is located three km west of the Siffleur Falls Trail Staging Area parking lot.

0.0	trailhead
0.2	end of the levee
0.6	cairn
0.7	junction
0.9	junction
1.1	junction
1.5	junction
2.0	junction
2.5	lichen-encrusted rock
3.5	trail flattens
5.7	ravine
7.3	top of Tuff Puff
14.6	trailhead

Snowfields at the top of Tuff Puff can linger until summer.

Continue along the footpath to the next junction with a path joining from the right. Continue straight ahead to a major intersection with a broad, braided path on the right. This is where you will turn right and begin to climb Tuff Puff. However, if at this point you are running low on water, continue straight ahead along the main footpath; within 200 m there is a stream where you can rest and refill your canteen. Return to the intersection and use any one of the braids to begin the climb.

It's a steep pull right from the beginning, and one that rarely lets up until you have reached the top of the ridge at the skyline. Wild strawberries and mountain chickweed struggle for survival on this hot, dry slope. Even the breezes give little relief from the intense heat on the lower part of the climb. Only after gaining some altitude do you enjoy the benefit of the prevailing winds that funnel through the valley. A short distance up the hill a path joins from the right. It is a braid that descends to the main footpath. Ignore it and continue climbing. From time to time the path nearly disappears, especially on rocky, exposed areas, but continue following the spine of the ridge. At another junction with a trail leading down to the right, continue climbing straight ahead. Such aerobic activity calls for a short rest at a rock outcropping, heavily encrusted with orange lichens called jewel lichens. You have gained some altitude now, so that the river valley stretches out below you. If you are lucky you will share the hillside with mountain sheep. There is a long pull ahead, but the unfolding scenery urges you to continue climbing.

Finally, the path leaves the open slope, bearing right through a grove of lodgepole pine. Traversing the hillside, the trail flattens a little, giving some respite. If you are undertaking this hike in the spring, snow patches may obscure the path through the trees, but the way is fairly obvious. After swinging to the left, the trail leaves the lodgepole pine behind as it begins its climb over another open, rocky ridge. An interesting aspect of this hike is watching the change in vegetation as you ascend. From the hot, dry, semi-desert floor of the Kootenay Plains, you climb through white spruce and pine forests. You know you have gained significant altitude when the path enters a second grove of trees. This one is of Engelmann spruce, which only grows at higher elevations. Once you are through the stand of spruce, the trail breaks out onto an alpine slope. In late spring, a variety of flowers dot the ridge, but where the path dips into a ravine snowfields may still linger. After crossing the ravine, the trail bears left up the slope and then disappears. Continue to work your way uphill, keeping the ravine to the left, and out onto a rocky spine. It's a hard pant to the top of the ridge, but when you finally reach the top the view is nothing less than spectacular. Above you are unnamed peaks. To the right is the valley of Two O'Clock Creek and its ridge behind. Below is the sweep of the North Saskatchewan River valley with the snowy peaks of the Rocky Mountains serving as its backdrop.

The Upper North Saskatchewan Valley

The Upper North Saskatchewan region runs west from Whirlpool Point to the Banff National Park boundary. This area is the transition zone between the montane aspen parkland characterized by the Kootenay Plains and the wetter, more thickly forested subalpine forests. Here grow Engelmann, white and black spruce, and lodgepole pine. The North Saskatchewan River is the dominant physical feature.

For about 15 years the upper North Saskatchewan, with its headwaters at Howse Pass, was a major transit route for fur traders between the British Columbia interior and the great plains to the east. Along its upper reaches a drama was played out with continental consequences. When fur traders first penetrated the area at the beginning of the 19th century, they were caught in the shifting balance of power between the plains and mountain Indians. It was this shifting balance that controlled their movements and strategies along the upper North Saskatchewan. The issue came down to guns.

Guns supplied by traders to the Indians allowed for easier and more successful hunting, as well as military dominance over any neighbour not so armed. By the late 18th century the Blackfoot on the plains, equipped with firearms, began to exert pressure on their western neighbours, the Kootenay, and began to push them back over the mountains. The Kootenay, aware that the guns were obtained through trade with the fur companies, tried to gain access to the trading posts along the Saskatchewan by bribing the Blackfoot with gifts of horses. The Blackfoot, aware that the Kootenay would then obtain firearms, refused to negotiate with them.

In 1798, two Kootenay Indians visited Fort Edmonton and described their country across the mountains as abounding in furs. On the strength of this report, the North West Company (NWC), soon followed by the Hudson's Bay Company (HBC), built forts near present-day Rocky Mountain House to serve the Kootenay Indians—if they could get past the Blackfoot confederacy, including the Peigan.

In October 1800, David Thompson sent two men, Le Blanc and La Gasse, to the Kootenay country to assess the fur resources and establish trading links. Le Blanc and La Gasse are credited with being the first white men to cross the Rockies via the North Saskatchewan River and Howse Pass. They made several trading trips between Rocky Mountain House and the British Columbia interior, but preferred the more direct route through Banff and Kananaskis. The Blackfoot blocked this route, so the traffic was redirected via the North Saskatchewan River and Howse Pass. This bypass took several years of pressure by the Peigan to close.

The Peigan first succeeded in driving the Kootenay from the upper North Saskatchewan, then they stopped them from travelling to Rocky Mountain House to trade.

They next blocked an attempt in 1806 by NWC trader Jaco Finlay, to establish a halfway post on the Kootenay Plains. Both the NWC and HBC then decided to move their goods directly through the blockade to the Kootenay. Both David Thompson for the NWC, and Joseph Howse for the HBC, made successful trips.

By 1809, Blackfoot fears were realized when they lost a bloody encounter with the newly-armed Salish, a transmountain tribe allied with the Kootenay. The Blackfoot sought revenge and wanted to destroy Rocky Mountain House and the traders within. The Peigan war chief Kootanae Appee, since he depended upon the supplies provided by the post, managed to save Rocky Mountain House, but stepped up the mountain blockade.

Thus it was in 1810 that the Peigan blocked David Thompson's brigade from ascending the North Saskatchewan, and forced him to establish a second bypass further north via Athabasca Pass. Thompson never returned to the upper North Saskatchewan, but the route was still used, albeit with greater difficulty. Alexander Henry the Younger resorted to subterfuge to shake the Peigan, before making his February 1811 dash to Howse Pass and back.

That summer the Peigan blockade increased to still greater intensity. Joseph Howse brought his fur brigade over Howse Pass and down the Saskatchewan, and made it through thanks to the diplomatic efforts of the HBC, but the company declined to face further Peigan hostility. There was one last trip over the Howse Pass. NWC partner John McDonald of Garth, in 1811, led a heavily-armed brigade over the pass to bring supplies to David Thompson, who had earlier crossed the Rockies via the Athabasca. From then on, both traders and travellers used the Athabasca, and the upper North Saskatchewan River was abandoned as the grand trunk route across the Divide.

The Peigan blockade was unsuccessful. The Kootenay obtained firearms anyway once the northern bypass over Athabasca Pass became fully established. The blockade was also breached from the west and south when trading posts were established along the Columbia and Missouri Rivers. The upper North Saskatchewan still remained a transit route for trade. Kootenay Indians crossed the mountains to the Kootenay Plains, and met with Stoneys and perhaps traders from Rocky Mountain House. Although the Kootenay did acquire guns, they never regained their lost hunting grounds along the eastern slopes of the Rockies. And the fur traders? There is perhaps one artifact of their presence along the upper North Saskatchewan.

Students from the St. John's School of Alberta, near Devon, were near the suspension bridge across the North Saskatchewan River, Labour Day weekend, 1993, when they found an old paddle. It was over two m long, with a flat and narrow blade about half its length. The wood was obviously very old and had moss growing on it. The original axe marks from its carving were still visible.

The paddle's age is undetermined, but it matches in design those shown in contemporary pictures of voyageurs and their canoes. As far as it is known, no other paddle of this type has been preserved as an artifact, thus making the St. John's School find unique. The students turned the paddle over to the Rocky Mountain House National Historic Site officials.

60 Loudon Creek – map p. 187

Duration ~ full day
Distance ~ 14.6 km
Level of Difficulty ~ long walk on hard-packed road followed by an easy bushwhack
Maximum Elevation ~ 1,430 m
Elevation Gain ~ 95 m
Map ~ 83 C/1 Whiterabbit Creek; 82 N/16 Siffleur River

Access ~ Park your vehicle at the Siffleur Falls Trail Staging Area parking lot 62 km west of Nordegg, or 21 km east of the Banff National Park boundary on Highway #11.

0.0	trailhead
0.6	suspension bridge
1.3	junction
2.0	cutline
5.1	Loudon Creek
5.4	trail leaves creekbed
6.0	ravine
6.2	top of bald hill
7.3	viewpoint opposite Mount Peskett
14.6	trailhead

A rather long walk along an old road should not discourage you from the pretty scenery that awaits you on the steep cliffs above Loudon Creek. To avoid dehydration on a hot day, refill your canteen at Loudon Creek.

~

Follow the broad, well-used trail as it leads down from the parking lot to the suspension bridge across the North Saskatchewan River. Cross the suspension bridge and continue along the trail to a fork. Turn right. After a short distance, the road climbs a little above the river to give satisfying views to the south and west. Continue straight ahead on the road past a cutline. If you are hiking in early spring, look across the highway, where you should be able to see two ice falls formed over rock ridges on the mountainsides. In summer this part of the hike can be a trudge, especially if the day is hot since there is little shade along the road.

After a three-km walk, you finally reach the cool welcoming waters of Loudon Creek. The old log bridge that used to span the creek has long been gone, but a ford to the right of the road offers access to the creek where you can refill your water bottle and enjoy a short rest before beginning the hike upstream. Looking up Loudon Creek, the distinctive peak of Mount Peskett rises on the right. For the fishermen among you, Loudon Creek contains small brook trout, Dolly Varden and cutthroat trout, but severe seasonal flooding renders Loudon Creek poor habitat for any fish species.

To begin the walk along Loudon Creek you need to find a game trail that leads upstream. Backtrack along the road for approximately 25 m. The trail is on the right through the bushes. The lower end of

Summit of Mt. Louden from the unnamed peak to the southwest. Courtesy of Tony Daffern.

the trail can be somewhat indistinct and if in doubt, hug the foot of the high banks on your left. After 300 m the path becomes much more obvious as it leaves the creek and climbs a low hill. The path takes a 90 degree turn around the shoulder of the hill and away from Loudon Creek. If you wish to gain some elevation for a good view, leave the path and scramble up the hillside. Return to the path. Do not turn left to continue along the trail, but drop down into a shallow ravine in order to gain access to the next ridge. A path leads up the spine of the ridge taking you high above the creekbed. The scenery becomes more and more exciting as the trail follows the edge of what are now steep banks above Loudon Creek. It is a delightful walk that leads through small meadows and stands of pines.

You want to end the hike at steep cliffs above the creek, with Mount Peskett to the southwest. There is a fine viewpoint of this mountain, as

well as of the glacier on Mount Wilson. This also makes an excellent spot for a short rest. Mount Peskett was first climbed in 1970.

The trail continues, descending to an unnamed creek, then disappearing, making it impractical to continue. Return the way you came.

HISTORICAL FOOTNOTES

Hector Nimrod (ca. 1900)

We know that he had long, graceful hands, hence his Stoney name "The-one-with-a-thumb-like-a-blunt-arrow." Good hands made for a good shooter and good shooters made good hunters. So good in fact, that when Sir James Hector hired this most famous hunter among the Stoney, and found that he could not pronounce his name, he christened him Nimrod, after the biblical king and mighty hunter. The name "Hector" came afterwards, possibly Nimrod's way of honouring his employer.

Nimrod was among the first of Stoney hunters and guides associated with the more famous non-native travellers in the Canadian Rockies during the 19th and early 20th centuries. Nimrod was with Hector and the Palliser Expedition for two seasons. He guided the group through the Canadian Rockies, including the Kootenay Plains, bagged game and likely shared his geographical and historical knowledge with Sir James Hector. Hector observed Nimrod's skill and resulting status: "Nimrod was the great man among the Indians on returning to camp, as a good hunter is always held in the highest estimation. He does nothing but idle and smoke in camp,

and may lord it over the rest as he pleases, as they are all afraid to offend him."

Nimrod left Hector. In 1859, Hector was planning to cross Howse Pass in September to reach Thompson River. Both Nimrod and Peter Erasmus were concerned about the lateness of the season and the chances of finding game. Erasmus declined to go with Hector, while Nimrod, it appears, went unwillingly. Nimrod left his family behind on the Kootenay Plains while he led Hector partway up the North Saskatchewan past Whirlpool Point. On the pretext of going hunting, Nimrod abandoned Hector's party and returned to his family. Together they went up the Siffleur River, crossed the Pipestone Pass and descended to the Bow River. There, Nimrod met another hunter, the Earl of Southesk, who at the time was down on his luck. Nimrod's group fed Southesk, and later accompanied the Earl to Edmonton to pick up gifts in appreciation for this charity.

As for Sir James Hector, he found his way across Howse Pass and tried to reach Thompson River. As predicted, it was too late in the season and Hector was forced to return.

WHAT'S IN A NAME?

Mount Peskett

An inspiration to the delinquent youths he tried to help, Rev. Louis Peskett (1931-1966) was Director of an Edmonton programme called Youth for Christ. He formulated the idea of building a youth camp in the Nordegg area in the 1960s, but did not live to see the completion of the Frontier Lodge Youth Camp. The minister died at the age of 35 from injuries received while camping with a group in the Valley of the Three Falls. While exploring a canyon, he was struck on the head by a falling rock. In a four-hour ordeal, he was carried out by stretcher to Highway #11, before being taken to hospital in Edmonton where he died several days later. The memory of his vision lives on in the 3,124 m-high peak named after him in 1968.

61 Whirlpool Point Loop – map p. 218

Duration ~ two hours
Distance ~ 3.2 km
Degree of Difficulty ~ easy walk with short climb
Maximum Elevation ~ 1,570 m
Elevation Gain ~ 205 m
Map ~ 83 C/1 Whiterabbit Creek

Everyone wants to discover for themselves why this rocky point of land is named Whirlpool Point. From the whirlpool this hike runs along an open forested ridge for a view of the entire upper North Saskatchewan River basin.

~

The track cuts through sandy soil and open forest as it leads down to the North Saskatchewan River.

Access ~ Park your vehicle by the large "happy face" rock on the east side of Whirlpool Point, at the roadside parking area on Highway #11, located 68 km west of Nordegg or 15 km east of the Banff National Park boundary. Your trailhead is a four-wheel drive track on the south side of the highway at the east end of the highway guard rail.

0.0	trailhead
0.1	road ends; footpath begins
0.3	highway riprap
0.6	junction
0.8	Whirlpool Point and stream-gauging station
1.0	logging road
1.1	cutback into slope
1.2	junction
1.5	ridge crest and rock outcrop
2.1	top of ridge
2.7	trail
3.1	borrow pit
3.2	trailhead

Opposite: This 1915 ferry over the North Saskatchewan, affectionately called "the bucket," operated in exactly the same way as the present one at Whirlpool Point. Courtesy of the Department of Environmental Protection, #9258.

Overlooking the whirlpool above the stream-gauging station.

The gnarled and wind-bent trees are limber pine, so-called because of the flexibility of their small branches that enable them to withstand the gale-force winds that blast through the valley. The path leads upstream as it skirts the river's edge. With the majestic Mount Peskett on the other side of the river serving as a backdrop, continue your pleasant, easy stroll through the pines.

The path ends at the east end of the highway riprap. Make your way through the riprap to the other side and go up the slope, bearing slightly to the right. You soon come to a junction of trails. Bear left and follow the footpath down to the river. For the best view of Whirlpool Point, continue upstream along the path, where there is an innocent-looking eddy that gives this bend in the river its name.

The North Saskatchewan flows quickly at this point, so quickly in fact that although fish can be caught in the river, various studies have not verified the presence of fish at Whirlpool Point. The fast-flowing waters, though, are useful for scientific studies. As part of a nationwide programme, Environment Canada erected a stream-gauging station to collect data on pollution, environmental impact and water management on the upper North Saskatchewan River. Water samples are collected by government workers who sit in a cradle and lower themselves to the middle of the river. They reach the shore by pulling themselves, hand over hand, back up along the cable.

219

Return to the junction and turn left to climb toward the highway. Almost immediately you reach a cairn dedicated to the Overlanders, who in 1940 were the first to blaze a route over Whirlpool Point en route to the Banff-Jasper Highway. Continue up the four-wheel drive track to the highway. Cross the highway and scramble up the sand and gravel slope left of the cliff, to an old logging road. Turn right onto the road. At a cutback into the slope, bear left. Here there is an abandoned corral. Walk through the corral to the open slope and find a game trail that leads up the ridge to a T-junction with another game trail. Turn right onto the trail as it leads to a crest in the ridge. Ten m past the crest, if you wish to climb to the top of the spine, pivot to the left onto another trail that takes you atop a rock outcrop. Bear to the right and begin to climb Whirlpool Point spine.

There is no distinct path, but remain on the spine of the ridge as you wend up through straggly pines and spruces. Occasionally turn around for better and better views of the valley. Majestic Mount Peskett, with its talon-like peak, gazes down on the many braids of the North Saskatchewan as it winds its way eastward. Pass a small rock cairn built by somebody who was either mistaken, or found no reason to continue to the end of the ridge. Continue as the slope dips steeply into a ravine. Within a surprisingly short time you reach the end of the ridge. A larger rock cairn marks the high point of the hike.

Return to the 1.5-km mark and turn left onto the path that parallels the highway below. It's a picturesque walk down through gnarled pines and ground-hugging junipers as far as a borrow pit, where you turn right to drop to the highway and your vehicle.

FLORAFACTS

Limber Pine

Scientific Name ~ *Pinus flexilis*

Also known as Rocky Mountain white pine, limber pine is a slow-growing, but long-lived species. Would it surprise you to know that some of the pine trees at Whirlpool Point could be as old as 1,000 years? A core sample of the outside 10 cm of one of these venerable pines showed that it was almost 400 years old. Since this sample represented less than 20% of the total radius of the tree, it could well be that this limber pine was a ripe 80 years of age when William the Conqueror landed in England in 1066.

The name "limber" is derived from the suppleness of the pine's young branches. Since limber pine prefer dry, exposed and windy rocky slopes and ridges, flexibility is key to its survival. Limber pine often are twisted and gnarled in appearance due to the effects of the wind.

The stand of limber pines at Whirlpool Point is one of two groves found along Highway #11. The other is at Windy Point. They represent the northernmost range of this species.

HISTORICAL NOTES

The Overlanders

The building of the David Thompson Highway has a chequered history. As early as the 1920s, the people of Rocky Mountain House wanted a road built west to Howse Pass. Much pressure was brought to bear on the government and, finally, a stretch from Rocky Mountain House to Nordegg was opened in 1931. No doubt the politicians thought that this would keep the people of Rocky happy. Little did they know the determination of the townsfolk, in particular of Ernest Ross, in completing the road all the way. It was in 1940 at a meeting with the Minister of Highways, Gordon Taylor, that a deal was struck. Taylor was trying to stall the completion of the highway by explaining that such a road would be prohibitively expensive due to the mountainous terrain. Ernest Ross retorted that he could drive his car from Nordegg to the Banff-Jasper highway now. To which Taylor replied that if Ross could drive his car through, he would build a road!

With four friends, Magnus Oppel, E. S. "Captain" Brett, Bill Shierholtz and Bill Ellenberg, Ernest Ross planned his assault on the area west of Nordegg. In his arsenal, Ross had a block and tackle, lots of rope, saws and extra blades, shovels, crowbars, a complete set of mechanic's tools, tents, blankets and a rifle. Finally, on October 1, 1940, the five set out on their adventure in a 10 year-old Ford roadster and a three-quarter ton truck carrying enough food for two weeks.

The first day saw them go all the way to the Cline River, close to where the David Thompson Resort now stands. Up early the next day, Ross located a ford across the Cline. After nearly losing his Ford roadster in the swift current, Ross kicked up sand as he roared across the Kootenay Plains at 80 km per hour. His fun was short lived upon their approach to the 180 m-high rock face that marks Whirlpool Point. The only way to surmount this obstacle was to go up and over it. Two days of clearing brush, inching the vehicles up the slope using the block and tackle, and then inching the vehicles down the other side, required the patience of Job, as one participant later recalled.

There was some confusion at first over how the block and tackle was supposed to work. Fortunately, they figured out that the tackle was supposed to be anchored to the car and not to the tree before they pulled the tree up by its roots!

Whirlpool Point marked the beginning of a hard 10-day slog that saw the men build corduroy across swamps and bridges across streams. Then, with only a few kilometres to go to the park boundary, the truck's axle snapped on a particularly rough piece of ground. There was nothing to do but to blaze ahead with the Ford. They set off the next day, taking with them only a can of tomatoes and a loaf of bread to eat. Fourteen hours later, they dragged themselves into the motel on the Banff-Jasper highway—only to find it closed and guarded by a watchman who would not give them so much as a drink of water.

What to do? On to Lake Louise! The night was pitch black and cold. One of Ross's companions promised to buy them all the largest steak, french fries and all the trimmings if they would only get to Lake Louise. When they did finally roll into town it was past midnight and the restaurants had all closed. The five stumbled to a house where they were greeted with screams from the hostess who took them for hobos, or worse. Once they stopped their teeth from chattering long enough to explain their predicament, they were plied with sandwiches and plenty of hot coffee. Then, it was off to a good night's (?) sleep in the ladies' waiting room at the railway station.

Taking delivery of a new axle, they retraced their steps, fixed the truck and repeated the harrowing journey down to Lake Louise. At the Banff-Jasper highway, the overlanders erected a sign "Rocky Mountain House 115 miles. Route now open." It was the 11th of October.

This was the first of the cavalcades that, year after year, risked swollen streams, swamps, forests and Whirlpool Point to convince the government to build a road. It was finally on August 2, 1975, that a cavalcade of 1,000 vehicles celebrated the opening of the David Thompson Highway.

Ernest Ross (on the right) and Bill Schierholtz tackling Whirlpool Point on the second Overlander trip in 1941. Courtesy of the Rocky Mountain House Museum.

ROCKY
MTN. HOUSE
115 MILES

The cairn at Whirlpool Point commemorating the feat of the Overlanders.

The original directional sign at the junction of the David Thompson "highway" and the Icefields Parkway. Courtesy of the Rocky Mountain House Museum.

62 Whirlpool Ridge – map p. 218

Duration ~ full day
Distance ~ 10.2 km
Level of Difficulty ~ long, steady climb to alpine area followed by a rock scramble
Maximum Elevation ~ 2,600 m
Elevation Gain ~ 1,100 m
Map ~ 83 C/1 Whiterabbit Creek

Access ~ Park your vehicle at the roadside parking area on the west side of Whirlpool Point on Highway #11, 69 km west of Nordegg or 14 km east of the Banff National Park boundary.

A steep, exhilarating climb carries you above the treeline to the top of Whirlpool Ridge for an unparalleled view of Whirlpool Point, Mount Peskett and the entire western portion of the North Saskatchewan River valley. The glaciers and snowcaps of Banff National Park mark the western boundary of the David Thompson corridor.

0.0	trailhead
0.4	reclaimed road
2.0	end of road
3.0	viewpoint
4.0	alpine meadows
5.1	cairns at top of Ridge
10.2	trailhead

~

On the opposite side of the highway from where you parked your vehicle are three large gravel cuts in the highway right-of-way. Walk past the

The much lower ridge walk of Whirlpool Point Loop lies far below you when on top of Whirlpool Ridge. Mount Peskett keeps guard over the west end of the David Thompson corridor.

westernmost cut to the next two slopes. These slopes are marked by horizontal cuts. Go up the left side of the ravine between these cuts to an old reclaimed roadway. Turn right onto the roadway. If you turn left you end up back on the highway. At one point, the roadway appears to end at the base of a slope. However, if you scamper up what appears to be a wide game trail you will regain the roadway once on top. Now, begin a series of switchbacks as the road climbs the west flank of Whirlpool Ridge. As reclaimed roadways go, this one is fairly easy to negotiate with little secondary growth and few boulders underfoot. After switching five times the roadway flattens a little as it skirts around the end of the hill. It's a pretty view with Mount Wilson and its gleaming glacier directly to the west. Fifty metres later the roadway switches again, then again, and yet a third time before you see the open spine of Whirlpool Ridge through the opening in the trees. Remain on the roadway as it cuts up the spine. The trees have now fallen away, offering splendid views of the North Saskatchewan River valley. The roadway ends abruptly and it is here that you begin to bushwhack up the Ridge.

No hiking trails mark the route, but the way up this open, windy spine is obvious. Mountain sheep claim this Ridge as their own, and you should be able to pick up their game trails, which lead you faithfully up the Ridge. Occasionally the trees close in a little to give some respite to the gale-force winds that can buffet you as you climb ever higher. Some of the twisted, gnarled pine trees must be quite old, a testimony to their strength and flexibility in face of the winds that can rip through the valley. You reach what appears to be the end of the Ridge, with a tantalizing scree and rock peak above. But this is merely a viewpoint both of the river valley below and of the peak that marks the immediate end of Whirlpool Ridge.

A shallow saddle separates you from the peak in front. Drop down into the saddle, then swing left to begin the climb. At first there is no

---

HISTORICAL FOOTNOTES

The Last Roundup

As you stand on Whirlpool Ridge and look down toward the North Saskatchewan River, you have before you the layout and strategy for the wild horse roundups that occurred in the area. The wild horses' range was split in half by Whirlpool Ridge. The animals would move back and forth between the Wildhorse Creek valley to the west and the slopes around the small tarn seen to the northeast. They crossed to one side or the other through the gaps seen lower down the ridge or along the river.

The tarn was favoured by the wild horses in summer. Here, there was grass, water and relief from flies. It was here that the roundup would begin. Riders drove the horses southwest toward Whirlpool Ridge. The animals, squeezed by the river and the Ridge, headed for one of the passes. In all the passes but one there were other riders waiting to head off the horses. In the remaining gap was a corral that would trap them. Such a corral still stands on the low end of Whirlpool Ridge (see Whirlpool Point Loop).

The last such wild horse roundup, according to one of its participants, local outfitter Ed McKenzie, was around 1955.

Ambitious scramblers may continue to the 2,635 m-high peak to the north. Courtesy of Gillean Daffern.

game trail to follow, but past a plateau or step in the Ridge you should be able to pick up a trail that goes up the slope. Once through rocks and low ledges you break out of the open pine forest to a series of beautiful green alpine meadows. If you are lucky, you can walk past mountain sheep resting or grazing here. Bear right to reach the last meadow and follow the game trail past a low, rocky ledge before swinging to the left to get onto the scree slope that leads to the top of the Ridge. Be aware that the winds can be fierce, so hang onto your hat for this last pull.

Two rock cairns mark this point on Whirlpool Ridge. Below, the view is nothing less than spectacular! To the northeast you can see an exquisite little tarn. It's been a tough little climb so take some time to enjoy the view and munch on your snacks before returning the way you came to the trailhead.

Ambitious scramblers can continue the ridge walk to the 2,635 m-high peak seen further to the north.

GEOFACTS

Whirlpool Point

The Front Ranges extend from the McConnell Thrust Fault at Windy Point west to the main ranges six km west of Whirlpool Point. Within the Front Ranges, there are several other minor thrust faults.

At Whirlpool Ridge, Precambrian rock of at least 600 million years old has been forced over rock of the Middle Cambrian and even younger strata, forming a very hard ridge. The North Saskatchewan River runs parallel to the ridge. The river has been able to erode only a narrow part of the ridge. The "whirlpool" in the river marks the point where the North Saskatchewan changes direction to cut through the ridge. You can see the extension of the ridge on the other side of the river.

Sir James Hector, of the Palliser Expedition, was the first to note the composition of Whirlpool Ridge: "Ascending the spur which forms the rocky point of the valley I found that it was composed of 200 feet of quartzite, overlaid by shales and limestones, and thin bedded sandstones composed of coarse grains of quartz with specks of green colouring matter. These sandstones exhibit much false bedding..."

63 Alexander Henry's Trail – map p. 218

Duration ~ two hours
Distance ~ 4.6 km
Level of Difficulty ~ easy walk with some light bushwhacking
Maximum Elevation ~ 1,370 m
Elevation Gain ~ 15 m
Map ~ 83 C/1 Whiterabbit Creek; 83 C/2 Cline River

Access ~ Park your vehicle on the west side of Whirlpool Point at the roadside parking area located 69 km west of Nordegg, or 14 km east of the Banff National Park boundary on Highway #11

A pretty stroll along the North Saskatchewan River, this hike is named after the fur trader and Nor'wester, Alexander Henry, who on February 8, 1811 dashed by these meadows en route to Howse Pass. Campers of all types find this area charming, as witnessed by the numerous informal campsites and sweat lodges that dot the meadows.

~

Walk east along the highway to the guardrail and take a trail to the right that leads down to the river. When you arrive at the North Saskatchewan turn right and walk upstream. This is a delightful walk. The snowcaps on the south side of the racing North Saskatchewan frame your view the entire way as you walk through the park-like meadows. At times the trail disappears, forcing you either to bushwhack along the river's edge or to walk down along the rocky shore. The trail soon leads to a grassy meadow. At its west end, find a distinctive footpath and follow it as it works its way up river. A footbridge across a small stream makes for an easy crossing. On the other side, you come to the first of a series of informal campsites that dot these meadows.

Bear left to return to the river. Continue up river for 300 m to Wildhorse Creek. In late summer, water levels have dropped enough to make your crossing of this gravel-bedded stream a hop, skip and a jump. Shortly after crossing Wildhorse Creek the path leads past three campsites within 200 m. At a fork, bear left keeping close to the river. Within 100 m you reach the campsite of the Elk River Outfitters. In autumn, the outfitters set up a base camp for their hunting expeditions. Other hunters, with horse trailers in tow, also use the campsites in this area and you may find your-

0.0	trailhead
0.1	North Saskatchewan River
0.3	meadow
1.4	stream
1.7	Wildhorse Creek
1.8	campsite
2.0	fork
2.2	Elk River Outfitters' campsite
2.6	trail ends
3.0	Elk River Outfitters' campsite
3.1	junction
3.5	junction
3.7	Wildhorse Creek
3.9	highway
4.6	trailhead

From a viewpoint you can gaze up the North Saskatchewan River to the snowcaps in Banff National Park.

self sharing the trail with camouflaged weekend deerstalkers. The road now swings to the right to connect with an old logging road. Across the river you can see the confluence of Spreading Creek with the North Saskatchewan. Past the Elk River Outfitters, the road becomes a footpath that ends in a meadow. Here, the North Saskatchewan makes a lazy curve, adding foreground interest to the inspiring view toward the snowcaps upstream. The wind-eroded embankments bear witness to the damage that the gales, which roar out of the mountains, can wreck upon this delicate rain shadow ecosystem.

Return to the Elk River Outfitters' campsite. Just beyond the campsite bear right at a junction with the old road. Within 400 m you will come to another junction. Continue straight on the old road. After recrossing Wildhorse Creek, the road swings back to the highway. Here, turn right and then back to your vehicle.

HISTORICAL FOOTNOTES

Sir James Hector (1834-1907)

The first person to record Whirlpool Point was Sir James Hector, the geologist and naturalist associated with the Palliser Expedition, 1857-1860. The expedition conducted a scientific and geographic survey of western British North America, in which it amassed astronomical, meteorological, geological and magnetic data, as well as descriptions of the geography, native inhabitants, flora and fauna, and capabilities for settlement.

In 1858 Sir James Hector attempted to reach Howse Pass, but was unsuccessful. Turning back, he passed Whirlpool Point on September 15th. He spent the next day at Whirlpool Point (which he called Pine Point), examining the pine trees and geological strata. He returned briefly the following year, where he noted a herd of several hundred bighorn sheep. This time he found and crossed Howse Pass.

HISTORICAL FOOTNOTES

Henry's Dash

If you wish to know exactly how tough fur traders were, then read Alexander Henry's account of his midwinter dash from Rocky Mountain House to Howse Pass and back in 1811.

The purpose of his dash was to escort several people across Howse Pass. The reason for the speed was the presence of the nearby Peigan. By 1811, the Peigan were intensifying their blockade of the fur traders' direct trade with the Kootenay. The Peigan were afraid, justifiably, that the traders would arm the Kootenay, thereby make them more formidable enemies. Alexander Henry began his journey with a trick. He told the Peigan at Rocky Mountain House that he was heading downstream, proceeded that way initially, then doubled back and dashed upstream.

He completed the journey in 11 days. He did it in subzero (Fahrenheit) temperatures, mostly on foot. The emphasis was on speed. The estimated round-trip distance was 600 km. His estimated average rate of travel was 55 km per day. Each day on the trail lasted about 12 hours. He usually began about 5:00 am, several hours before dawn and ended past dusk at about 5:00 pm. The route was along the frozen North Saskatchewan River.

The travellers and dogs depended upon caches of food left by hunters who were several days ahead. When the hunters were unsuccessful or the food caches penetrated, then everyone in Henry's party did without, since they carried little food themselves. On the trail where the snow was deep, men ran ahead on snowshoes to break trail for the dogs. There were accidents. One morning before dawn, one man fell into the river. On another occasion, a dog team fell through the ice. One of the hunters suffering from swollen knees was left behind with provisions.

And there was the abuse. Wrote Henry: "I awoke my men to prepare for departure, but as they had not slept more than two hours, fatigue was still heavy upon them. Their motions were therefore slow; but what grieved them most was having nothing to eat before starting. This made them surly; they first quarrelled among themselves and then gave full vent to their ill humour upon the poor dogs, which they beat most cruelly."

This was the beginning of Alexander Henry's last day. Camped near the mouth of Shunda Creek on the North Saskatchewan, his party left at 2:00 am, arriving at Rocky Mountain House at 2:30 pm. In twelve and a half hours, on foot, very hungry and very cold, on their 11th day of winter travel, they covered about 80 km!

Alexander Henry (?-1814)

Alexander Henry the Younger is not to be confused with his uncle of the same name called "the Elder." Alexander Henry the Younger's journals, as edited by Edward Coues, are the best reading among all the traders and travellers in the Canadian northwest. His lucid description of his February 1811 dash from Rocky Mountain House to Howse Pass and back does credit to any modern travel writer.

Henry was David Thompson's superior at Rocky Mountain House. Thompson's 1810 decision in the face of Peigan pressure to abandon an attempt to cross the Rocky Mountains via Howse Pass frustrated Henry. Henry urged Thompson to use the Howse Pass route. Instead Thompson chose the more northerly Athabasca Pass.

Henry might have been one of the last people to use Howse Pass as a fur trade route. He died in 1814 in a boating accident on the Columbia River.

64 Wildhorse Creek – map p. 218

Duration ~ two days
Distance ~ 15.2 km
Level of Difficulty ~ very steep ascent to pass and a steep descent to Landslide Lake
Maximum Elevation ~ 2,515 m
Elevation Gain ~ 1,130 m
Map ~ 83 C/1 Whiterabbit Creek; 83 C/2 Cline River

Access ~ Park your vehicle north of Highway #11 at a signed abandoned gravel pit 900 m west of Wildhorse Creek. The gravel pit turn-off is 71 km west of Nordegg or 12 km east of the Banff National Park boundary. The trail begins on either side of the old gravel pit.

The British Army Training Unit, Suffield, used to send their members jogging up this trail under full packs, so you know you are in for a challenge. The climb up Wildhorse Creek to the pass overlooking Landslide Lake is steep, but the views of the North Saskatchewan River valley and Landslide Lake are worthwhile. Good campsites at the lake invite a stay of several days, if you have the time.

0.0	trailhead
0.1	braid
0.3	braids
1.4	Wildhorse Creek
2.9	gravel wash
3.0	Wildhorse Creek and campsite
3.3	scree slope
3.7	top of notch
4.3	top of pass
7.6	Landslide Lake
15.2	trailhead

~

The trail, a four-wheel drive track, begins innocently enough, winding slowly uphill through aspens and poplars. At a braid, continue straight ahead or to the left. There are several more braids that occur over the next 200 m or so. Ignore them all and continue along the main track as it begins to climb to the northeast. By the time the trail comes out to the slope above Wildhorse Creek, you have left the deciduous trees behind and are climbing along a footpath through lodgepole pines. This is the last chance to fill your water bottle, so if you have not done this drop to the creek; you'll be glad you did, especially if the day is warm.

To this point, it has been a slow but steady ascent. Now, you begin the climb in earnest. It's quite a puff, so take time to enjoy the scenery as it unfolds behind you. To the left you can see Whirlpool Point and Ridge, and on the other side of the North Saskatchewan River, Mount Peskett and Spreading Creek. Continue your relentless ascent. The trail winds in and out of open forest. Because you are on the north bank of the North Saskatchewan River, ground covering is thin and the sun's rays radiate off the thin soil, a tiring addition to the hike. You may also

Looking back up to the pass from Landslide Lake. Courtesy of Alfred Falk.

have to contend with winds that gather strength as the day progresses.

The pitch of the trail flattens where you cross an avalanche slope. Young pine and spruce trees have taken hold here, making the crossing a little rough. Once across, reenter the forest as you continue to climb north-north-east. Within a short distance you break out of the treeline and onto a gravel slope. By now you can see most of the way up the creek valley. Bearberry bushes and willows have replaced the trees by the time you reach Wildhorse Creek, a mere rivulet at this point, making your crossing a hop and a skip—if you have the energy left! At the only truly level piece of ground between the trailhead and Landslide Lake there is, not surprisingly, an informal campsite. This makes an excellent place to rest and to refill your water bottle. There will be no other water until you reach the meadows before Landslide Lake.

The view from the campsite is inspiring. Below is the trailhead and directly above is the mountain you have to climb. Once you have rested, begin what feels like a nearly vertical ascent over scree toward two notches. The trail disappears about 100 m above the campsite, so hikers make their way up as best they can. There are two notches, both located a little to the right. Head for the notch on the left. On top, pick up the trail again as it traverses a talus slope. The trail is quite distinct; nevertheless, the Alberta Forest Service has erected rock cairns every 50 m or so. The biggest rock cairn is at the summit of the pass.

A beautiful sight lies at your feet. The brilliant aqua-green lake sits like a gem in a setting of high, precipitous mountains. Even by mid-summer snowfields demarcate the sweep of the mountainside and linger in the shadows at the south end of the lake. After enjoying the view, pick up the trail that begins an equally steep descent to the lake. Rock cairns help you find the way down. As you descend, the scree and gravel give way to krummholz spruce, and then to a variety of wildflowers that paint the meadows in a profusion of colour. Finally the trail reaches the spruce trees. At this point, the trail becomes indistinct and there are no more rock cairns to guide you. It is best to work your way through the meadows and bog to the stream that feeds the lake. Do not cross the stream, but stay on the right side where you again pick up the trail. When you reach the lake, bear to the right again along the lakeshore. The first of three good campsites can be found within 100 metres.

Return the way you came, or exit from the north side of the lake via the Landslide Lake Recreation Trail.

HISTORICAL FOOTNOTES

Horses on the Plains

Horses have been associated with the Kootenay Plains since a noteworthy barbecue in 1808, hosted by David Thompson. In June, Thompson and his group came over Howse Pass to the Plains, but had run out of food. Unable to find any game, they killed and ate several of their packhorses.

Thompson and the North West Company fur traders used the Kootenay Plains as grazing ground for their horses prior to packing freight over Howse Pass. On return trips, they unloaded these horses at the Plains. The freight was put into canoes for the downstream trip to Rocky Mountain House, and the animals were either left to graze or were taken back to Rocky Mountain House as well.

Sir James Hector, when travelling through the Kootenay Plains area in 1858, reported that the Stoney Indians possessed horses. But it wasn't until the beginning of the 20th century that horses became a major presence on the Plains. In the winter of 1902-1903, Tom Wilson established a ranch with 40 animals. At the peak of his operation there were up to 300 packhorses wintering in the area. These animals supplied the growing packing and guiding business based in Banff-Lake Louise. Each fall they were herded north across the Pipestone Pass and down the Siffleur River to the Plains. They spent the winter there in free-running herds. In the spring a crew rounded up horses that were at least three years old, broke them to saddle or to pack, and returned them to Banff-Lake Louise.

Tom Wilson's ranching operation eventually came into conflict with local Stoney Indians who also owned horses. Wilson attempted to exclude the Stoneys and their animals from the Plains by obtaining a grazing lease. He was unsuccessful and eventually left. The dispute over the grazing of horses on the Plains continued, now between the Stoneys and the Alberta government.

For reasons of ecological control and the preparation of the Kootenay Plains area for commercial grazing leases, Alberta Forestry began removing free-roaming horse herds from the Plains. In the case of the wild herds, this meant that they were killed. During these campaigns, Stoney-owned animals were also killed and the Government was accused of harassment. As the regional focus changed from commercial grazing leases to tourism and environmental protection, the policy of removing horses from the Plains continued.

The Kootenay Plains was officially closed to grazing in 1967.

65 Thompson Creek Campground –

Duration ~ one hour
Distance ~ 2.6 km
Level of Difficulty ~ some short, steep sprints
Maximum Elevation ~ 1,400 m
Elevation Gain ~ 30 m
Map ~ 83 C/2 Cline River

The Thompson Creek campground is very large. To accommodate the many campers, a second camping, or overflow area, has been constructed to the west. Campers created and continue to use a hiking path that leads up a low hill above the overflow camping area. Beautiful views of snow-caps to the west and north greet you before you climb over to another ridge for an equally inspiring view of the North Saskatchewan River.

~

From the trailhead walk north along the campground road to the intersection with the road leading to the overflow camping area. Turn left onto this road. Within a short distance you come

Access ~ Park your vehicle at the parking area beside the cookhouse at the Thompson Creek campground, located 80 km west of Nordegg and three km east of the Banff National Park boundary on Highway #11.

0.0	trailhead
0.1	Thompson Creek
0.2	junction
0.4	campsite #47
1.0	junction
1.3	viewpoint
2.6	trailhead

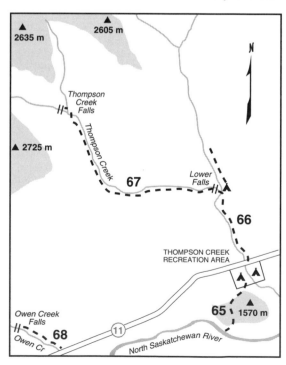

The southern-most slopes of Mount Cline rear above the spruce trees at the Thompson Creek campground.

to Thompson Creek. The creek was named after either David Thompson, a fur trader and map maker with the North West Company, or Charles S. Thompson, a member of the Appalachian Mountain Club who was in the area approximately 1900. Cross Thompson Creek and continue along the road to a T-junction where there are washrooms and a water pump. Vehicular traffic must bear to the right along the campground road, but go left and walk against the campground traffic as far as campsite #47. Just past the campsite are two footpaths. One leads sharply to the left to return to Thompson Creek and then back to the caretaker's cabin in the primary camping area. Ignore this path in favour of a distinct trail that leads up the ridge in front of you. It's

a short but steep sprint to the top. Look behind to the north for marvellous views of the lower slopes of Mount Cline.

Follow the trail as it swings around the shoulder of the ridge, descends and then climbs another ridge. There are many braids in the trail near the top of this second ridge. Look carefully and bear a sharp right on the first trail that leads downhill. At the bottom of the slope, the trail enters the cool pine and spruce forest, a relief on a hot day. The trail leads to a low ridge overlooking the North Saskatchewan River. It's a pretty scene, one to be savoured as you walk upstream or downstream along the open ridges. Find several upright logs that mark the trail back through the woods to your trailhead.

David Thompson (1770-1857)

As a fur trader, explorer, surveyor and author, David Thompson is well established in the pantheon of Canadian heroes. His name and reputation have been drafted to a number of present-day local initiatives, such as the David Thompson Highway, the David Thompson Resort, the David Thompson Country tourist zone and the David Thompson Days festivities at Rocky Mountain House.

It was in the hope of establishing a lucrative trade with the Kootenay Indians, the original residents of the Kootenay Plains, that the North West Company established Rocky Mountain House in 1799. However, hostilities between the Kootenay and the Peigan forced the flight of the Kootenay across the mountains. All attempts to have the Kootenay come to Rocky Mountain House were stymied by the Peigan. It became apparent that if there was to be any trade with the Kootenays, the traders would have to go to them. This was David Thompson's job. When he arrived at Rocky Mountain House in 1800, Thompson sent two men, La Gasse and Le Blanc, across Howse Pass to establish trade with the Kootenays.

His own first attempt to follow La Gasse and Le Blanc in 1801 failed. Thompson then left Rocky Mountain House and did not return until 1806. That year, Jaco Finlay established a trading outpost on the Kootenay Plains and cut a trail across Howse Pass for Thompson. On June 25, 1807, Thompson and his party crossed Howse Pass. He spent almost a year exploring, surveying and trading in present-day British Columbia, Idaho and Montana. He recrossed Howse Pass and reached the Kootenay Plains on June 22, 1808. Thompson repeated the trip across Howse Pass two more times, finally returning to Rocky Mountain House in the spring of 1810. That year, the Peigan moved to block any further trans-mountain trade.

A race between American traders and the North West Company to establish a trading post at the mouth of the Columbia River was lost to the Americans when Thompson panicked in face of Peigan hostility. In July, the canoe brigade, which was moving upriver ahead of Thompson, was turned back by the Peigan. Thompson, badly frightened, hid for a month. Despite assurances by Alexander Henry that the route was now clear, Thompson headed north and crossed the Athabasca Pass in January 1811. He arrived at the mouth of the Columbia on July 14, only to discover that the Americans had already arrived.

There were several consequences to David Thompson's inaction. Many years later, during the Oregon Dispute over the boundary between Canada and the United States, the Americans successfully claimed the lower Columbia River because they were there first. But for Thompson's month of hiding near Rocky Mountain House, the course of history might have been different. Of more immediate importance to the North West Company was the abandonment of Howse Pass in favour of Athabasca Pass. As a result, the Kootenay Plains ceased as a transit stop on the trunk route across the mountains.

There is a touch of irony since the same business community in Rocky Mountain House and central Alberta, which has taken up David Thompson as its "hook," has also been lobbying unsuccessfully for a road through Howse Pass, the route that Thompson abandoned.

66 Thompson Creek – map p. 232

Duration ~ one hour
Distance ~ 2.4 km
Level of Difficulty ~ easy walk
Maximum Elevation ~ 1,415 m
Elevation Gain ~ 45 m
Map ~ 83 C/2 Cline River

For those who are staying at the Thompson Creek campground there are several hikes that can be enjoyed. This easy 20-minute walk brings you to a delightful little waterfall.

~

Find the trail behind the toilets that leads across the grass to Highway #11. Cross the highway and pick up the trail as it continues up the right side of the creek. With the jagged peaks of the south ridge of Mount Cline above you, begin this pretty

Access ~ Park your vehicle at the cookhouse at the Thompson Creek campground, located 80 km west of Nordegg and three km east of the Banff National Park boundary on Highway #11. Your trail begins behind the toilets located across the roadway from the cookhouse.

0.0	trailhead
0.1	Highway #11
1.2	small gorge and waterfall
2.4	trailhead

The waterfall on Thompson Creek makes this short walk perfect for younger families.

Jaco Finlay (ca. 1768-1828)

David Thompson is known as the great geographer of the northwest. But the trail blazer, the man who established the track that Thompson first followed up the North Saskatchewan and over Howse Pass, was a North West Company fur trader, guide and interpreter named Jacques-Raphael Finlay. His friends called him "Jaco."

Jaco Finlay's involvement with David Thompson, the Kootenay Plains and the upper North Saskatchewan began in 1806 when he was ordered by Thompson to leave Rocky Mountain House, make a trail passable for packhorses across the continental divide, and build canoes on the Columbia River. Finlay, therefore, became the first non-native after Le Blanc and La Gasse to ascend the North Saskatchewan and cross Howse Pass, which he did in the summer of 1806. Also that year, Finlay established a small trading post on the Kootenay Plains. Peigan pressure forced its abandonment in 1807. This outpost to Rocky Mountain House was the first non-native residence built in the area.

walk up Thompson Creek. In autumn, the gold of the poplars contrasts with the dark green of the lodgepole pine and white spruce. The trail winds in and out of the forest with interesting views of gravel slopes across the creek.

The trail cuts through the forest for 100 m before regaining the creek embankment. The streambed has changed. What was a broad, gravel streambed with several braids is now a single stream that cuts through rock. This soon becomes a mini gorge, where Thompson Creek begins its long task of slicing through the bedrock. You can hear the waterfall before climbing a rocky ridge where you can see it. Two branches of Thompson Creek join at this location, the waterfall being on the left-hand branch just metres upstream of the confluence.

Alpinists have two options at this point. The right-hand branch leads to a pass between Cline and Resolute mountains. From here they may either ascend Resolute Mountain, or attack the Whitegoat Peaks further on. The left-hand branch leads to another pass, from which they ascend Mount Cline.

At this point, you can return the way you came. Or, if you wish to loop back on the other side of the creek, step down to the right-hand branch of Thompson Creek. Cross the creek (rocks make this an easy crossing) and scramble up the outcrop beside the waterfall. You are now walking up the left-hand branch of the creek. Above the waterfall, the trail becomes indistinct. Bushwhack upstream approximately 25 m and cross Thompson Creek. Turn left and find the trail that leads downstream. This trail is a little rougher than the one on the other side, with some deadfall. Nevertheless, it remains a good trail that leads you back to Highway #11 in short order. At the highway, turn left, cross the bridge and find the path that leads back to the toilets and your vehicle.

67 Thompson Creek Falls – map p. 232

Duration ~ full day
Distance ~ 10.8 km
Level of Difficulty ~ rough trail with some bushwhacking
Maximum Elevation ~ 1,830 m
Elevation Gain ~ 460 m
Map ~ 83 C/2 Cline River

A spectacular 35 m-high waterfall plunging off an escarpment is the sight that will greet you at the end of this somewhat rough hike up Thompson Creek.

~

From behind the toilets, find the path that leads to Highway #11. Cross the highway and pick up the trail that leads upstream. A kilometre of easy walking brings you to the confluence of

Access ~ Park your vehicle at the cookhouse at the Thompson Creek campground, located 80 km west of Nordegg and three km east of the Banff National Park boundary on Highway #11. The trail begins behind the toilets located across the roadway from the cookhouse.

0.0	trailhead
1.2	small waterfall and Thompson Creek crossing
4.0	gravel slope
4.8	gravel wash and Thompson Creek crossing
5.2	stream
5.4	Thompson Creek Falls
10.8	trailhead

Dwarfed by the Thompson Creek Falls, one of your scribes enjoys the view.

Joseph Howse (1774-1852)

Joseph Howse was a Hudson's Bay Company fur trader, explorer and linguist, who passed through the Kootenay Plains several times en route to Howse Pass and the British Columbia interior. He was the first Hudson's Bay man to cross the Rocky Mountains. Howse Pass was named after him by his chief competitor, David Thompson. Ironically, much of the documentation about Howse's activities was recorded by Thompson.

Joseph Howse was sent across the Rocky Mountains in 1809 to inspect the region for its fur trade potential, and report on North West Company activity. Howse left Edmonton House July 18th on a lightning excursion. He followed the North Saskatchewan, crossed Howse Pass, explored a portion of the Columbia River, then quickly returned. Thompson met Howse returning east on August 9th along the upper North Saskatchewan west of the Kootenay Plains. Relations between Thompson and Howse seemed cordial, since Thompson gave Howse a letter to deliver.

Howse's trade assessment was a positive one. His second and last expedition across the divide lasted a year and included exploration and trade. He went up the North Saskatchewan in June, 1810. His return to Edmonton House in mid-July, 1811 was a difficult one. The Peigan at the time were bent on blocking the transmountain fur trade. One chief declared: "if they again met with a white Man going to supply their Enemies, they would not only plunder & kill him, but that they would make dry Meat of his body."

The Hudson's Bay Company managed to conciliate the Peigan, who then allowed Howse's brigade to pass unchallenged through the Kootenay Plains and North Saskatchewan. The investment (trading goods, stores, wages and Peigan bribes) in this yearlong adventure was £576; the value of the furs brought back was £1,500. Despite the profit, the Hudson's Bay Company never mounted another transmountain fur trading expedition until its merger with the North West Company in 1821. The hostility of the Peigan to the trade was too great.

---

the two branches of Thompson Creek. A chute on the left-hand branch of the stream marks the conclusion of the Thompson Creek hike. To continue up Thompson Creek to the waterfall first cross the right-hand branch of the creek and scramble up the low, rocky outcrop by the chute. The trail is fainter and marred by deadfall. Twenty m above the chute cross the left-hand branch of Thompson Creek and find the trail that continues upstream.

For the next two km the trail weaves between old rocky streambeds and the moss-covered forest floor. Deadfall blocks the trail on occasion, forcing you to bushwhack around in order to pick up the trail again. Pretty yellow avens form a deceptively soft-looking mat over the gravel wash along the stream. You have to watch your footing or run the risk of turning an ankle. Also, the trail across the aven-covered rocks is faint at best; if in doubt continue to walk up beside the stream. Pick up the trail again where deadfall or a steep bank blocks the path, forcing you into the forest.

As you climb upstream the terrain begins to change. The fairly open stream begins to narrow. Walking is slow as you stumble over rocks and through thickets of willows and young lodgepole pine and white spruce. Now and again you pick up the trail that continues to alternate between the stream and the forest.

After a somewhat tedious hike views open up upstream. At the same time the trail reappears, leading past gravel cliffs. The trail, now quite distinct, climbs steeply before traversing the slope above the creek. The trail leads over talus and avalanche slopes. A small rock cairn marks a meltwater chute on the left and your first distant view of the Thompson Creek Falls. Even from this distance you can see the horse tail spray from the waterfall as it plunges over a headwall on the lower slope of the unnamed peak that looms over you on the left. Cast a glance behind you, too, for a breathtaking vista of the braided North Saskatchewan River backdropped by Mount Murchison on the right and other, unnamed, majestic peaks of the main ranges.

Alpinists at this point scramble up the gravel wash to the rock wall, then traverse to the right to reach Thompson Creek above the Falls. From here they continue upstream to camp beside one of two tarns before preparing their ascent of Mount Cline.

Cross the rushing waters to the right side of Thompson Creek. Pick up the trail and continue upstream. Where the creek takes a sharp 90 degree curve to the left, a tributary stream joins Thompson Creek. It is here that you have the first unobstructed view of the beautiful waterfall. Even in autumn there is a heavy flow of water, so you will not be disappointed.

From the tributary to the base of the waterfall is a bushwhack up old streambeds, through willows and over rocks. Is it worth it? You betcha! Return the way you came.

GEOFACTS

Hanging Valleys

Like many waterfalls in the Rockies, the Thompson Creek Falls plunge over cliffs that mark the abrupt end of a valley higher up. Hence the term "hanging valley."

Glaciers have held the mountains in their icy grip more than once. As glaciers flowed down the main valleys, "tributary" or side glaciers flowed from valleys higher up, eventually joining the main glacier. The main glacier was thicker than the tributary glaciers, enabling it to gouge deeper and wider valleys than glaciers in the side valleys. The melting of these massive ice sheets exposed a much altered landscape. Valley configuration had changed. What were once winding, V-shaped valleys were now straighter and wider, sporting the classic U-shape. Meltwaters from the tributary glaciers in the valleys above continued to follow the earlier drainage. This has resulted in spectacular waterfalls cascading from a higher valley. Usually associated with hanging valleys are gorges below the cliffs. This is not the case with Thompson Creek.

You can just catch a glimpse of the upper valley above the Thompson Creek Falls.

68 Owen Creek Gorge – map p. 232

Duration ~ one hour
Distance ~ 2.2 km
Level of Difficulty ~ easy walk with some light bushwhacking
Maximum Elevation ~ 1,465 m
Elevation Gain ~ 80 m
Map ~ 83 C/2 Cline River

Access ~ Park your vehicle on the north side of Highway #11 at Owen Creek located just within the Banff National Park boundary, or 83 km west of Nordegg. Park along the east bank of the creek.

Even though Owen Creek is technically 100 m within the Banff National Park boundary and therefore beyond the parameters of this book, we have included this quick scramble since its deep gorge and churning waters are of considerable interest.

~

Although faint and hard to find at first, a footpath leads upstream from the trailhead along the edge of

0.0	trailhead
0.3	informal campsite
0.4	first gorge
1.0	second gorge
1.1	waterfall
2.2	trailhead

Owen Creek gorge.

the creek. You may lose the trail where it dips down onto a gravel wash by the edge of Owen Creek, but 20 m beyond you pick it up again where it climbs onto the bench just above the stream. There are several informal campsites in this area. Owen Creek trail is an access point into the Michele Lakes. Despite the short distance (about 10 km), the walk to the lakes is a long and rough backpack. Only intrepid hikers and fishermen lusting after the rare golden trout, which is stocked solely in high-elevation lakes in the Rockies, persevere along this difficult track.

Take heart, though. This short jaunt is not particularly difficult and its gorge, although not very long, is remarkably narrow and deep. You begin to understand this when the trail appears to end where Owen Creek tumbles out the lower end of the canyon. The footpath continues on the right, leading up the embankment. On top you suddenly find yourself looking down into a very deep gorge. Scoops carved out of the rock over the eons by the swirling water pockmark the gorge walls. Continue along the trail for another 50 m to a natural bridge across the narrow chasm. You can hear the waters, forced through this slit in the rock, churning below.

Beyond this point, the trail becomes rougher with deadfall and boggy areas. Pass the top of the gorge where Owen Creek begins its plunge. The trail continues to where Owen Creek is carving out a second canyon. It's quite a pretty sight to see the water slicing over the smooth rocks. A short, rough hike over deadfall soon brings you to a pretty little waterfall that is crisscrossed with deadfall.

Return the way you came.

Mt. Cline from the Whitegoat Peaks. Courtesy of Tony Daffern.

HISTORICAL FOOTNOTES

First Ascent of Mount Cline

The first recorded ascent of Mount Cline (3,361 m) was in July 1927. The five-man party included Alfred Castle, a lawyer from Hawaii, and his son Alfred Jr., J. H. Barnes, Swiss mountaineering guide Rudolph Aemmer and Jimmy Simpson of Banff, who acted as outfitter and guide on the approach to the mountain.

The approach route Simpson took was up Owen Creek. He then crossed over to the west branch of Thompson Creek above the Thompson Creek Falls to two small lakes at the head of the valley. From the lakes they worked their way up to a col, then on toward the summit. Simpson, who had just celebrated his 50th birthday, found the ascent nerve-racking. Aemmer was working his way across a difficult gap in the ridge. Meanwhile, both Simpson and Castle watched Aemmer with concern. Castle asked Simpson: "Do you want to die this sudden?" "I don't feel quite like it," replied Simpson. "Well, we'll see what this damn fool guide does," said Castle.

Both men and the rest of the party eventually followed Aemmer to the summit. For Simpson, it would be the last major climb in his career.

69 Sunset Pass – map p. 242

Duration ~ two days
Distance ~ 34.6 km
Level of Difficulty ~ steep ascent to pass followed by a long, steady walk
Maximum Elevation ~ 2,175 m
Elevation Gain ~ 737 m
Map ~ 83 C/2 Cline River

Access ~ Park your vehicle at the Norman Creek staging area on Highway #93 in Banff National Park. The staging area is 17 km north of the junction of Highways #11 and 93.

There are two accesses to Pinto Lake. Most hikers choose the Sunset Pass route rather than up the Cline River because it cuts off a full day of hiking. So, even though the Norman Creek staging area lies outside the parameters of the David Thompson corridor, this access is recorded here.

~

There is no opportunity to "warm up" on this hike! Almost immediately, the well-used footpath leading from the staging area begins to switch up the slope through lodgepole pine forest. There are few rests along this pull until you reach the top of the pass. The first respite comes at 1.4 km when you reach a fork in the trail. Turn right for 20 m to catch a fine view of the Norman Creek gorge and waterfall. Return to the main trail and continue switching up the slope. The next rest point comes 600 m later, when you have another opportunity to catch a glimpse of Norman Creek. As you continue to climb, views to the west across Highway #93 begin to open up. The third chance to catch your

0.0	trailhead
1.4	viewpoint, Norman Creek
2.0	viewpoint, Norman Creek
2.7	viewpoint, Alexandra River
4.6	junction
6.0	Sunset Pass
6.2	Norman Creek
6.5	campsite
8.1	junction and Norman Creek
10.7	Banff National Park boundary
11.6	viewpoint over Pinto Lake
16.5	bog
16.7	junction
16.9	bridge
17.0	bridge
17.3	main campsite at Pinto Lake
34.6	trailhead

Mount Coleman from Sunset Pass meadows. Courtesy of Gillean Daffern.

breath is at a viewpoint overlooking the alluvial flats of Alexandra River now far below you.

At a fork in the trail, there is a sign for Pinto Lake, Norman Lake and Sunset Pass pointing to the right. If you bear to the left you climb to a fire tower, making a fine day hike from Norman Creek campsite. However, you should go to the right as you continue climbing. Making sure not to trip over the contour lines, you have two more short, steep pitches to tackle before, suddenly, you're at Sunset Pass. Behind and stretching far below is the North Saskatchewan River valley. Beyond are the mountains along the Continental Divide with pockets of ancient glaciers clinging to their peaks. To the northeast stretch the meadows of Sunset Pass and the impressive peak of Mount Coleman at your nine o'clock. Ahead, past the meadows, is the boundary of Banff National Park.

Continue along the trail, crossing Norman Creek by means of a well-made log bridge—a sure sign that you are in a national park! There is a Park-designated campsite 100 m later. The trail swings along the right side of the huge meadows going up and down over hills and through dells. Norman Lake lies to the left on the other side of the meadows at the base of Mount Coleman. There is a fork in the trail and a small rock cairn at a crossing of Norman Creek. Going to the right takes you to a ridge walk overlooking Pinto Lake. Keep to the left. The trail marches through willows and alders to the end of the meadow, where it climbs the first of a series of low, rocky ridges. Along the way you pass a sign marking the boundary of Banff National Park. Another sign announces: "Area cleaned by volunteers. Keep clean." This refers to a volunteer programme of the Alberta Wilderness Association whereby its members hike into the back country with the express purpose of cleaning sites and packing out any garbage they find. Help them in their job and leave only your footprints behind. Three tough pulls carry you to the top of a sharp ridge overlooking the topaz-blue waters of Pinto Lake. Before beginning the steep descent, take time to savour the beauty of the tree-carpeted valleys tucked beneath the surrounding high scree slopes and rugged mountain peaks.

The trail leads down through the scree and then begins a long, winding traverse that eventually takes you to the top of a steep pitch. Switch down the pitch through pine and spruce forest. There are no views. Once the path flattens it is only a short distance to a bog beside a blocked junction. Bear right across the bog and come to a junction. If you go left across the rivulet you begin the hike down the Cline River. Bear right upstream. The path cuts along the edge of the Cline River, already a 10 m-wide waterway. Two log bridges and a short jaunt bring you to the main campsite beside the river and the lake. Surrounded on three sides by high scree cliffs and glacier-topped peaks, Pinto Lake is a delightful conclusion to a long day. Picnic tables, toilets and fire pits are touches of luxury at the campsite.

Return the way you came, or follow the Cline River down to Abraham Lake. There are three day hikes from the campsite: the Pinto Lake Lookout, Pinto Lake Loop and Cline River Falls.

WHAT'S IN A NAME?

Sunset Pass

Previous Name ~ Pinto Pass

Sunset Pass takes its name from its location. It lies west of Pinto Lake. In the evening, as the sun sets, light streams onto Pinto Lake from between the mountains framing the pass.

The first recorded visitor to Sunset Pass was A. P. Coleman in 1893. Coleman did not cross it, but simply ascended it from the east side. Mary Schäffer was the first to cross what she called Pinto Pass, in 1906. The descent to Pinto Lake was a difficult one due to heavy snow cover. "We found an old game trail down which man and horse slid with what agility they could," she wrote. The next year, while camped at Pinto Lake and running out of food, Schäffer watched her guides Billy Warren and Sid Unwin ascend the pass as they headed for a food cache along the North Saskatchewan River. The scene of the men and horses along the skyline captivated her. As they went out of sight, Schäffer turned around and found her meagre breakfast of bannock burned "black as a pot."

At the end of a steep ascent the broad, flat meadows of Sunset Pass beckon.

HISTORICAL FOOTNOTES

The Pinto

In retrospect, it may not have been such a good deal. In 1892, A. P. Coleman's brother, Lucius, purchased 13 pack ponies from the Stoney Indians at Morley for $10 to $25 apiece. Included in the many-coloured bunch was The Pinto. He was a horse that always seemed to find a way to stand out among his cantankerous tribe of fellow packhorses. Coleman found that The Pinto was always getting into trouble. In his book he wrote: "As usual, the first attempt at packing [the horses] resulted in a 'circus', ugly old Pinto especially making trouble. It took two hours of hard riding to induce him to enter the corral, and then he bucked and tore the post he was tied to out of the ground when the saddle touched his back, but afterwards he was of lamb-like meekness."

Besides his bad temper, Pinto was a klutz. He fell on his back, crashed into trees and took false steps at the most inopportune times. During his second season in 1893 with the now steaming Coleman, Pinto fell into the Whirlpool River and had to be rescued from a sandbar by boat. Then he went missing. "But our loads were now light and none of us was sorry to lose him, so we left him behind. Though he was more trouble as a packhorse than all the others put together, we immortalized him by giving his name to an exquisite lake near the head of Cataract [Cline] River."

What happened to ugly, old Pinto after his master abandoned him near the Athabasca River is unknown. It was a terrible thing for Coleman to do. Whatever the horse's fate, he has his monument, beautiful Pinto Lake. And nearby, looking down, no doubt in disapproval, is A. P. Coleman's monument, Mt. Coleman. A. P. Coleman and The Pinto. Together again. Forever.

Pinto Lake.

FURTHER READING

Below is a list of readings for those whose interest in the flora, geology and/or history of the David Thompson corridor has been piqued. This list does not constitute a complete bibliography of sources used by the authors. Consulted primary documents found at the Provincial Archives of Alberta, the Glenbow Archives or the Archives of the Canadian Rockies, newspapers, government reports and published works not easily obtained have not been listed here. Rather, these are suggested readings that should be readily available at public libraries and bookstores.

Cavell, Edward. (ed.) *A Delicate Wilderness: The Photography of Elliott Barnes 1905-1913*. Banff: Altitude Publishing/Whyte Foundation, 1980.

Coleman, A.P. *The Canadian Rockies: New & Old Trails*. London: T. Fisher Unwin, 1911.

Coues, Elliott. (ed.) *New Light on the Early History of the Greater Northwest*. The Manuscript Journals of Alexander Henry, Fur Trader of the Northwest Company and of David Thompson, Official Geographer and Explorer of the same Company, 1799-1814. Exploration and Adventure among the Indians on the Red, Saskatchewan, Missouri and Columbia Rivers. Minneapolis, Minnesota: Ross & Haines, Inc., 1897.

Fraser, Esther. *The Canadian Rockies: Early Travels and Explorations*. Edmonton: Hurtig Publishers Ltd., 1969.

Gadd, Ben. *Handbook of the Canadian Rockies: Geology, plants, animals, history and recreation from Waterton/Glacier to the Yukon*. Jasper: Corax Press, 1986.

Gough, Barry M. (ed.) *The Journal of Alexander Henry the Younger, 1799-1814*. 2 Volumes. Toronto: The Champlain Society, 1988-1992.

Green, John. *On the Track of the Sasquatch. Book One*. Harrison Hot Springs, B.C.: Cheam Publishing, 1968.

Hart, E.J. *Jimmy Simpson: Legend of the Rockies*. Banff: Altitude Publishing, 1991.

Hopwood, Victor G. (ed.) *David Thompson: Travel in Western North America 1784-1812*. Toronto: Macmillan Company of Canada Limited, 1971.

Hunter, Don with René Dahinden. *Sasquatch*. Toronto: McClelland & Stewart Inc., 1973.

Karamitsanis, Aphrodite. *Place Names of Alberta: Mountains, Mountain Parks and Foothills. Volume I*. Calgary: Alberta Culture and Multiculturalism and Friends of Geographical Names of Alberta Society and University of Calgary Press, 1991.

Nordegg, Martin. *The Possibilities of Canada Are Truly Great: Memoirs 1906-1924*. Toronto: Macmillan Company of Canada Limited, 1971.

Outram, James. *In the Heart of the Canadian Rockies*. New York: The Macmillan Company, 1905.

Palliser, John et al. *The Journals, Detailed Reports, and Observations Relative to the Exploration...of that Portion of British North America...During the Years 1857, 1858, 1859 and 1860.* London: H.M. Stationary Office, 1863.

Rich, E.E. *The Fur Trade and the Northwest to 1857.* Toronto: McClelland and Stewart Limited, 1967.

Schäffer, Mary T. S. *Old Indian Trails Incidents of Camp and Trail Life, covering Two Years' Exploration through the Rocky Mountains of Canada.* New York: G.P. Putnam's Sons, 1911.

Smith, Cyndi. *Off The Beaten Track: Women Adventurers and Mountaineers in Western Canada.* Lake Louise: Coyote Books, 1989.

Snow, Chief John. *These Mountains Are Our Sacred Places: The Story of the Stoney Indians.* Toronto: Samuel Stevens, 1977.

Southesk, The Earl of. *Saskatchewan and the Rocky Mountains: A Diary and Narrative of Travel, Sport, and Adventure, during a Journey through the Hudson's Bay Company's Territories, in 1859 and 1860.* Edinburgh: Edmonston and Douglas, 1875.

Spry, Irene M. (ed.) *The Papers of The Palliser Expedition 1857-1860.* Toronto: The Champlain Society, 1968.

Stenson, Fred. *Rocky Mountain House National Historic Park.* Toronto: NC Press Limited in cooperation with Parks Canada and the Canadian Government Publishing Centre, Supply and Services Canada, 1985.

Stutfield, Hugh and J. Norman Collie. *Climbs & Exploration in the Canadian Rockies.* London: Longmans, Green and Co., 1903.

Tyrrell, J.B. *Report on a Part of Northern Alberta and Portions of Adjacent Districts of Assiniboia and Saskatchewan, embracing the Country lying South of the North Saskatchewan River and North of lat. 51°6', between long. 110° and 115°15' West.* Montreal: Dawson Brothers, 1887.

Tyrrell, J.B. (ed.) *David Thompson's Narrative of his Explorations in Western America 1784-1812.* Toronto: The Champlain Society, 1916.

White, J. *Place-names in the Rocky Mountains between the 49th Parallel and the Athabasca River.* Transactions of the Royal Society of Canada. X (3rd series): 501-535, March 1917.

Whyte, Jon. *Indians in the Rockies.* Banff: Altitude Publishing Ltd., 1985.

Wilcox, Walter Dwight. *Camping in the Canadian Rockies: an account of camp life in the wilder parts of the Canadian Rocky Mountains, together with a description of the region about Banff, Lake Louise, and Glacier, and a sketch of the early explorations.* London: G.P. Putnam's Sons, 1896.

Wilson, Thomas E. *Trail Blazer of the Canadian Rockies.* Calgary: Glenbow-Alberta Institute Historical Paper No. 3, 1972.

WHAT ELSE IS THERE TO DO?

GOLF COURSES

Nordegg Golf Club
Nordegg. One km south of Highway #11 on Nordegg's main street.
Telephone ~ 721-2003.
Services ~ nine holes. Pro shop.

Pine Hills Golf Course
Located off Highway #11X either from Highway #11 north of Rocky Mountain House, or from Highway #11A off 52 Avenue in Rocky Mountain House.
Telephone ~ 845-7400.
Services ~ 18 holes. Pro shop.

MUSEUMS AND HERITAGE CENTRES

Bighorn Dam
28 km west of Nordegg off Hwy #11.
Hours ~ mid-May to mid-September daily 8:30 am-4:30 pm. Group tours available including tours of the powerhouse.

Mandelin Antique Museum
16 km southwest of Rocky Mountain House on Highway #752.
Hours ~ mid-May to mid-September, 10 am-6 pm, Thurs. through Mon.
Displays of phonographs, telephones, stoves, bells, radios and barbed wire.
Smithy work demonstrated.
Admission charge.

Nordegg Heritage Centre
Nordegg. One km south of Highway #11 on Nordegg's main street.
Hours ~ 9 am-5 pm daily (closed on weekends during winter months).
Displays relating to Nordegg's mining history. Gift shop.
Tours of Nordegg's historic townsite and mine, departing 2 pm daily.
No admission charge to Centre.

Rocky Mountain House Museum
4604 - 49 Avenue, Rocky Mountain House. Located behind the Tamarack Motel on Highway #11.
Hours ~ Summer hours (May long weekend to Labour Day): Monday to Saturday 10 am-7 pm. Sunday 1 pm-7 pm. Winter hours: Monday-Friday 10 am-5 pm, Saturdays 1 pm-5 pm. Closed Sundays.
Displays of pioneer exhibits dating to 1900.
Admission charge.

Rocky Mountain House National Historic Park
Highway #1A west, Rocky Mountain House.
Hours ~ Summer hours: mid-May to Labour Day 10 am-8 pm daily. Winter Hours: Labour Day to Thanksgiving 10 am-5 pm weekdays; 10:30 am-6 pm weekends. Open weekdays only the rest of the year.
Displays on the fur trade, exploration of the west and native peoples. Two trails explore the archaeological sites of the fur trade fort.

TRAIL RIDES

Diamond Jim and Sons Mountain Rides
Mailing Address ~ PO Box 394, Rocky Mountain House, T0M 1T0.
Telephone ~ 845-6859/ 845-4537.
Services ~ Hourly rides along Blackstone, Wapiabi and Big Horn Rivers.

Baldy Mountain Trail Rides
Mailing Address ~ PO Box 684, Rocky Mountain House, T0M 1T0.
Local Address ~ Nordegg, behind the Nordegg Resort Lodge.
Telephone ~ 721-2030 (Nordegg) or 845-4437 (Rocky Mountain House).
Services ~ Hourly rides 9 am-12 noon, 1:30-6 pm to East Bush Falls, toward Baldy Mountain, and down the valley past the rock quarry.
~ Full-day rides (five-seven hours) to Coliseum Mountain, "T-Bone" and "V.I.P." tours.
~ Afternoon rides (three-four hours) to Box Canyon.
~ Wagon rides (two hours) toward Baldy Mountain and to the old ghost town and mine site of Nordegg.

McKenzies' Trails West
Mailing Address ~ PO Box 971, Rocky Mountain House, T0M 1T0.
Local Address ~ Cline River. Across Highway #11 from the David Thompson Resort.
Telephone ~ 845-6708.
Fax ~ 845-4389.
Services ~ Hourly rides 9 am, 11 am, 1 pm, 3 pm, 5 pm.
~ Half-day rides 8 am and 2 pm.
~ "The Last Frontier" a six-day trip to Job Creek valley.
~ "The Explorer" a 12-day trip to the Brazeau River.
~ "Howse Pass" a three-day trip to the west side of Howse Pass.

Sam Sands and Son
Summer Packtrips
Mailing Address ~ PO Box 1985, Rocky Mountain House, T0M 1T0.
Telephone ~ 845-5956/845-5712.
Services ~ Three- to 10-day fishing, photography or riding trips.

WATER SPORTS

Alpenglow Mountain Adventures
Mailing Address ~ General Delivery, Nordegg, T0M 2H0.
Telephone ~ 721-2050.
Services ~ Rafting and Canoeing: full-day and overnight trips on North Saskatchewan River between Nordegg and Rocky Mountain House.
~ Kayaking

Jet-Boat Adventures
Mailing Address ~ D & B River Runners Ltd., R.R. #2, Rocky Mountain House, T0M 1T0.
Telephone ~ 845-4085/729-3977.
Services ~ Full-day trip from Rocky Mountain House to The Gap.

Voyageur Adventure Tours Ltd.
Mailing Address ~ 4808 - 63 St., Rocky Mountain House, T0M 1T4.
Telephone ~ 845-7878.
Services ~ Half-day (15 km), full-day (45 km) and overnight (100 km) guided tours using 10-passenger voyageur canoes.

WILDERNESS COURSES

Alpenglow Mountain Adventures
Mailing Address ~ General Delivery, Nordegg, T0M 2H0.
Telephone ~ 721-2050.
Services ~ Courses on rock climbing and rappelling. Guided day hikes, caving and overnight backpacks.

Centre For Outdoor Education
Mailing Address ~ General Delivery, Nordegg, T0M 2H0.
Telephone ~ bookings 1-800-474-8632; information 721-2208.
Services ~ supervisor's programme on rock and wall climbing, mountain leadership and cave leadership.

Frontier Lodge

Mailing Address ~ PO Box 1449, Rocky Mountain House, T0M 1T0.
Telephone ~ 721-2202.
Services ~ Five-day courses on rock climbing, canoeing. Other courses and tours include mountain biking and bicycle touring. Frontier Fat Tire Festival every July featuring guided rides, self-guided rides, mass ride, heli-biking and early-bird rides. In conjunction with the Fat Tire Festival, the Black Mountain Challenge race. Guided backpacks, heli-hiking. Wilderness camp for ages 11-13.

HELICOPTER FLIGHTS

Shunda Helicopter Service Ltd.
Mailing Address ~ PO Box 463, Rocky Mountain House, T0M 1T0.
Local Address ~ The David Thompson Resort, located 150 km west of Rocky Mountain House on Highway #11.
Telephone ~ 845-2534.
Services ~ scenic mountain flights, heli-hiking, heli-fishing, charter flights.

A PLACE TO SLEEP

CAMPGROUNDS

Beaverdam

Location ~ five km east of Nordegg or 132 km west of the Banff National Park boundary on Highway #11.
Operator ~ Alberta Forest Service.
Number of Sites ~ seven walk-in sites, tents only.
Services ~ water, toilets, firewood, canoeing, fishing, pump water, cookhouse.

Beaverdam Overflow

Location ~ five km east of Nordegg or 133 km west of the Banff National Park boundary on Highway #11.
Operator ~ Alberta Forest Service.
Number of Sites ~ 31.
Services ~ water, toilets.

Crescent Falls

Location ~ 18 km west of Nordegg or 65 km west of the Banff National Park boundary off Highway #11.
Operator ~ Alberta Forest Service.
Number of Sites ~ 26.
Services ~ water, toilets, firewood, hiking/equestrian trails, fishing.

David Thompson Resort

Location ~ 46 km west of Nordegg or 37 km east of the Banff National Park boundary on Highway #11.
Operator ~ David Thompson Resort.
Number of Sites ~ 134.
Services ~ water, washrooms, showers, firewood, T.V. reception, playground, heated pool, whirlpool, frisbee golf, volleyball, horseshoes.

Dry Haven

Location ~ 11 km west of Nordegg or 88 km east of the Banff National Park boundary on Highway #11.
Operator ~ Alberta Forest Service.
Number of Sites ~ eight.
Services ~ water, toilets, cookhouse, firewood.

Fish Lake

Location ~ four km west of Nordegg or 128 km east of the Banff National Park boundary on Highway #11.
Operator ~ Alberta Forest Service.
Number of Sites ~ 92.
Services ~ water, toilets, firewood, cookhouse, canoeing, fishing, hiking trails.

Goldeye Lake
Location ~ eight km west of Nordegg or 126 km east of the Banff National Park boundary on Highway #11.
Operator ~ Alberta Forest Service.
Number of Sites ~ 44.
Services ~ water, toilets, firewood, cookhouse, canoeing, fishing, hiking.

Harlech
Location ~ 13 km east of Nordegg on Highway #11.
Operator ~ Alberta Forest Service.
Number of Sites ~ 17.
Services ~ water, toilets, cookhouse, firewood.

Snow Creek Group Camp
Location ~ 17 km west of Nordegg on Highway #11.
Operator ~ Alberta Forest Service.
Number of Sites ~ 15.
Services ~ water, toilets, firewood, cookhouse.

Thompson Creek
Location ~ 80 km west of Nordegg or three km east of the Banff National Park boundary on Highway #11.
Operator ~ Alberta Forest Service.
Number of Sites ~ 55.
Services ~ water, toilets, firewood, cookhouse, fishing, hiking trails.

Two O'Clock Creek
Location ~ 61 km west of Nordegg or 22 km east of the Banff National Park boundary on Highway #11.
Operator ~ Alberta Forest Service.
Number of Sites ~ 20.
Services ~ water, toilets, firewood, cookhouse, hiking trails.

Upper Shunda Creek
Location ~ 300 m west of Nordegg or 132 km east of the Banff National Park boundary on Highway #11.
Operator ~ Alberta Forest Service.
Number of Sites ~ 21.
Services ~ water, toilets, firewood, cookhouse, fishing, hiking trails.

BEDS AND SERVICES

Alpine Motel
Address ~ PO Box 148, Rocky Mountain House, T0M 1T0.
Location ~ 4905 - 45 Street, Rocky Mountain House.
Telephone ~ 845-3325.
Fax ~ 845-3526.
Services ~ 31 units, kitchenettes.

Big Horn Motor Inn
Address ~ PO Box 1447, Rocky Mountain House, T0M 1T0.
Location ~ on Highway #11 in Rocky Mountain House.
Telephone ~ 845-2871.
Services ~ 40 units, courtesy coffee, licensed dining room, cocktail lounge.

Bighorn Stoney Service Centre
Location ~ on Highway #11, 18 km west of Nordegg near the turn-off to Crescent Falls.
Services ~ groceries, handicrafts.

Chinook Inn
Address ~ PO Box 1, Rocky Mountain House, T0M 1T0.
Location ~ Highway 11 at 59 Avenue, Rocky Mountain House.
Telephone ~ 20 units, some non-smoking units, courtesy coffee, laundry and dry-cleaning service.

The Crossing
Address ~ Bag Service 333, Lake Louise, T0L 1E0.
Location ~ near the junction of Highways #11 and #93.
Telephone ~ 761-7000.
Fax ~ 761-7006.
Season ~ 1 March-15 November.
Services ~ 66 units, licensed dining room, cafeteria, pub, sauna, whirlpool, groceries, gas bar, gift shop.

David Thompson Resort

Address ~ PO Box 819, Rocky Mountain House, T0M 1T0.
Location ~ 50 km west of Rocky Mountain House on Highway #11.
Telephone ~ 721-2103.
Season ~ 1 May-15 October.
Services ~ 45 units, cafeteria, pub, whirlpool, outdoor swimming pool, gas bar, gift shop, mini golf, video arcade, fishing supplies, groceries, laundry.

The House Motel

Address ~ PO Box 1047, Rocky Mountain House, T0M 1T0.
Location ~ on Highway #11 opposite Walking Eagle Motor Inn.
Telephone ~ 845-3388.
Services ~ 24 units, kitchenettes, courtesy coffee.

Inn Town Bed and Breakfast

Address ~ 5316 - 55 Street, Rocky Mountain House, T0M 1T4.
Telephone ~ 845-2616.

Mountview Hotel and Motel

Address ~ PO Box 1255, Rocky Mountain House, T0M 1T0.
Telephone ~ 845-2821.
Services ~ 32 units, cafe, licensed dining room, cocktail lounge, pub.

Nordegg Resort Lodge

Address ~ General Delivery, Nordegg, T0M 2H0.
Location ~ one km south of Highway #11 on main street of Nordegg.
Telephone ~ 721-3757/721-3733.
Services ~ 38 units, kitchenettes, laundry, licensed dining room, cafe, pub, gas bar, groceries, fishing supplies.

Shunda Creek Hostel

Address ~ Northern Alberta District Hostelling Association, 10926 - 88 Avenue, Edmonton, T6G 0Z1.
Telephone ~ 439-3089.
Location ~ three km north of Nordegg on Highway #11 along Shunda Creek Recreation Area road.
Services ~ accommodates 47 people, family rooms, laundry, communal kitchen, whirlpool.

Tamarack Motor Inn

Address ~ PO Box 2860, Rocky Mountain House, T0M 1T0.
Location ~ 4904 - 45 Street, Rocky Mountain House.
Telephone ~ 845-5252.
Fax ~ 845-3825.
Services ~ 49 units, licensed dining room, cocktail lounge, pub, sauna, whirlpool.

Voyageur Motel

Address ~ PO Box 1376, Rocky Mountain House, T0M 1T0.
Telephone ~ 845-3381.
Fax ~ 845-6166.
Services ~ 28 units, laundry, courtesy coffee, kitchenettes.

Walking Eagle Motor Inn

Address ~ PO Box 1317, Rocky Mountain House, T0M 1T0.
Telephone ~ 845-2804.
Fax ~ 845-3685.
Services ~ 63 units, licensed dining room, pub, cocktail lounge, courtesy coffee, gift shop.

ALBERTA FORESTRY TRAIL GUIDE

Alberta Forestry has published a trail guide to the Rocky/Clearwater Forest. The trails listed tend to be long. Trail descriptions in some cases may bc dated and hiking times are often approximate.

Here is a brief description of some of the trails listed:

ALLENBY TRAIL
14.5 km in 5 hours
Begins at the Ram Falls Recreation Area and ends about 14.5 km downstream along the South Ram River.

AYLMER TRAIL
19 km in 7.5 hours
Begins at the Bighorn Dam parking area and ends downstream at the junction of the Forestry Trunk Road and the North Saskatchewan River at Aylmer parking.

BIGHORN TRAIL
38.5 km in 15.5 hours
Begins at Crescent Falls Recreation Area and ends on the Blackstone River just west of the Blackstone Gap.

CLEARWATER TRAIL
40 km in 14.5 hours
Begins at the Elk Creek Recreation Area and ends at Indianhead Lodge in Banff National Park.

ESKER TRAIL
14.5 km in 5 hours
Begins at Lynx Creek on the Forestry Trunk Road and ends on the North Ram River about seven km east of the North Ram Recreation Area.

FORBIDDEN CREEK TRAIL
26.5 km in 10 hours
Begins about 2.5 km east of the Forty Mile Forestry Cabin on thc Clearwater River and ends on the Clearwater Trail several kilometres east of Indianhead Lodge.

HEADWATERS TRAIL
62 km in 24.5 hours
Begins at the Bighorn Dam parking area and ends at the Clearwater Trail several kilometres east of Indianhead Lodge in Banff National Park.

HUMMINGBIRD/CANARY/ONION CREEK CIRCUIT TRAILS
variable distances
Begins at the lower Hummingbird Falls. An abandoned road may be followed to Onion Lake or the Headwaters Trail via Canary, or Hummingbird Creek may be used.

JOB CREEK/CORAI CREEK TRAIL
44 km in 17 hours
Begins at Highway #11 near the Cline River bridge and ends at Job Lake.

LOST GUIDE CANYON TRAIL
14.5 km in 7 hours
Begins at its junction with the Ranger Creek Trail, goes to Lost Guide Lake and ends at the Clearwater Trail about five km from the Forty Mile Forestry cabin.

MONS-CHUNGO TRAIL
26.5 km in 10.5 hours
Begins at the Chungo Road/Chungo Creek junction and ends on the Blackstone River about five km west of the Blackstone Gap.

NORTH RAM TRAIL

29 km in 10 hours

Begins at the end of the Kiska Tower Road and ends at Headwaters Lake (Farley Lake).

RANGER CREEK TRAIL

24 km in 9 hours

Begins seven km west of Ram Falls Recreation Area and ends in the headwaters of Ranger Creek near the Banff National Park boundary.

SIFFLEUR TRAIL

26 km in 11 hours

Begins at the Siffleur Falls parking area and ends at the south boundary of the Siffleur Wilderness.

SMALLPOX TRAIL

17 km in 6 hours

Begins on the Forestry Trunk Road about four km northeast of the North Ram Recreation Area and ends on the North Saskatchewan River about seven km east of the Bighorn Dam.

SOUTHESK TRAIL

17 km in 6.5 hours

Begins at the Blackstone Gap and ends at Dowling Ford on the Brazeau River.

SOUTH RAM RIVER TRAIL

24 km in 8 hours

Begins on the Forestry Trunk Road about seven km west of the Ram Falls Recreation Area and ends at the Headwaters Forestry Cabin.

WHITERABBIT TRAIL

27 km in 8 hours

Begins at the Siffleur Falls parking area and ends at the Headwaters Forestry cabin.

For further information and a copy of the Guide contact:

Alberta Forest Service
Rocky/Clearwater Forest
Box 1720, Rocky Mountain House
Alberta, T0M 1T0. (403) 845-3394

PHOTO CREDITS

Archival photographs obtained from the Whyte Museum of the Canadian Rockies, the Forest Technology School of the Department of Environmental Protection, the Glenbow Archives, the Provincial Archives of Alberta and the Rocky Mountain House Museum have been selected to enhance some of the Historical Footnotes. We also wish to thank Robin Chambers, Gillean and Tony Daffern, Alfred Falk, John Farley, Chris Hanstock, Karl Keller, Koni MacDonald and Doris Magnus who have generously allowed use of their photographs. All other photographs in this book were taken by the authors.

ACKNOWLEDGMENTS

The authors would like to gratefully acknowledge all those who have helped in some way in this endeavour: to Laurie Berry, Linda Blom, John Campbell, Robin Chambers, Alfred Falk, John Farley, Karl Keller, Dave Koshman, Chuck Labatiuk and Ulrike Spohr who joined us in our quest for trails old and new; to Reg Banks of the Centre For Outdoor Education, Colin Belton of St. John's School of Alberta, Heather Clement, formerly of Shunda Creek Hostel, Clayton Grosso of Baldy Mountain Trail Rides, Ed McKenzie of McKenzies' Trails West, Dennis Morley of Nordegg Historic Heritage Interest Group, and Joyce and Doug Ritchie of Frontier Lodge, who shared their local knowledge with us; to Terry Smith and Bob Young of the Department of Environmental Protection and the staffs of the Archives of the Canadian Rockies, Glenbow Archives, Provincial Archives of Alberta and the Rocky Mountain House Museum for their help in locating documents pertinent to the David Thompson corridor; to Peter Murphy of the University of Alberta and Harry Edgecomb, retired Forest Rangers, for their review of our forestry sidebars; to Julie Hrapko, botanist, and Ron Mussieux, geologist, both of the Provincial Museum of Alberta for help in their respective fields; to George and Doris Magnus for their warm hospitality and sharing of information; and lastly, to Elaine, George and Josh Nye of Red Deer who cheerfully looked after Duster when we were on the trail.

ABOUT THE AUTHORS

Jane Ross is trained as an historian and has worked in the heritage resources field for 20 years. She has written several social studies textbooks and historical monographs. Jane has hiked in Baffin Island, New Zealand and the Canadian Rockies. She coauthored *Hiking the Historic Crowsnest Pass.*

Dan Kyba is the owner of Kyba & Associates, a marketing research firm based in Edmonton. He loves the outdoors and has hiked in Baffin Island, the Himalayas, New Zealand, Papua New Guinea and the Canadian Rockies. He is also an amateur historian specializing in eastern Europe.

Courtesy of Koni MacDonald.

INDEX OF TRAILS